STANDARDS AND ACCOUNTABILITY IN SCHOOLS

DEBATING ISSUES
in American Education

STANDARDS AND ACCOUNTABILITY IN SCHOOLS

VOLUME EDITOR

THOMAS J. LASLEY, II
UNIVERSITY OF DAYTON

9

VOLUME

DEBATING ISSUES
in American Education

SERIES
EDITORS

CHARLES J. RUSSO
ALLAN G. OSBORNE, JR.

⑤SAGE reference

Los Angeles | London | New Delhi
Singapore | Washington DC

Los Angeles | London | New Delhi
Singapore | Washington DC

FOR INFORMATION:

SAGE Publications, Inc.
2455 Teller Road
Thousand Oaks, California 91320
E-mail: order@sagepub.com

SAGE Publications Ltd.
1 Oliver's Yard
55 City Road
London EC1Y 1SP
United Kingdom

SAGE Publications India Pvt. Ltd.
B 1/I 1 Mohan Cooperative Industrial Area
Mathura Road, New Delhi 110 044
India

SAGE Publications Asia-Pacific Pte. Ltd.
3 Church Street
#10-04 Samsung Hub
Singapore 049483

Publisher: Rolf A. Janke
Acquisitions Editor: Jim Brace-Thompson
Assistant to the Publisher: Michele Thompson
Developmental Editors: Diana E. Axelsen, Carole Maurer
Production Editor: Tracy Buyan
Reference Systems Manager: Leticia Gutierrez
Reference Systems Coordinator: Laura Notton
Copy Editor: Patricia Sutton
Typesetter: C&M Digitals (P) Ltd.
Proofreader: Victoria Reed-Castro
Indexer: Mary Mortensen
Cover Designer: Janet Kiesel
Marketing Manager: Carmel Schrire

Printed in the United States of America.

Library of Congress Cataloging-in-Publication Data

Standards and accountability in schools / volume editor, Thomas J. Lasley, II.

p. cm. – (Debating issues in American education; v. 9)

A SAGE Reference Publication.
Includes bibliographical references and index.

1. Education—United States—Finance. I. Thro, William E.

ISBN 978-1-4129-8766-0 (cloth : alk. paper)

1. Education—Standards—United States. 2. Educational accountability—United States. I. Lasley, Thomas J.

LB3060.83.S66 2012
371.14'40973—dc23   2011027018

12 13 14 15 16 10 9 8 7 6 5 4 3 2 1

CONTENTS

ABOUT THE
EDITORS-IN-CHIEF

Charles J. Russo, JD, EdD, is the Joseph Panzer Chair in Education in the School of Education and Allied Professions and adjunct professor in the School of Law at the University of Dayton. He was the 1998–1999 president of the Education Law Association and 2002 recipient of its McGhehey (Achievement) Award. He has authored or coauthored more than 200 articles in peer-reviewed journals; has authored, coauthored, edited, or coedited 40 books; and has in excess of 800 publications. Russo also speaks extensively on issues in education law in the United States and abroad.

Along with having spoken in 33 states and 25 nations on 6 continents, Russo has taught summer courses in England, Spain, and Thailand; he also has served as a visiting professor at Queensland University of Technology in Brisbane and the University of Newcastle, Australia; the University of Sarajevo, Bosnia and Herzegovina; South East European University, Macedonia; the Potchefstroom Campus of North-West University in Potchefstroom, South Africa; the University of Malaya in Kuala Lumpur, Malaysia; and the University of São Paulo, Brazil. He regularly serves as a visiting professor at the Potchefstroom Campus of North-West University.

Before joining the faculty at the University of Dayton as professor and chair of the Department of Educational Administration in July 1996, Russo taught at the University of Kentucky in Lexington from August 1992 to July 1996 and at Fordham University in his native New York City from September 1989 to July 1992. He taught high school for 8½ years before and after graduation from law school. He received a BA (classical civilization) in 1972, a JD in 1983, and an EdD (educational administration and supervision) in 1989 from St. John's University in New York City. He also received a master of divinity degree from the Seminary of the Immaculate Conception in Huntington, New York, in 1978, as well as a PhD Honoris Causa from the Potchefstroom Campus of North-West University, South Africa, in May 2004 for his contributions to the field of education law.

Russo and his wife, a preschool teacher who provides invaluable assistance proofreading and editing, travel regularly both nationally and internationally to Russo's many speaking and teaching engagements.

Allan G. Osborne, Jr. is the retired principal of the Snug Harbor Community School in Quincy, Massachusetts, a nationally recognized Blue Ribbon School of Excellence. During his 34 years in public education, he served as a special education teacher, a director of special education, an assistant principal, and a principal. He has also served as an adjunct professor of special education and education law at several colleges, including Bridgewater State University and American International University.

Osborne earned an EdD in educational leadership from Boston College and an MEd in special education from Fitchburg State College (now Fitchburg State University) in Massachusetts. He received a BA in psychology from the University of Massachusetts.

Osborne has authored or coauthored numerous peer-reviewed journal articles, book chapters, monographs, and textbooks on legal issues in education, along with textbooks on other aspects of education. Although he writes and presents in several areas of educational law, he specializes in legal and policy issues in special education. He is the coauthor, with Charles J. Russo, of five texts published by Corwin, a SAGE company.

A past president of the Education Law Association (ELA), Osborne has been an attendee and presenter at most ELA conferences since 1991. He has also written a chapter now titled "Students With Disabilities" for the *Yearbook of Education Law*, published by ELA, since 1990. He is on the editorial advisory committee of *West's Education Law Reporter* and is coeditor of the "Education Law Into Practice" section of that journal, which is sponsored by ELA. He is also on the editorial boards of several other education journals.

In recognition of his contributions to the field of education law, Osborne was presented with the McGhehey Award by ELA in 2008, the highest award given by the organization. He is also the recipient of the City of Quincy Human Rights Award, the Financial Executives Institute of Massachusetts Principals Award, the Junior Achievement of Massachusetts Principals Award, and several community service awards.

Osborne spends his time in retirement writing, editing, and working on his hobbies, genealogy and photography. He and his wife Debbie, a retired elementary school teacher, enjoy gardening, traveling, attending theater and musical performances, and volunteering at the Dana Farber Cancer Institute in Boston.

ABOUT THE
VOLUME EDITOR

Thomas J. Lasley, II is executive director of Learn to Earn Dayton at the Dayton Foundation and a professor at School of Education and Allied Professions at the University of Dayton. From 1998 until 2010, he served as dean at School of Education and Allied Professions, University of Dayton. He completed his baccalaureate (1969), master's (1972), and doctoral degree (1978) at the Ohio State University. Lasley has published in excess of 70 articles in professional journals and also has published a wide variety of op-eds in both regional and national newspapers (*Education Week, Columbus Dispatch,* and the *Dayton Daily News*). He has authored or coauthored 13 books. He was instrumental in helping cofound the Dayton Early College Academy, which is a unique educational partnership between the University of Dayton and the Dayton public schools, and was the first early college of its type in the state of Ohio. He serves on a variety of nonprofit boards or committees including Think TV Network (education chair), Dayton Digital Technology High School (president of the board), the United Theological Seminary (trustee), the Ohio College Access Network (chair), Young People Succeeding (co-champion), and The Ohio Early College Association (executive director).

ABOUT THE CONTRIBUTORS

Susan R. Bodary is a partner with Education First Consulting and a nationally recognized education policy expert. She has spent her career working at the local, state, and national levels to advance college and career readiness, college completion, STEM (science, technology, engineering, and math) talent development, and a 21st-century workforce readiness.

Elizabeth Lasley Cameron received a BA in integrated language arts from Ohio University and a master's in literature from the University of Dayton. She taught English at Federal Hocking High School in Athens, Ohio, with union representation. She currently teaches English at the Dayton Early College Academy in Dayton, Ohio, a charter and nonunion school.

Kerry C. Coovert is an assistant professor at the University of Dayton. She is currently a member of the Middle Childhood Education Program and works primarily with reading courses and diversity across the curriculum. She has worked with students, teachers, and schools in grades K–12.

Mary E. Diez is professor and dean of the School of Education at Alverno College in Milwaukee, Wisconsin. A former president of the American Association of Colleges for Teacher Education, she chairs the association's task force on teacher education as a moral community.

Daniel Fallon was chair of the education division at Carnegie Corporation of New York. He designed and led Teachers for a New Era initiative. Fallon is professor emeritus of psychology and public policy at the University of Maryland at College Park, where he also served as vice president for academic affairs and provost.

Suzanne Franco is an associate professor in the Educational Leadership department at Wright State University in Dayton, Ohio. Her research interests are school accountability, assessment, teacher preparation, and urban educational leadership. She has worked with value-added scores both on the state level and with individual districts in Ohio.

Martha S. Hendricks is an associate professor of education at Wilmington College. Her research interests include urban education, educational reform, and the development of novice teachers.

Sarah Kelly is a program officer at New Visions for Public Schools in New York City. She has worked for the Boston Teacher Residency program and is a former New York City Teaching Fellow. Kelly has a BA in English from Colgate University and an MEd in secondary English from the City University of New York.

Rodney Kennedy has been the lead pastor at First Baptist Church Dayton since 2003 and is the director of Baptist House of Studies at the United Theological Seminary in Dayton, Ohio. He received his PhD in rhetoric and homiletics and is the author of *The Creative Power of Metaphor* and *Sermons From Mind and Heart.*

Kathryn Kinnucan-Welsch, EdD, is professor and associate dean for Undergraduate Learning and Community Partnerships in the School of Education and Allied Professions, University of Dayton. Her interests include the professional development of teachers, including teacher preparation and instructional coaching as professional development.

Theodore J. Kowalski is the Kuntz Family Endowed Chair in Educational Administration at the University of Dayton. A former school superintendent and college of education dean, he recently received the 2011 Distinguished Service Award from the American Association of School Administrators in recognition of research and scholarly books.

Edward Liu is director of Organizational Learning at Boston Teacher Residency. Formerly an assistant professor of educational administration at Rutgers University, high school history teacher, and founding director of Summerbridge Portland, now writing, Liu is coauthor of *Finders and Keepers: Helping New Teachers Survive and Thrive in Our Schools.*

James W. Mahoney has been an educator for over 35 years and, since 2001, has served as executive director of Battelle for Kids (BFK), a national nonprofit that provides strategic counsel and solutions to educational improvement challenges. BFK partners with school districts to improve student progress, teaching effectiveness, and to recognize teaching excellence.

Jamie Davies O'Leary is a senior Ohio policy analyst and associate editor at the Thomas B. Fordham Institute. She has a master's in public affairs from Princeton University and spent 2 years working in Camden, New Jersey, as a Teach For America teacher.

James L. Olive is an assistant professor in the Department of Leadership Studies at Ashland University. His research areas of interest include the support of marginalized students as well as the intellectual and identity development of all postsecondary students.

Emmy L. Partin is director of Ohio policy and research at the Thomas B. Fordham Institute, overseeing its Ohio-focused education research, policy, and advocacy work. A graduate of The Ohio State University, she previously worked in education policy and public affairs for the Ohio Department of Education and Governor Bob Taft.

William L. Phillis has served as executive director of the Ohio Coalition for Equity & Adequacy of School Funding since April 1992. Previously, he served as assistant superintendent of public instruction for the state of Ohio for 16 years and as a teacher, principal, and superintendent for 18 years. He has written articles on a bimonthly basis for the *Ohio School Law Journal* for about 25 years.

William A. Proefriedt, a former high school English teacher, is professor emeritus at Queens College, the City University of New York (CUNY). He is the author of *High Expectations: The Cultural Roots of Standards Reform in American Education* and presently serves as a mentor in CUNY's Faculty Fellows Publication Program.

C. Daniel Raisch is an associate professor and associate dean in the School of Education and Allied Professions at the University of Dayton. His research interests include school finance, school law, and educational leadership. His consulting interests include strategic planning and administrator and board member relationships. He has published several journal articles and is coeditor of *The Encyclopedia of Educational Reform and Dissent.* He was a public school educator for 30 years, 25 as an administrator and 18 as a superintendent.

Dennis M. Reardon presently serves as a member of the State Board of Education, Ohio. In December 2008, he retired from the Ohio Education Association as its executive director, the position he held since 2001.

Terry Ryan is vice president for Ohio Programs and Policy at the Thomas B. Fordham Institute. He leads all Ohio operations for the Institute and is a research fellow at Stanford University's Hoover Institution. He is coauthor, with Chester E. Finn, Jr. and Mike Lafferty, of *Ohio Education Reform Challenges: Lessons From the Front Lines*, and he coauthored the book *The Unfinished Revolution* with the English educator John Abbott.

Janet Santos, a senior policy research analyst at Jobs for the Future (JFF), conducts research on state policies enabling the development of education models that incorporate college-level courses into secondary school curricula. Before joining JFF, Santos was an intern at the Annenberg Institute for School Reform and served as a program associate at The Education Alliance at Brown University. Santos earned her MA in urban education policy and a BA in history from Brown University.

Philip Smith is a philosopher of education interested in the relationship between education and culture, with particular concern in the tension between the inclinations of individuals to act in their own self-interests and the need to work for the larger interests of the group. Smith has specialized in neopragmatic critiques of John Dewey and the progressive educational tradition. He has taught at The Ohio State University and served as visiting professor at several institutions, including Harvard University.

Tracey R. Smith is a doctoral student and adjunct faculty member at the University of Dayton and a past governor appointed member of the State Board of Education in Ohio. She served on the Ohio Department of Education Achievement Committee, which tackled educational issues and was responsible for the revision of state standards, and the adoption of Common Core standards. She now works at the Greene County Educational Service Center as director of curriculum.

Jesse Solomon, director, Boston Teacher Residency, taught secondary math for 10 years. He founded The Teachers' Institute at City On A Hill, was an instructor at the Harvard Graduate School of Education (HGSE), and is a National Board certified teacher. Solomon holds a BS in mathematics from MIT and an MEd from HGSE.

Sandra A. Stroot is the senior associate dean of the College of Education and Human Ecology, The Ohio State University. Over the last decade, Dr. Stroot's work has targeted education reform initiatives that impact both school and university settings. Most recently, she is working closely with the Ohio Department of Education to help develop a Resident Educator Program, to support beginning teachers during their first 4 years of teaching in the state of Ohio. Dr. Stroot has contributed to over 10 books that focus on teacher education policy and practice, and she has published a wide variety of articles in professional journals. Dr. Stroot is active as an associate editor for two professional publications and on several boards including the Partnering Anthropology with Science and Technology (PAST) Foundation (president) and the Board of Governors for the Phi Delta Kappa Educational Foundation.

Bob Taft received his MPA from Princeton University and his LLD from University of Cincinnati and taught school in Tanzania as a Peace Corps volunteer. He served as governor of Ohio from 1999 to 2007, focusing on standards-based school reform. He is currently a distinguished research associate at the University of Dayton, lecturing on education policy and political science.

Richard W. Van Vleck is president of Oak Point Capital, LLC, and holds a PhD in business administration. He has been engaged in education for 30 years, as board president of an independent K–12 college preparatory school, advisor to an inner-city public high school, consultant to the Ohio Board of Regents, and adjunct professor of business administration at the University of Dayton.

Joel Vargas, vice president at Jobs for the Future (JFF), leads efforts to develop and expand early college designs that prepare underserved students for postsecondary success and research to inform policymakers, intermediary organizations, and advisory groups on policies enabling their development and scale-up. Vargas has authored multiple publications and has been recognized as one of the thinkers in "A Look at Higher Education's Next Generation of Thinkers" by the *Chronicle of Higher Education*. He received an EdD from Harvard Graduate School of Education.

Kate Walsh has served as the president of the National Council on Teacher Quality (NCTQ) since 2002. She previously worked for The Abell Foundation in Baltimore, the Baltimore City Public Schools, and the Core Knowledge Foundation. Her work covers a broad spectrum of educational issues, with a primary focus on the needs of children disadvantaged by poverty and race. Walsh has authored many papers on teacher quality and serves on the Maryland State Board of Education.

Joseph Watras is a professor of Foundations of Education at the University of Dayton. He served in the Peace Corps in Niger, West Africa, and in the Teacher Corps in Honolulu, Hawaii. Among his publications are five books on the history of education. Several of his articles appeared in such journals as *History of Education, Journal of Ethnographic and Qualitative Research, Theory and Research in Social Education,* and *The International Review of Education.*

John White is an assistant professor of social studies education at the University of Dayton. He has published articles and book chapters on the development of international curricula in history and the social sciences and on the history of Catholic schools in the United States.

Shaun C. Yoder is a senior consultant at Education First Consulting, managing multistate projects in STEM education, teacher and leader effectiveness, and school turnaround. A graduate of Anderson University, he previously directed the Ohio Business Alliance for Higher Education and the Economy, an affiliate of the Ohio Business Roundtable, and worked in education policy and public affairs for Governor Bob Taft, the Ohio Board of Regents, and the Ohio Senate. He began his education career as a teacher in Ohio's public schools.

Susan Tave Zelman is vice president for state partnerships for Houghton Mifflin Harcourt. Previously, she served as senior vice president for the Corporation of Public Broadcasting. For 10 years, she was the Superintendent of Public Instruction for the state of Ohio. She is the author of numerous publications that deal with educational policy and practice and the recipient of three honorary degrees.

INTRODUCTION

The standards and accountability debate has been a prominent part of the educational and political landscape for the past several decades. Public faith in schools in the United States has been repeatedly and openly questioned by a wide range of social and educational critics. In the 1950s, that questioning occurred with the launching of the Russian satellite Sputnik: Were we competing with the Russians? In the 1960s, concerns surfaced when sociologist James Coleman and others began to document that public schools were simply not creating equitable opportunities for all young people: Who was responsible for ensuring a quality education for each child? In 1983, the *Nation at Risk* report was released, and politicians asserted that America's public schools were simply not effective: Specifically, were schools in the United States educating young people to be competitive in a globalized world? In 1994, President William J. Clinton signed into law Goals 2000, a document that provided a mandate for defined academic standards and specific performance measures; and in 2002, President George W. Bush promoted and supported the No Child Left Behind (NCLB) law, which for the first time mandated testing in reading and math for every student in grades 4 through 8: What standards and assessments were needed to ensure that all students were making adequate academic progress? Finally, and most recently, the Obama administration promulgated its own educational legislative fix (Race to the Top) to reward states endeavoring to establish strong standards and reward excellent teaching.

All of these efforts were intended to enhance the quality of schools throughout the United States and to create educational conditions where young people could be more competitive with peers, nationally and internationally. Indeed, embedded within the current accountability rhetoric is a strong focus on mitigating the degree to which U.S. students are falling behind their counterparts in other countries. Educational reformers have called for change, and standards and accountability are two of the critical pillars associated with making schools more effective; a third "pillar," but not one to be discussed in this volume, is educational choice. In essence, reformers assert that with academically rigorous standards and with assessment and accountability protocols to measure student progress relative to those standards and with choice, or the parents' right, to determine where a child will be educated and who will teach "my child," the policy ingredients are in place to ensure a more productive and internationally competitive education system.

Reform sounds simple on the surface, but the standards and accountability goals are ones that easily and perhaps necessarily become compromised or impacted by several conditions. Some of those "mitigating" conditions will be discussed here as a means of contextualizing the point–counterpoint essays presented in this volume.

Condition 1: The focus on student achievement limits the ability of policymakers to appreciate and value the social and pedagogically complex nature of the teaching act.

Teaching is an inherently social and moral activity. Teachers interact with students daily, and through each verbal and nonverbal interaction, they both share part of themselves and learn something about their students. With the accountability movement, there has been a concomitant and seemingly necessary fixation on student achievement. To paraphrase Gary D. Fenstermacher and Virginia Richardson (2010), high-stakes accountability negatively impacts a teacher's ability to create the type of social relationships that are necessary for both moral development and democratic understandings.

Schools, in essence, have an important responsibility in terms of cultural transmission, and a critical part of that transmission process is having classrooms within which the moral, aesthetic, and democratic nature of the human experience can be negotiated in thoughtful ways by teachers and students. The emphasis on accountability does not prevent such knowledge transmission, but it does make it potentially more difficult to foster essential social bonds in an environment where high-stakes test performance is premised as the sine qua non of excellence.

Condition 2: The absence of common, universal standards regarding what students should know and be able to do in reading, mathematics, and science, as well as other key disciplinary areas, has created a "proficiency variance."

The No Child Left Behind legislation (2002) mandated that all students evidence proficiency in reading and mathematics by 2014. Such a prescription sounds straightforward, but the reality is that how states define *proficiency* begins to dictate their apparent success in fulfilling the federal mandate. The unintended consequence of the federal prescription (for all children to be proficient) was a move by individual states to "adjust" the proficiency bar. In essence, states began to differentially define what it means to be proficient such that a student in one state, say South Carolina, may have to read or compute at a very different performance level than, for example, a student in Oklahoma.

Unfortunately, the focus on accountability has also often created an emphasis on teacher evaluation approaches that are not healthy from either a policy or a practice perspective. Specifically, some seek to tie the success of a classroom teacher to a single variable: student test scores. As this chapter is being written, the *Los Angeles Times* is under heated criticism for its decision to make public (on August 29, 2010) student test scores as a means of profiling teacher effectiveness. Quite obviously, union leadership was outraged (threatened to strike) because of the *Times'* decision. But, interestingly, the criticism of the practice created some unusual bedfellows (e.g., Rick Hess from the conservative American Enterprise Institute). Hess represents a critical voice about much of what occurs in traditional public schools. He is a choice proponent (recall that "choice" is one of the reform pillars for conservatives) and an advocate for real change in how schools operate and how educational professionals are prepared. But, curiously, he came out rhetorically swinging vis-à-vis the overreliance on Los Angeles's student test data. Instead of using teacher effectiveness data as a tool, Hess asserts that the *Times* treated them as a weapon. In his words,

> sadly, this little drama is par for the course in K-12. In other sectors, folks develop useful tools to handle money, data, or personnel, and then they just use them. In education, reformers taken with their own virtue aren't satisfied by such mundane steps. So, we get the kind of over caffeinated enthusiasm that turns value-added from a smart tool into a public crusade. (Just as we got NCLB's ludicrously bloated accountability apparatus rather than something smart, lean, and a bit more humble.) When the shortcomings become clear, when reanalysis shows that some teachers were unfairly dinged, or when it becomes apparent that some teachers were scored using sample sizes too small to generate robust estimates, value-added will suffer a heated backlash. And, if any states get into this public I.D. game (as some are contemplating), we'll be able to add litigation to the list. This will be unfortunate, but not an unreasonable response—and not surprising. After all, this is a movie we've seen too many times.

Hess and many others would not argue against the use of student test scores as a metric for assessing teacher performance. What they do criticize is an overreliance on test scores such that they become a defining aspect of the teaching act.

What is now evidenced is variability across states in terms of defined standards as well as the degree to which students have to demonstrate knowledge and skills relative to those defined standards. Such variation makes it difficult to determine how one student (e.g., in South Carolina) compares to another student (e.g., in Oklahoma). On state mandated measures, both students might be viewed as proficient. Yet if both students were to take a national metric of performance, such as the National Assessment of Educational Progress (NAEP), then their proficiency might be evaluated quite differently (i.e., South Carolina has strong state proficiency standards; Oklahoma has quite weak ones). As a result, a "basic" level reader in South Carolina may be a "proficient" reader in Oklahoma.

Paul E. Peterson and F. M. Hess (2008) rated three states (Massachusetts, South Carolina, and Missouri) as having world class standards, while other states (e.g., Georgia and Oklahoma) set proficient levels far below the NAEP proficiency requirement.

One very significant variable that will likely mitigate this second "proficiency variance" condition is the push by the National Governors Association and the state education chiefs to promulgate a set of common state academic standards. The standards are referenced by some of the authors in this volume, and clearly, as more states embrace those standards, there will be concomitant efforts to ensure comparable proficiency requirements relative to those standards across the adopting states.

In essence, with the common academic standards, participating states will (or at least should) work together to create comprehensive assessment systems to measure and evaluate student performance (a circumstance that is already emerging with the announcement of the Partnership for Assessment of Readiness for College and Careers, or PARCC), and the emergence of this more comprehensive approach will better ensure that students, regardless of where they live, are exposed to and able to demonstrate the content knowledge and academic skills they need to be academically successful, especially in mathematics and English language arts. The common academic standards are not a silver bullet, but they do represent a chance to mitigate the way in which, up to now, geography has dictated what content students are expected to learn and the degree to which they are expected to learn it.

Condition 3: The inability of traditional teacher preparation programs to prepare an effective teacher for every classroom in the United States.

The focus on quality teaching is not new in American education but the understanding of how important good teachers are to achievement is now a well documented phenomenon. Several decades ago, the popular view was that parents (home environment) served as the most significant predictor of student performance. By the start of the 21st century, however, researchers began to document that though parents influence how much intellectual and social capital a student brings to school, it is teachers who influence the actual amount of academic growth that occurs in the classroom. Highly effective teachers produce real growth (1½ years or more) but ineffective teachers often are unable to produce anything close to one year of academic growth. The research conclusions represent a consensus about the importance of the teacher: Teachers make a difference!

The real controversy has come into play with regard to how to prepare highly effective teachers (and prepare more of them) and how to identify the ineffective teachers (and move them out of classrooms). The solutions proffered on how to prepare better teachers and how to dismiss ineffective ones are filled with practical problems and ideological bias. Conservative reformers often argue for creating more teacher preparation channels (and expanding alternative human capital development options such as Teach For America) while those within the traditional education establishment are characterized as defenders of the extant education monopoly—a monopoly that limits an infusion of human capital into classrooms. For example, there are many educators who assert that deregulation (or even overregulation) will not permit better quality teachers to enter the workforce; they suggest, instead, that change can come from within the system of programs now operating in states and that any effort to "open" credentialing options simply further compromises efforts to have an effective teacher within every PreK–12 classroom in the United States.

There are also calls by reformers for more quality control relative to who enters the teaching field and to what happens to prospective teachers once they enter a teacher preparation program. The Washington, D.C.–based National Council on Teacher Quality has now promulgated a set of standards that directly addresses the idea of attracting and recruiting higher quality candidates into teaching (e.g., students who graduate in the top half of their high school classes). Countries that recently have educationally outperformed the United States (e.g., Finland and Singapore) attribute part of their excellence to the quality of the people they attract into the teaching profession. Finland, for example, draws its teacher talent from the top 5% of the high school graduates; the United States draws disproportionately from the bottom third of the high school graduates.

The debate about how to ensure an effective teacher in every classroom is probably best captured by contrasting the voice of Linda Darling-Hammond (2010), who argued that effective teachers can be prepared (and are probably best prepared) by traditional teacher education programs, to that of Barbara Velton (2010), who extolled the power of the now popular Teach For America (TFA) program.

Darling-Hammond (2010) asserted that quality teachers emerge from quality training and extensive preparation. In her words,

> in Scandinavian countries like Finland, Sweden, Norway, and the Netherlands, all teachers now receive 2 to 3 years of graduate-level preparation for teaching, generally at government expense, plus a living stipend. Typically, this includes a full year of training in a school connected to the university, like the professional development school partnerships created by some U.S. programs, along with extensive coursework in pedagogy and a thesis researching an educational problem in the schools. (p. 45)

Velton and others who argue for TFA assert that such programs work because "recruits" are directly mentored in the specific teaching area for which they will (and eventually do) have classroom responsibility. Traditional programs prepare for generic circumstances: The prospective teacher is trained to teach anywhere the credential qualifies. The TFA approach immerses the neophyte in the culture of the school assignment and, as a result, the TFA teachers are able to more directly apply what they are "short-coursed" pedagogically to use in the situation where they will use it. The traditional candidate is trained for all classrooms that a license applies. As you can see, there is shared concern with preparing highly effective teachers; there is sharp disagreement on how best to accomplish the goal.

Condition 4: The inability of traditional teacher preparation programs to ensure a high quality teacher for our neediest students.

Condition 4 is clearly connected to Condition 3. The inability to ensure the adequate and effective preparation of all new teachers means that some students are not being taught by those on the high end of the professional bell curve. Every parent wants the best possible teacher for his or her child. Unfortunately, there are vast differences in the quality and effectiveness of the classroom teachers in U.S. classrooms: Some teachers create real value-added gains in the students they teach; others are unable to effect such growth.

Part of what readers will see in the essays within this volume includes the very different ways in which policymakers are endeavoring to solve the "quality" issue. As alluded to earlier, those on the ideological right tend to look toward programs such as TFA or the New Teacher Project (TNTP) to infuse talent into U.S. classrooms. For them, quality starts with ensuring that those recruited to teaching have the intellectual abilities to handle the complex demands of teaching. The premium for conservative critics is placed on the intellectual talents of the prospective teacher candidate—the candidate is expected to learn the pedagogical skills *in situ*.

One recent article in the popular press captured this intellectual asset emphasis by declaring that in many respects, it was harder for a Harvard graduate to get into TFA than it was for him or her to be admitted to law school. The research on whether TFA graduates actually foster academic achievement is mixed and, not surprisingly, ideological. Critics of TFA point out that TFAers turn over quickly; one of the few real knowns about teacher quality is that more experienced teachers (regardless of how they received that experience) are more effective than teachers with less experience (especially just 1 or 2 years of experience). In essence, those critical of TFA assert that TFA teachers simply do not have a commitment to the profession and to young people and that they leave before they can really allow their expertise to mature to a point where they can impact the students they teach.

Those within the education establishment (the *traditionalists*) see quality emerging by enhancing the teacher education practices that already are in place. True, they agree that recruiting good candidates is important, but the defenders of traditional teacher education emphasize that with more academically rigorous clinical experiences and with more focused and purposeful disciplinary preparation, quality can be achieved and, more important, the candidates will have a commitment to the profession sufficient to stay in teaching for longer periods of time.

What remains unquestioned by almost all is that students of color and those who are economically challenged are much more likely to have a "prepared" teacher who is unable to create real value-added learning than are those who live in more socioeconomically advantaged circumstances, but the teacher expertise is only one part of the school excellence equation.

The complexities of securing high quality teachers for all students are often an outgrowth of another mitigating condition: the inability to ensure a high quality leader who can create a culture of learning at a school and who can identify effective and ineffective teachers.

Condition 5: The inability of schools to recruit and retain high quality educational leaders compromises efforts to foster educational excellence in schools.

To ensure that quality teachers are in U.S. classrooms, it is imperative that schools have the right administrators in leadership positions. For years, weak teachers have been conveniently moved from school to school because administrators simply did not want either to deal with the paperwork necessary to dismiss a weak teacher or they were unwilling to deal with the concomitant conflict that accompanied efforts to fire an ineffective classroom teacher.

School leadership is essential to the emergence of any quality school. Emerging research commissioned by the Wallace Foundation and conducted by the University of Minnesota's Center for Applied Research and Educational Improvement highlights the significance and attributes of quality school leaders. High performing school principals are instructional leaders who know how to leverage all the professional assets within a school to create programs that make a difference. They also engage in data-driven decision-making protocols to assist them (and their teachers) in thinking through the nature and essence of best classroom practices.

The question confronting policymakers is, how do schools go about securing these high-end principals and what is the best way to educate them? Similar to the circumstance with teacher preparation, there are a range of answers about how best to educate future school leaders. Those within the educational establishment tend to argue for established university-based preparation programs. They would assert that the preparation programs now in place have the capacity and expertise to prepare effective school leaders. Those critical of extant practices argue either for deregulation of the preparation practices or for the use of alternatives that would permit the intellectual talents of those from other disciplinary areas (e.g., business) to bring their unique gifts and abilities to address the complex problems facing schools.

So the question becomes, how can schools secure the best leadership possible and, equally important, how can schools better ensure that quality administrators, once employed, are retained in positions long enough to really make a difference? The Wallace Foundation study (see Samuels, 2010) clearly documents not only the attributes of effective principals (e.g., instructional leaders who can leverage and enhance the talents of all the teaching staff) but also the importance of keeping those leaders in place for extended periods of time.

The essays in Chapter 8 capture some of the controversy around how best to prepare effective school leaders as well as how to better attract and recruit quality talent to school leadership positions.

Condition 6: The inability to fund schools in ways to ensure that every child has access to adequate and sufficient educational resources and opportunities.

Few issues create more debate than whether schools are over- or underfunded. Many from the world of business perceive that for far too long education has been, for example, expanding its administrative infrastructure without concomitantly reducing its costs. Critics argue that the public schools constantly demand more funding but there is a real failure on the part of the schools to show results that justify those costs.

The questions around school funding often revolve around the issue of adequacy. That is, what type of funding is needed to ensure adequate funding for every student? Complicating the answer to this question is the fact that "adequacy" is often contingent on the unique needs of the students being served. A student who comes from an affluent family, who is an independent learner, and who does not require substantial or even any supplementary support services needs one type of funding support from the local school district, while a student who comes from either a poor family in an urban setting or a special needs student in a rural setting might need a very different level of financial support.

In fact, there is a whole set of variables that defines the issue of adequacy. Allan R. Odden and Lawrence O. Picus (2008) identified some significant components to adequacy funding. For example, given what the state expects in terms of curriculum and curriculum delivery, what are the explicit implications in terms of what needs to be provided for students to successfully engage with the learning opportunities provided or, given what level of proficiency a student needs to demonstrate on the state's assessment protocols, what are the implications for what needs to be available in order for each student, except for those who are most significantly and severely disabled, to experience success? In essence, any effort to succinctly define adequacy would meet with failure because adequacy is tied up with a wide variety of issues around what a student needs and what a state expects.

Property taxes continue to produce the largest amount of local revenue for education. As a result, wealthy school districts are advantaged over poor districts; they can simply produce more revenue for the students they educate. Some states adjust formulas to address the differential needs that students bring to the school, but even with those adjustments, there are problems with ensuring that the dollars are available at the level needed for each student to be properly and effectively educated. The problem has been especially acute recently because of state budget deficits across the United States. States have imposed cuts, and those cuts, though impacting all districts, often take away services from students that families with more capital can compensate for by using personal resources. Indiana, for example, recently significantly reduced the delivery of music and art education in response to state budget challenges. Poor families have limited ability to secure, on their own, services of art or music teachers to work with their children. Affluent families, on the other hand, have a choice: They can use personal resources and make a decision to secure assistance when appropriate curricula are not available at or provided by the local school.

As you can see, even in good times, there are challenges associated with making certain that every child has the educational opportunities that a quality educational program provides. In economically difficult times, those challenges are exacerbated, and it becomes even more difficult to ensure anything close to adequate and sufficient resources for educating every child. That said, many conservatives would argue that schools fail to deliver such services simply because they are poorly managed or at least focused too fully on social issues at the expense of basic education programs. You will read two essays in this volume (see Chapter 14) where the authors capture quite cogently these arguments about whether schools have or do not have sufficient funds and whether the resources for adequacy for all children are available to educators and for families.

Condition 7: The "will" to make necessary changes to ensure equity is often compromised by politics of educational policy and practice.

Over the past several decades, education has become increasingly political. The importance of educating young people has always been part of political rhetoric, but in the modern era, the politics of education announced itself with Sputnik in 1957. Americans suddenly felt threatened by the emerging Soviet advantage in the race to space, and everyone frantically looked for answers for why the United States had apparently lost its educationally strategic advantage.

In part, it became a debate between those arguing for student-centered instruction (the progressives using the ideas of John Dewey) and those asserting the need for more teacher-centered and traditional instruction (conservative thinkers such as Hyman Rick or Albert Bector). Joseph Watras (see Chapter 1) captures some of this debate in his description of the shortcomings of accountability efforts and of how the Eight Year Study was used to help identify the best way (student-centered or teacher-centered instruction) to educate students in the United States.

The debate about how best to educate America's children continues to rage today; each U.S. president and every state governor has a clear education agenda. Over the past couple decades, the agenda debate has focused heavily on standards and the need for specifying for teachers what students should learn and when they should learn it. The first President Bush initiated the standards movement in 1989; President Clinton then modified the Bush "agenda" to create Goals 2000 (see D. M. Sadker, M. P. Sadker, & Zittleman, 2008). The goals were ambitious and broad (e.g., the United States will be first in the world in math and science by the year 2000), but they became part of the public school agenda.

The second President Bush transitioned the emphasis on standards to a focus on testing. Besides the With No Child Left Behind (2001) law, the United States legislatively mandated annual testing, academic proficiency for students (as measured by the individual states), report cards to publicly inform communities about each school's progress, and highly qualified teachers in every classroom to ensure curriculum delivery.

The Bush agenda was then "tweaked" by the Obama administration with Race to the Top in 2009. The Obama focus endeavored to make student academic growth (value-added) a clear part of the teacher evaluation process. Highly effective teachers are those who can foster at least 1.5 years' academic growth, and the Obama agenda focused on rewarding states that found ways to identify and even incentivize the work of the best classroom teachers and, concomitantly, to find ways to rid classrooms of those who were ineffective.

As the agendas of different U.S. presidents and state governors have emerged, the political debates about education have become more strident. Union leaders in many states opposed the Obama (Race to the Top) agenda because they decried the emphasis on testing and apparent inability of assessments to be used across all disciplinary areas (e.g., measuring academic growth in music or art would be highly problematic).

As politicians, educators, and policymakers heatedly debate how best to educate America's children, America's children continue to matriculate through schools across the country. The constant policy changes and practice compromises make it difficult for classroom educators to know what to expect and to know how they will be evaluated. The consequence is an education system that fails to meet the standards of practice necessary to ensure that every child receives an adequate and effective education. The question is, are there sufficient dollars available to reform the education system that exists in the United States today even if some of the policy conundrums are successfully addressed?

Condition 8: The inability to engage communities in solving the educational problems for all students who populate schools.

For several decades, the United States has held a dominant position in world economics and politics. Much of that dominance could be attributed to the education system, especially the higher education system, in the United States. Though the quality of K–12 education has been heatedly discussed, the prominence of American postsecondary institutions has gone largely unquestioned.

In fact, since the very beginning of America's efforts to educate every child and Horace Mann's advocacy for the "common school," the United States has confronted a fundamental challenge in terms of educating all its young people. The affluent have, by and large, been served well by the extant system. The offerings provided by schools coupled with the intellectual capital that students bring to school enabled the vast majority of socioeconomically advantaged students to achieve to their potential. The problem confronting educators and policymakers has been how to educate those who come from less privileged backgrounds, regardless of their race or ethnicity.

Education continues to be a key to personal economic success. According to the U.S. Census Bureau (American Community Survey: 2005–2009), of those in the adult U.S. population (25 or older) with less than a high school diploma, 24% live in poverty; for those with an associate's degree (or at least some college) or a higher college degree, 8% and 3.7%, respectively, live below the poverty line.

The achievement gap for students of color as compared to White students continues to be a reality despite significant efforts to reduce academic performance differences. Regardless of what report one accesses in terms of student achievement, the distinct and profound difference between wealthy and poor students or students of color and White students quickly becomes apparent. The result of these differences for poor students and students of color are lower high school completion rates (e.g., 65% of poor children earn a diploma; 91% of the upper income students do so); weaker college preparedness (e.g., 21% of poor children are college ready; 54% of the upper income students are prepared); and college enrollment (e.g., 63% of the poorest students enrolled; 91% of the affluent students matriculate) (see Hoffman, Vargas, Venezia, & Miller, 2007). The problem for the United States is one of available human capital. If it is true that many of the jobs of the future do not even exist now, then it is also quite true that the United States will need a highly educated workforce to adequately address its uncertain future. The jobs of the future may not be well defined, but it is clear that an uneducated and unskilled workforce will not be adequate to address the economic challenges.

The Lumina Foundation has set a goal for 60% of Americans to hold some type of high quality, marketable degree by 2025 (at present, less than 40% hold such degrees). President Obama challenged the country to lead the world in terms of college degrees by 2020. Whether it is the Lumina goal or the president's challenge, the theory of action appears clear: If the United States is going to continue as a world political and economic leader, then it needs to have a well educated population, and achieving that goal means that schools will have to find better ways to educate all students, not just the economically or socially advantaged and not just those who embrace the importance of education. What will be needed are citizens who have the skills to contribute to the social welfare; they cannot be dependent on others for their financial welfare.

SUMMARY

Taken together, these eight mitigating conditions illustrate the complexity of 21st-century education policy and practice. Dealing with those conditions fosters a wide variety of solutions focused on attracting better teachers into classrooms and making schools more accountable for educating all students.

In this volume, you will see through a series of point–counterpoint arguments not only how different educators and policymakers perceive that problems should be addressed but also why they advocate for particular changes. There are no policy silver bullets and few, if any, simple solutions. Rather, there is an inherent complexity to almost every policy position, whether measuring student academic growth or licensing individuals for classrooms who are "well educated" but who lack pedagogical preparation. There are also unintended and unforeseen consequences to many apparently logical policy solutions.

The purpose of this volume is for readers to see the diverse perspective and to then use those diverse views to help shape a more informed personal understanding of what could and should be done to make classroom practices more effective and schools more accountable.

Thomas J. Lasley, II
University of Dayton

FURTHER READINGS AND RESOURCES

Darling-Hammond, L. (2010). Teacher education and the American future. *Journal of Teacher Education, 61*(1–2), 35–47.

Fenstermacher, G. D., & Richardson, V. (2010). What's wrong with accountability? *Teachers College Record* (ID No.: 15996). Retrieved July 2, 2010, from http://tcrecord.org

Hess, R. (2010). *LAT on teacher value added: A disheartening display.* Retrieved August 18, 2010, from http://blogs.edweek.org/edweek/rick_hess_straight_up/2010/08

Hoffman, N., Vargas, J., Venezia, A., & Miller, M. S. (2007). *Minding the gap.* Cambridge, MA: Harvard Education Press.

Lumina Foundation: http://www.luminafoundation.org

National Council on Teacher Quality. (2010). *Rating the nation's education schools.* Washington, DC: Author.

Odden, A. R., & Picus, L. O. (2008). *School finance: A policy perspective.* Boston: McGraw-Hill.

Peterson, P. E., & Hess, F. M. (2008). Few states set world-class standards. *Education Next, 8*(3), 70–73.

Sadker, D. M., Sadker, M. P., & Zittleman, K. R. (2008). *Teachers, schools and society* (8th ed.). Boston: McGraw-Hill.

Samuels, C. A. (2010). *Study: Effective principals embrace collective leadership.* Retrieved July 23, 2010, from http://www.edweek.org/ew/articles/2010/07/23/37principal.h29 html?tkn=TPSFHsBZuHO

Velton, B. (2010). *Learning on other people's kids.* Charlotte, NC: Information Age.

Will educational accountability enhance the ability of schools to foster student academic growth?

POINT: Bob Taft, *University of Dayton*

COUNTERPOINT: Joseph Watras, *University of Dayton*

OVERVIEW

The two essays in this chapter focus on the whole notion of accountability and how it influences and potentially fosters student academic growth and development. Few issues in schooling have been more dominant in the literature over the past decade than educational accountability. There have been multiple "silver bullets" offered by policymakers and pundits, but with all of the rhetorical flourishes, there still continue to be as many questions as there are answers.

One of the most significant mechanisms used in judging the effectiveness of teachers and schools in the United States is testing. How much have students learned, and does the amount they learn correlate with what one would predict they could or should learn during an academic year? Teachers often feel vulnerable because historically there has been considerable misalignment between the taught and tested curriculum, especially in schools or states that rely heavily on standardized tests to assess the quality of teaching and learning that occurs in the classroom. Those advocating for enhanced accountability and testing suggest that such assessment measures are essential in a globalized economy: They maintain that schools in the United States must be competitive and held accountable for the failures of far too many students who clearly are not college and career ready when they graduate from high school.

Those advocating against enhanced accountability assert that tests are an inadequate and insufficient measure of student learning and that far too much time is already being taken to assess what students have or have not learned. The key issue is whether school leaders will be able to enhance student academic growth if more thoughtful and rigorous accountability approaches are implemented by states at both policy and practice levels.

In this chapter, the authors approach the accountability topic from two somewhat different perspectives. In the first essay, Bob Taft (University of Dayton and governor of Ohio 1999–2007) describes the positive impact of accountability on student growth as well as some of the arguments against a strong focus on accountability mechanisms. Taft describes the unique nature of the American school as he also outlines how academic standards and curriculum alignment efforts have the potential to enhance student achievement as well as to potentially close the persistent achievement gap that plagues so many of our nation's schools. At the same time, Taft describes how things such as teaching to the test and an excessive emphasis on reading and mathematics have the potential to compromise the educational integrity of what teachers are attempting to accomplish in classrooms throughout the country.

In the second essay, Joseph Watras (University of Dayton) focuses on educational accountability in a somewhat different fashion. Watras notes that accountability has been part of a real national desire to organize schools more efficiently and in doing that there have been concomitant efforts to measure what was happening in schools as well as to reduce the variations between and among student academic performance within the U.S. classroom. In his analysis, Watras offers a more historical perspective while he describes the multiplicity of efforts that have been evidenced to design educational processes that are more business-like in nature and clearer in terms of outcomes. Watras also focuses on the fact that throughout the past 100 years a wide variety of progressive practices have been put in place to drive schools toward more accountability and enhanced efficiency as he carefully articulates examples of these in the essay.

Taken together, the two essays describe from a policy perspective (Taft's point essay) and a historical and theoretical view (Watras's counterpoint essay) the different ways in which educators in the United States have struggled to make schools more accountable and the outcomes of educational practice more defined. There are two questions that readers should focus on as they read the two essays. First, what specific ideas appear to be emerging that have the potential for helping each young person achieve to his or her full intellectual, social, and emotional potential? Second, from an historical perspective, where have there been successes that would suggest that the current pro-grams such as No Child Left Behind have the potential for truly enhancing the quality of educational practice in the United States?

Thomas J. Lasley, II
University of Dayton

POINT: Bob Taft
University of Dayton

E *ducational accountability* means, first of all, the establishment of clear, state level academic standards defining what students should be able to know and do in each subject area at each grade level. States then set performance levels that students and school systems are expected to meet based on statewide assessments aligned to the standards. As this piece is being written, a majority of the states have embraced common standards in mathematics and English language arts; the action on the part of their states represents real movement toward enhanced national educational accountability.

Schools and boards are held accountable for the performance of their students through published report cards; these report cards have consequences for good or poor performance for schools and students. The latter may include interventions and changes in school management as well as the right for students to attend other public or private schools. In addition, students may be denied high school diplomas for failing to pass state graduation tests.

A POSITIVE IMPACT ON STUDENTS' ACADEMIC GROWTH

Aligned systems of academic standards, assessment, and accountability are one essential component of an effective strategy for raising the bar for student learning, enabling U.S. students to compete with those from other nations and giving all students an opportunity for success after high school.

The standards-based education reform movement is just beginning to gain maturity. Nevertheless, it has already had a positive impact on the academic growth of students.

What Schools Should Be About

School report cards based on state standards and assessments keep educators and the school community focused on their primary mission, which is the academic preparation of students, providing useful, comparable information on how well schools are fulfilling that mission and where they need to improve. The athletic and social aspects of school life remain important, but report cards provide a more relevant indicator of school effectiveness. After all, how should the quality of education be measured other than by the academic performance of students?

Rigor, Relevance, and Consistency of Instructional Content

All 50 states have adopted specific grade level academic standards. These standards provide a level of rigor, relevance, and consistency that often did not exist in prior times when each school and teacher may have had a different idea about what should be taught. The process of creating standards has forced state and local educators to examine what students should master to be successful in college and on the job. Many states have had their standards reviewed by national groups such as Achieve, which has expertise in rigor and relevance.

States continue to upgrade their standards. Achieve reports that 45 states have either aligned their high school standards with college and workplace requirements or are planning to do so. Achieve worked with 14 states to develop a rigorous algebra II end-of-course exam. Finally, as noted earlier, 48 states and territories (Texas and Alaska are the exceptions) are involved in the development of a *Common Core* of state standards in English language arts and mathematics in grades K–12 that will be internationally benchmarked and aligned with college and workplace expectations.

Alignment of Curriculum

It is clear from many studies that school officials have made significant efforts to align their curricula and instruction to state standards in various subjects and that teachers welcome this kind of guidance and consistency in what is to be taught.

For example, teachers at Norfork Elementary, an award winning school in Arkansas, indicate that before state standards, units were not coordinated across grade levels. In one case, a science teacher at the school spent 6 weeks at the end of each year on Greek mythology because it was a topic she liked.

Now, teachers have clearer goals for what to teach and can spell out what they need from their colleagues who teach in lower grades. A study for the Center on Education Policy found that statewide standards led to stronger horizontal alignment among teachers in the same grade and closer vertical alignment across grade levels. A standardized curriculum is also an obvious benefit in urban school districts where 20% to 30% of students may change schools each year.

There is much anecdotal evidence that specific standards have led teachers to revise their curricula and texts to align with the standards and assessments. Teachers increasingly go beyond the textbook, drawing on a variety of materials to tailor courses to meet more rigorous standards. School boards have developed curriculum guides, frameworks, and pacing sequences and mapped curricular materials to the standards.

Closing the Achievement Gap

A central purpose of standards-based reform is to address large achievement gaps in mathematics and reading assessments based on income, race, and ethnicity. As an example, African American and Hispanic 12th graders were reading at the level of the average White 8th grader in 2005, according to the National Assessment of Educational Progress (NAEP). These gaps extend to high school and college graduation rates as well, undermining efforts to provide equal opportunity for all Americans. The federal No Child Left Behind (NCLB) Act, which requires all states to establish educational accountability systems, provides that its goal is "to close the achievement gap . . . so that no child is left behind."

Educational accountability reforms have highlighted the lagging achievement of students with disabilities, English language learners, and low income and minority students. NCLB criteria require assessment data to be disaggregated by these subgroups of students and holds schools accountable for making progress with each subgroup. As a result, educators have higher expectations for students than before and must develop strategies for advancing their learning.

Turning Around Failing Schools

Educational accountability systems established by states better ensure that it is no longer possible for schools to underperform indefinitely without intervention. This is an important change because so many students of color are concentrated predominately in these lower achieving schools.

NCLB law and laws in many states set up a series of consequences for failing schools. For example, NCLB provides that schools failing to meet the *Adequate Yearly Progress* (AYP) assessment for 2 consecutive years must have school improvement plans in place. Further, after AYP is not met for 4 consecutive years, schools must take *corrective action* to replace staff, extend instructional time, or restructure the schools. More severe sanctions are triggered after that. For example, in Florida, Ohio, and Wisconsin, students in persistently failing schools receive vouchers to attend private schools.

Many systems and schools have accessed federal or state monies to intervene in failing schools, receiving assistance for school improvement plans, added training for teachers, increased instructional time in reading and mathematics, or other reforms. However, there is insufficient funding and staffing at state and district levels to provide this help to all schools in need of improvement. There is also lack of data to determine the overall impact of school interventions. Proposed reforms at the federal level would limit interventions to the lowest performing 5% of schools.

Assessments Provide Useful Data to Improve Schools and Instruction

Standardized assessments provide information that can be useful for school improvement. Across the country, there is a new emphasis on data-driven decision making and professional training in the use of data to drive instruction.

Educational leaders have the ability to use assessment data to benchmark the performance of their schools against others with similar socioeconomic profiles and set goals for school improvement. Leaders can also identify and adopt best practices of schools that perform better on state assessments. School reform advocate groups, such as the Education Trust and The Thomas B. Fordham Institute, have used assessment data to identify, describe, and recognize schools with large numbers of low income students who are achieving outstanding academic results. Achievement test results can be helpful in evaluating *school choice* initiatives such as charter schools and school voucher programs.

Test data are used by district leaders to recognize schools that achieve significant gains and to identify schools that need to be reorganized or closed. Data from assessments can be used to evaluate the success or failure of initiatives designed to improve instruction or restructure schools. Data from assessments in the early years of schooling are useful for identifying struggling students early enough in their school careers to intervene and bring them up to grade level.

In most states, principals and teachers can obtain data on the performance of their students on individual test items compared to state averages and look for causes and solutions in cases where large numbers of students gave incorrect answers. Teachers also use assessments to identify gaps in curriculum and instruction and determine where they need to modify their instructional strategies.

Annual standardized testing in reading and mathematics, as required by NCLB in grades 3 through 8, has enabled the use of *value-added* measures, which provide a more powerful lens for viewing student and school performance. Until recently, school rating systems have been based primarily on achievement or how many students may be *proficient* in a subject at a given point in time. Results on this kind of measure tend to be due more to a student's family background than to the effects on learning produced in a school. By contrast, value-added measures compare expected student growth in learning to actual growth over a year's time to isolate the impact of the school (and particularly the teacher) on learning. It becomes possible to determine whether during a school year students are achieving a year's worth of growth in particular subjects and grades. Value-added measures are providing educators with valuable information for designing school improvement strategies.

Research has shown that the quality of the teacher is the most important in-school factor determining the level of student achievement. Value-added information, when properly attributed down to the classroom level, is useful as one factor in evaluating teacher performance and in the effort to make sure that every child has an effective teacher. There is a strong push at the national level, and in a number of states, to require school boards to base teacher evaluations at least in part on the academic performance of their students.

Innovative Practices

Many principals and teachers have responded to the demands of accountability by reforming instructional practices in innovative ways. There has been a strong interest in *assessment for learning,* frequent interim assessments during the school year, followed by reteaching material or regrouping students according to need. Much teacher professional development has covered this topic, as well as how to differentiate instruction, to meet the needs of all students. The development of common standards and assessments has facilitated the formation of *professional learning communities* where teachers work together to share best practices and collaborate on curriculum. School leaders have restructured the academic calendar so that core content areas, such as reading and mathematics, can be taught in more depth while providing teachers with time to analyze assessment results and adapt teaching practices accordingly.

Educational Accountability and Test Score Results

Educational accountability efforts appear to be making a difference: Overall, achievement test results have improved in recent years for students across the United States. The Center on Education Policy (CEP) examined student achievement scores on state reading and mathematics tests from 2002 through 2008, concluding that student achievement in those two subjects had generally increased. For example, CEP found gains in more than 80% of grade levels and subjects at the proficient-and-above levels established by the states. The CEP uncovered fewer gains at the high school level as compared to elementary and middle school levels. Other CEP studies discovered more gains than declines on state tests for minority students, students with disabilities, and English language learners over the same period of time.

Another study reviewing test scores in 66 large urban school districts found significant improvement on state tests in mathematics and reading at 4th and 8th grade levels from the 2000–2001 school year to 2006–2007. Some progress was made in reducing the racial-ethnic achievement gap although urban school achievement remained below average state achievement levels.

Some observers criticized studies that look only at results on state assessments because the rigor of state standards varies widely and some states have reduced the cut scores used to determine proficiency from year to year. Indeed, one of the criticisms of NCLB has been that it allows states to define what it means to be proficient. A more objective measure of student achievement across states is NAEP, which is both rigorous and consistent from year to year and in which all states must participate. Using those data, there is some good news: NAEP results show improvement in reading and mathematics scores for 9- and 13-year-olds when comparing 1994 (reading) and 1996 (mathematics) to 2008 although no significant improvement for 17-year-old students.

For example, the percentage of 4th graders performing at *below basic* (the lowest of three categories) on NAEP in mathematics declined from 36% in 1996 to 18% in 2009 and in reading declined from 40% in 1994 to 33% in 2009. At the 8th grade level, the decline in mathematics was from 38% to 27% and the decline in reading from 30% to 25%. There were corresponding increases in the percentage of students at or above proficient in each subject.

Other studies have examined the effects of stronger accountability systems on student achievement. One study, based on state level NAEP results, concluded that the increase in mathematics achievement was greater in states with stronger systems of educational accountability in place during the 1990s. Another study compared states that had *report card accountability* and *consequences for poor performance* to those that had just report card accountability. It found increases in NAEP scores by students in the former states with stronger accountability systems.

Although minority student scores continue to lag White students by substantial margins, there has been slow but measurable progress in reducing the achievement gap. A study by the Center on Education Policy concluded that the gap in mathematics and reading scores on state assessments narrowed across a substantial majority of grade levels and subjects between 2002 and 2008. NAEP results show that reading and mathematics gaps between White students and both Black and Hispanic students narrowed between the 1970s and 2008. Since 1996, NAEP's results show the gap in reading, but not in mathematics, has narrowed for 9-year-olds whereas it has not narrowed in either subject for 13- and 17-year-olds.

A recent study using NAEP results to compare states with and without strong accountability systems prior to NCLB concluded that NCLB has narrowed the gap for Black, Hispanic, and low income students in 4th grade mathematics and for Hispanic and low income students in 8th grade mathematics.

ARGUMENTS AGAINST EDUCATIONAL ACCOUNTABILITY: A RESPONSE

Teaching to the Test

Some critics charge that standardized assessments result in teaching to the test rather than enabling students to gain the knowledge and abilities they really need. However, this argument misses the principal purpose of assessments that have consequences attached to them—to encourage the teaching of a rigorous curriculum based on state standards that are aligned to what students need to be able to know and do to succeed after high school. Tests should and can be properly aligned to a state's academic standards and test questions can be designed to measure higher order thinking skills as well as basic knowledge. Test questions can also be changed from year to year, so schools can't give students specific answers to specific questions to prepare them for the tests.

Tests can always be improved to measure what matters. Achieve and other groups are working on developing *next generation* assessments to align with the more rigorous Common Core standards that are being adopted by the states.

It is also worth noting that test-taking skills are relevant to later success in life. Selective colleges and graduate schools use standardized testing as part of the admissions process. Passing tests is a part of certification or licensure process for professions such as law and accounting. The armed services and many employers use standardized tests for hiring purposes. Finally, authoritative analyses comparing national achievement among countries confirm the positive impact on learning of standardized, curriculum-based examinations.

Excessive Emphasis on Reading and Mathematics

Insofar as the NCLB requires and a number of states test only in reading and mathematics, some educators contend that other subjects such as science are neglected. In fact, there is evidence that less time becomes available for social studies and the arts when schools spend more time on the basic subjects.

Nevertheless, many states test and rate schools and districts based not only on reading and mathematics but also on science, writing, and social studies. In addition, there are proposals to reform NCLB law to allow states to incorporate other subjects besides reading and mathematics into their assessment and accountability systems for NCLB purposes.

Most important, reading and mathematics are *gatekeeper subjects* whose mastery is essential for the learning of other subjects and also for success in postsecondary education and on the job. It is especially important for schools to spend sufficient time and attention on these subjects in the early years of schooling, which is when most statewide assessments occur. A U.S. Department of Education study found that students not mastering reading and mathematics by the 8th grade are unlikely to become proficient in them by the end of high school.

Adverse Impact on Certain Students

When schools are rated based on the percentage of students scoring above specific proficient scores, there could be a tendency for schools to pay more attention to students who are close to that score, neglecting both advanced and lower performing students. A 2010 study by the Center on Education Policy, however, found no strong evidence that NCLB is having that kind of effect. Moreover, a number of states rate schools based not only on the percentage of students who are proficient but also on value-added measures and performance indexes, which reflect the achievement gains of all students.

The Dumbing Down of Standards

Some studies have concluded that NCLB sanctions have had the effect of encouraging some states to weaken their standards or lower the cut scores that define *proficiency*. This result appears to be a legitimate criticism of NCLB. However, as noted above, almost all states (48) are involved in the Common Core standards initiative, which includes a commitment by states to adopt more rigorous expectations for mathematics and language arts.

In addition, federal reform proposals would eliminate the unrealistic target of 2014 set by NCLB as the date by which all students in all states must be proficient. This reform would reduce the incentive for states to lower standards and cut scores.

As can be seen, educational accountability is a complex and highly debated topic. The whole issue revolves around how to ensure that every child graduating from every school has the same chance of success in life. To ensure equal opportunity for all students, educators must have in place clear and common expectations of what students should know and also have implemented the assessments to ensure that those expectations are met. Making teachers and schools accountable for results is an important and necessary step toward educational excellence in American education.

COUNTERPOINT: Joseph Watras
University of Dayton

Employers use some assessment method to determine how well their employees perform. Although this statement represents accountability, it does not indicate the many aspects that the term may include. Insofar as the aim of assessment is to ensure that workers are productive, the process may include determining that the rewards for individuals depend on their accomplishments. In some schemes, employers may try to help ineffective workers learn better skills. In other cases, accountability may extend to some verification of the worth of the product.

Educators have used many forms of accountability. Throughout the 20th century, the movement toward accountability was part of the progressive desire to organize schools more efficiently. For a group of administrative progressives, this meant that school leaders had to take on practices found among successful business corporations. The problem was that the business model, and the measurements it encouraged, tended to reduce the acceptable variations in education that often create a misplaced emphasis on issues such as efficiency.

ACCOUNTABILITY AS EFFICIENT ORGANIZATION

In the latter half of the 19th century, people adopted new ideas about democracy and about the proper roles of government. Before the American Civil War, people resisted state control of schools because they considered the autonomy of their communities to be the best protection of democracy. After the War, they began to look to larger organizations such as state and national governments to introduce modern managerial forms that promised to treat people equitably.

People changed their attitudes because the conditions of their lives had changed. After the Civil War, the United States spread across the continent, and rural communities gave way to industrial cities. One result of these changes was the growth of large corporations. These enormous trusts introduced methods of managing the manufacture and the distribution of their products. Some of these corporations, such as U.S. Steel, instituted factory methods that eliminated the need for skilled labor, which resulted in lower wages for the workers. Because the corporations did not need workers with special skills, the laborers found it difficult to form unions. The corporations claimed these changes led to lower prices for consumers; however, critics argued that these corporations produced inferior goods, distributed tainted foods, and polluted the environment. At any rate, the corporations made enormous profits.

As the 19th century ended, people turned to state and federal governments to restrain corporations. The results included the creation of the Interstate Commerce Commission in 1887 and the Sherman Antitrust Act in 1890. In the following years, progressive politicians tried to reduce social problems by using the corporations' methods of organization. The hope was ironic because it implied that there were technical or bureaucratic solutions to technical or bureaucratic problems.

School superintendents thought that they could solve educational problems if they imitated the patterns of organization found in large corporations. The first effort was to consolidate leadership in the hands of an expert, namely, a school superintendent, but it was an effort that met with mixed success. For example, although there were only 29 city superintendents in the United States by 1870, there were 226 cities with populations exceeding 8,000 people. In a short period, most city schools started to turn to some form of central organization. By 1927, the *Educational Directory* listed nearly 3,000 superintendents of city schools.

As the office of superintendent gained popularity, school superintendents agreed that city school districts should follow scientific methods of operation to prevent waste and ensure the best education of the children. The second step was to divide the school districts into departments with specially trained experts in charge of the various aspects. For example, in 1895, the National Educational Association's (NEA's) Committee of Fifteen endorsed dividing city school officials into two central departments. One department would supervise business affairs, and the other department would ensure that classroom instruction followed a scientific basis. The report recommended that for schools to operate efficiently, the superintendents of these departments had to have adequate authority and demonstrate quick public accountability.

According to the NEA report, the superintendent of instruction had to ensure that teachers carried out instruction in professional ways. This meant that the personal wishes or biases of the board members or the community leaders could not influence the selection of teachers; however, the board could state the qualifications that prospective teachers must meet and ask the superintendent of instruction to create a list of candidates for teaching who qualified. The criteria should include a course of 4 years in a city high school, an examination by the board of examiners, and a year's course in the city's teacher training school. Once the superintendent of instruction selected the teachers, he or she had responsibility to supervise their work or assign assistants to conduct the surveillance, with particular attention to such qualities as neatness, teaching power, reliability, and amiability.

Universities adopted courses of teacher training that facilitated the desires of superintendents to move toward the efficient operation of schools. For example, in 1918, Charles Judd, head of the Department of Education at the University of Chicago, removed courses in the history of education and philosophy from the curriculum. In their place, he introduced courses in the scientific study of education. Judd (1934) argued that school administrators had to understand the scientific study of education if they were to make decisions to improve education. He complained that in many districts, lay board members had control over such issues as school building design, selection of texts, and the working conditions of teachers. The problem was that these lay people refused to make decisions based on expert knowledge. The solution was for school administrators to have the freedom to make decisions based on systematic, scientific studies of education. Judd intended to give them training in those areas, and he began assigning graduate students to find the most effective ways of teaching various subjects.

To ensure that teachers taught school subjects in efficient and effective ways, the NEA created three committees on the Economy of Time in Education. They published reports in 1913, 1916, and 1918. These committees tried to determine which courses would enable students to contribute to life in a democracy, what the content of those courses should be, and how teachers should carry out the instruction.

These studies resulted in several curriculum innovations. For example, in 1916, W. W. Charters reported his work in determining the minimum essentials in grammar instruction. He found studies that listed the most common errors students made. After arranging the errors in order of frequency, Charters (1917) classified them according to type. He asked teachers to consider which facts the students should learn to correct those errors. In this way, he had the teachers select the curriculum that would help their students speak and write grammatically correct English.

The studies on the economy of time in education (on enhanced educational accountability) did not improve instruction except in trivial ways. According to Ellen Condliffe Lagemann (1989), this difficulty permeated educational research. Surveying the development of educational research, Lagemann noted that John Dewey developed an innovative idea that connected educational research with important social changes. Although some educators were enamored of Dewey's ideas, Lagemann contended that most educators disliked Dewey's idea of education. Although scholars in philosophy, sociology, and social psychology believed that education could advance democracy, Lagemann found that most public elementary and secondary school educators believed that educational scientists such as Edward Lee Thorndike would discover the ways to tailor instruction to the psychology of the child and to transmit those insights to teachers. She concluded that scientists such as Thorndike turned the study of education into a technical field separated from philosophy. Since the researchers were to work separately from the teachers, Thorndike's model replaced the idea of a sharing community among educators and ultimately reinforced the inferiority of education as a field and, concomitantly, implicitly created the notion of schools as places in need of "control" or accountability.

When Lagemann (2000) tried to explain why school administrators tended to imitate corporations, she thought that sexism played an important role. The researchers like Judd and Thorndike were men, and they hired graduate students who were men. The teachers were women, and they were supposed to follow the methods of instruction discovered by the male researchers; they needed to be supervised and "controlled."

Other commentators found different reasons to explain why school administrators embraced ideas that did not match the educational needs of the community. For example, George Counts (1922/1969) surveyed the social composition of school board members. The typical city school board had six members. Counts found that, oftentimes, one member was a woman, usually a homemaker. The other five were professional men such as bankers, lawyers, physicians, or business executives. Occasionally, one member was a salesperson, a clerk, or a laborer. From his survey, Counts contended that the business elite controlled city schools. It was reasonable to think they would select superintendents who followed their ways of thinking and would create schools that were focused on efficient results rather than the development of the whole child.

A student of Counts, Raymond E. Callahan, agreed that educators adopted the business mentality; however, he suggested another reason for the dominance of this mind-set. When Callahan began his research, he wondered why educators adopted business practices. Schools were not factories, and education was not a business. Nonetheless, because city schools were large operations, Callahan thought it reasonable for administrators to borrow some ideas from large corporations. As he finished his research, he was surprised at how strongly school administrators held to the business ideology. He could not find among them any sense of professional autonomy. According to Callahan, school administrators were extremely vulnerable to public criticism. They surrendered to business models to protect themselves and to appease their critics. After all, he noted, school administrators had to seek approval of property taxes to fund the schools. Public disapproval could lead to financial problems. Implicitly, the need for accountability grew because public approval was needed.

Callahan argued that when school administrators tried to make instruction efficient, they found themselves adopting practices that saved money but made it difficult for students to learn. An obvious example was class size. Because teachers' salaries dominated the budget, larger classes offered cost efficiency. Further, experts claimed that effective teaching could take place with large classes as well as with small ones. While teacher associations resisted these changes, educational researchers undertook studies that showed, for example, student achievement in classes of 50 students equaled the levels of achievement in classes of 20. Other researchers recommended changing the training of teachers to facilitate their instruction of large classes.

Although Callahan described educational administration as a mindless, imitative field, he pointed to prominent school administrators who were exceptions. Notable among these exceptions was Jesse Newlon who had been superintendent of Denver Public Schools in Colorado, president of the NEA, and a professor at Teachers College. As a member of the Commission on the Social Studies created by the American Historical Association, Newlon wrote a major text, *Educational Administration as Social Policy.* Callahan added that Newlon was unable to turn educational administration into a substantive field despite his many efforts in that direction.

As superintendent in Denver, Newlon attracted national attention by involving teachers in curriculum development. He appointed committees of teachers to revise courses of study, and he gave them time during the school day to perform the work. Although Newlon left Denver schools in 1927, his innovations remained in place. According to Craig Kridel (1999), it was the innovations that Newlon brought to Denver that caused the Progressive Education Association (PEA) to include those schools in the organizations' influential Eight-Year Study in 1932.

Progressive education had an ambivalent influence on education and business ideals. Yet the Eight-Year Study offered the best proof that effective education was a democratic affair. It did not derive from efforts to regiment schools or from an effort to find the best practices for all teachers to follow or, one could extrapolate, to make them more accountable.

The Eight-Year Study began in 1930 when 200 members of the PEA met in Washington, D.C., to discuss ways to bring about changes in high school programs. According to the director of the project, Wilford M. Aikin, the members of the PEA felt they had succeeded in opening elementary schools to opportunities for more student freedom and activity. They believed the secondary schools remained more subject matter oriented and controlled by business ideals. Thinking the difficulty was the desire of high school teachers to prepare students for college entrance, the PEA secured agreements from more than 300 colleges to accept the graduates from high schools participating in the study who had the recommendation of the high school principal and who presented some record of abilities such as scores on aptitude tests.

In 1932, the directing committee recruited schools from every section of the country to participate in the study. The range of educational policies in the schools extended from conservative to radical. Fourteen were public schools or entire public school systems, and 16 were private. Since the public schools were usually large and could include an entire district, the majority of the students in the study attended public schools.

The study involved many aspects and many prominent educators. A Study of Adolescents explored the needs of youth as a basis for curriculum theory. Subcommittees for curriculum areas generated instructional ideas and involved teachers in summer workshops where they considered if or how the curricula could fit their situations. One famous educational researcher, Ralph Tyler, worked with the evaluation staff to seek ways to measure the results of curriculum innovations.

The design of the evaluation was simple even if the process was difficult. The team matched the students from the schools involved in the study with similar students from traditional high schools and compared their success in college. In all cases, the results were favorable; however, the most radically organized schools enjoyed the most success. In these radically organized schools, students had the freedom to choose their own activities, to pursue them under the leadership of teachers, and to share their accomplishments with the entire school. This early research indicated that the freedom to choose, a basic democratic tenet, took precedence over the need to make all schools the same, with common standards and assessments.

One of the most successful and most radical schools was the Ohio State University school. In this lab school, the subject matters had little separate identity. In general, the students enrolled in core courses that included several subject matters related in functional ways. Not only did the students work cooperatively on these projects, but the administrators, the counselors, the teachers, and the parents worked also in cooperative, democratic relationships. In addition to frequent conferences among these parties, faculty representatives served on more than 12 committees that took responsibility for various areas of governance. Even student evaluation involved a medley of measures. Organized in cumulative folders, the measures included records of accomplishments, performance on achievement tests, anecdotal records of teachers, and reactions of parents.

Although historians disagree on the influence of the Eight-Year Study, Daniel and Laurel Tanner contended that the study continued as a positive force in educational literature through the 1990s. They found three reasons for the extensive vitality of the study. First, up to that time, it was the only comprehensive longitudinal experiment in U.S. education. Second, it focused on the perennial problem of developing a curriculum that served students' needs and met the function of general education. Third, the study buttressed subsequent movements such as the tendency to use evaluation as a means of improving teaching and curriculum development.

ACCOUNTABILITY AND SCHOOL IMPROVEMENT

In recent years, the influence of the federal government has repeated the errors of educators who pursued the ideal of efficiency without limits. According to Donna A. Breault (2010), the problems arose through the reauthorization of the Elementary and Secondary Education Act as No Child Left Behind (NCLB). Breault claimed that the measures of accountability sought to close the achievement gap between students from low income homes and those from comfortable families.

The NCLB law requires state departments of education to identify standards of achievement in areas such as mathematics, reading, and science and the level of improvement that would qualify as adequate yearly progress. Failure to meet this level of performance would bring about various sanctions. School officials might have to allocate more resources to the students from low income families. The faculty might have to implement a new curriculum model, or the administrators might have to replace faculty members. Breault also complained that the NCLB program required that textbook publishers develop curriculum according to scientifically based principles. This meant that the publishers had to conduct empirical tests to determine the effectiveness of the materials.

This model of accountability repeated the desires of educators such as Judd or Thorndike who wanted to locate the best practices and diffuse them through the schools. It is a model based on the view that teachers determine what students learn. Although teachers might be influential, students have their own aims, and they vary within a school building or a state system of education. The trick is for students to fulfill their aims in ways that open them to the many opportunities to learn and grow in a democratic society.

The Eight-Year Study offered a way to work around these problems. Instead of teaching children specific subject matter, the Ohio State University school taught them how to learn. In the process, the students learned a great deal of subject matter. Those results might not appear on standardized achievement tests, but they did appear in the students' abilities to be socially sensitive, self-confident, and to think critically. Those skills are just as important today, perhaps more so, than they were 80 years ago. They were skills developed not by heavy-handed federal and state accountability mechanisms but by thoughtful teachers who knew how to help students explore their own intellectual interests.

FURTHER READINGS AND RESOURCES

Breault, D. A. (2010). Accountability. In C. Kridel (Ed.), *Encyclopedia of curriculum studies* (Vol. 1, pp. 3–5). Thousand Oaks, CA: Sage.

Callahan, R. E. (1962). *Education and the cult of efficiency: A study of the social forces that have shaped the administration of the public schools.* Chicago: University of Chicago Press.

Center on Education Policy. (2009). *Is the emphasis on "proficiency" shortchanging higher- and lower-achieving students?* Washington, DC: Author.

Charters, W. W. (1917). Minimum essentials in elementary language and grammar. In H. Wilson (Ed.), *The sixteenth yearbook of the National Society for the Study of Education: Part I. Second report of the committee on minimum essentials in the elementary school.* Bloomington, IL: Public School.

Counts, G. (1969). *The social composition of school boards.* New York: Arno Press. (Original work published 1922)

The Education Trust. (2009). *Ed trust honors schools with dispelling the myth awards* (Press Release). Washington, DC: Author.

Evers, W., & Walberg, H. (Eds.). (2002). *School accountability.* Stanford, CA: Hoover Institution Press.

Fordham Institute. (2010). *Needles in a haystack: Lessons from Ohio's high-performing, high-need urban schools.* Columbus, OH: Thomas B. Fordham Institute.

Judd, C. H. (1934). *Education and social progress.* New York: Harcourt, Brace.

Kridel, C. (1999). Jesse Homer Newlon. In R. J. Altenbaugh (Ed.), *Historical dictionary of American education.* Westport, CT: Greenwood Press.

Lagemann, E. C. (1989). The plural worlds of educational research. *History of Education Quarterly, 29*(2), 185–214.

Lagemann, E. C. (2000). *An elusive science: The troubling history of educational research.* Chicago: University of Chicago Press.

National Center for Education Statistics. (2009). *The nation's report card: Trends in academic progress in reading and mathematics 2008.* Washington, DC: U.S. Department of Education.

Tanner, D., & Tanner, L. (1990). *History of the school curriculum.* New York: Macmillan.

Thernstrom, A., & Thernstrom, S. (2003). *No excuses: Closing the racial gap in learning.* New York: Simon & Schuster.

Will common academic standards make the United States more educationally competitive?

POINT: Terry Ryan, *Thomas B. Fordham Institute*
COUNTERPOINT: John White, *University of Dayton*

OVERVIEW

In recent years, debate has raged about the efficacy of national "common" standards for schools. Some asserted that such common standards were essential to ensuring the international competitiveness of American schools. Others argued that such nationalizing of the curriculum would compromise the autonomy of local school districts. At present, the local and state control of the curriculum have created a circumstance where students in different states and different communities within those states quite literally have varied expectations about what to learn and what proficiency levels are required means relative to defined curriculum outcomes.

The focus on the Common Core State Standards Initiative is being led by the National Governors Association Center for Best Practices and the Council of Chief State School Officers. The intention is to create K–12 standards with common academic expectations across the 50 states. As of this writing, most states have adopted them, but several states had still not moved to adopt them for a variety of reasons. Advocates for the standards view them as a way to align K–12 and college–workforce expectations. In recent years, more attention has been given to whether students are really college and career ready. One mechanism for ensuring the preparedness of all students is the adoption of standards designed to mitigate the influence of geography. In other words, the geographic location of a school in a globalized economy should not dictate what teachers and administrators expect of students.

In essence, can the United States be competitive globally if some form of common academic curriculum across the states does not exist? That question is answered in quite different ways by educators and policymakers across the country. In this chapter, readers will be able to see two very different opinions to address the question.

In the first essay, Terry Ryan, vice president of the Thomas B. Fordham Institute, asserts that common standards are an essential ingredient to a quality education system. The common curriculum and clearly defined standards across states, Ryan maintains, is a prescription for improved educational opportunities for all children. Ryan believes that with common standards it will no longer matter, at least to the degree evidenced in the past, where a child is educated because defined standards across regions and states will enable educators to structure learning experiences and expectations that are not geographically or demographically dependent. True, high standards will not guarantee student academic excellence, but Ryan argues that they will create a foundation on which more common learning experiences can be created and those common learning experiences should translate into more students who are college and career ready at the point of their high school graduation.

John White (University of Dayton) does not object to the idea of common standards but rather contends that there are simply too many mitigating factors that will compromise any efforts to implement the standards effectively. The notion of a Common Core is not new. White carefully outlines the historical record to illustrate the number of ways in which "thought" leaders in this country have attempted to create a common curriculum for students in the United States. He also documents the different ways in which research fails to support the ability of common standards to achieve the type of goals that proponents find so compelling. Finally, he documents the political process that has evolved and ultimately that resulted in the current focus on Common Core standards, now embraced by over 40 states. White's conclusion is that the Common Core will politicize education; the Common Core will not result in significant enhanced student performance and student achievement.

As you read the arguments for and against the common academic standards, consider these questions: What is the best way to ensure that all students are prepared to compete academically and professionally in a globalized economy? And, even if common standards emerge, what problems surface as educators seek to assess what students know relative to defined standards?

Note: For more information on the assessment issue, readers are encouraged to Google the Partnership for the Assessment of Readiness for College and Careers, or PARCC.

Thomas J. Lasley, II
University of Dayton

POINT: Terry Ryan
Thomas B. Fordham Institute

Will common academic standards make the United States more educationally competitive? Absolutely, if the standards are strong, rigorous, clear, coherent, and consistent and if states develop and implement assessment systems that are well aligned to these higher standards. In fact, getting academic standards right—specifying the knowledge and skills that teachers should teach and children should learn—is at the heart of just about everything that matters in K–12 education. Standards wield significant influence over what happens inside classrooms, and high quality academic standards that are the same across state lines offer the best shot at ensuring quality education for all American students whether they live in Massachusetts, Ohio, or Oregon.

Or as Mike Feinberg and Dave Levin (2009), the founders of the high performing Knowledge Is Power Program (KIPP) network of schools wrote for *The Washington Post* in early 2009,

> perhaps the single greatest lever for raising expectations and achievement for all children in America would be the creation of national learning standards and assessments. With KIPP schools operating in 19 states, we have seen how the maze of state standards and tests keeps great teachers from sharing ideas, inhibits innovation, and prevents meaningful comparison of student, teacher and performance. (p. A17)

The basic idea here is simple. States specify what students need to know by subject and grade, instructional programs are built around those standards, teachers teach to the standards, and schools, teachers, and students are held accountable for meeting the standards through annual testing. Where this is done well, student achievement has gone up.

Massachusetts, for example, committed itself to dramatically raising its academic standards in the 1990s and to holding its teachers and students accountable to these new standards through rigorous testing. Student achievement in Massachusetts soon surpassed that of any other state, and by 2007, the math scores of Bay State 4th graders rivaled those of traditionally top scoring Taiwan and Japan on the world's largest assessment of international achievement, the Trends in International Mathematics and Science Study (TIMSS). These results were so impressive that many refer to it as the "Massachusetts education miracle."

Even so, the United States has been plagued by a patchwork of 50 different state standards. A few states such as Massachusetts and Indiana have excellent standards but most have mediocre to weak ones. The Thomas B. Fordham Institute rated the nation's varied state academic content standards in 2006 and 31 states received a C, D, or F for their English standards while 46 states were graded C or below in mathematics.

The situation gets worse. These weak academic standards have been supported by assessment systems that inflate student achievement scores, so it looks like our children are learning more than they actually are. Consider the achievement results from one state, Ohio. In 2009, 72% of 8th graders in Ohio were proficient in reading based on the state's test, but they were only 37% proficient according to the National Assessment of Educational Progress, the so-called nation's report card. Doesn't this fact suggest a clear need for reform?

U.S. Secretary of Education Arne Duncan (2009) captured the challenge concisely when he told a gathering of governors the following:

> Common sense also tells you that kids in big cities like Newark and San Francisco, or small towns like Tarboro, North Carolina, are no different from each other. Standards shouldn't change once you cross the Mississippi River or the Rocky Mountains. Kids competing for the same jobs should meet the same standards. . . . We need standards that will get them ready for the day after graduation. That means they must be rigorous. Today, our standards are too low and the results on international tests show it. Worse yet, we see the signals in the international economy as more and more engineers, doctors, and science and math Ph.D.s come from abroad.

THE COMMON CORE

The need for some form of national standards has been obvious to education reformers since at least 1959 when President Dwight D. Eisenhower called for "national goals" in education, including "standards." By the late 1990s, both President George H. W. Bush and President Clinton had suggested them. Politics killed these earlier attempts because the political right opposed the notion of *national* and the left despised *standards.*

As the *New Republic* opined in early 2010, "for decades conservatives deployed their usual ideological objections to all things federal, and they especially worried that national education standards would give Washington an excuse to force liberal ideas on students. Meanwhile, on the left, teachers' unions feared that national standards would mean (gasp) more accountability and less autonomy for educators."

Despite such political headwinds, Chester E. Finn, Jr. and my colleagues at the Thomas B. Fordham Institute have been making the case for national standards for more than a decade. But as recently as 2006, there was serious doubt that such an effort could actually launch. In a report titled *To Dream the Impossible Dream: Four Approaches to National Standards and Tests for America's Schools*, its authors Chester E. Finn, Jr., Liam Julian, and Michael J. Petrilli observed,

> Two large obstacles loom. The first is political: a winning coalition must be assembled, probably a presidential contender—no small change, considering that the failed attempts of the 1990s to create national standards and tests left a bad taste in many politicians' mouths. The second obstacle is substantive: until policymakers can envision what a system of national standards and tests might look like, how it would work, and how its various logistical challenges might be addressed, this idea will remain just that. (p. 1)

In June 2010, the dream came closer to reality with the release of the Common Core standards in English language arts and mathematics. That effort was led by the National Governors Association and the Council of Chief State School Officers. The Common Core effort emerged from the states themselves and was developed using the expertise and input of a wide variety of education stakeholders and content experts. The speed at which all of this happened was nothing short of astonishing, as were the political alliances and shifts along the way. Walter Isaacson (2009) described the import: "Common, coherent, grade-by-grade standards promote effective professional development . . . A shared understanding of what students should know and be able to do enables the best kind of professional development: collegial efforts to share best practice." By the end of 2010, it was expected that at least 41 states would voluntarily have adopted the Common Core standards.

Despite such support from a variety of state leaders, conservative critics argued the Common Core was a move toward the nationalization of public education and would ultimately result in states and communities losing control of their schools. They pointed to the Obama administration's use of the Race to the Top competition to twist the arms of states to sign up to the Common Core standards or risk not receiving the competitive federal grant dollars. David Shreve from the National Conference of State Legislatures captured the angst when he told *The Wall Street Journal,* "The history of the federal government is to take something good and co-opt and corrupt it. . . . The whole idea of this as a national effort directed by the federal government scares a lot of our members" (see Branchero, 2010, "Governors Group").

At least one state, Virginia, subsequently dropped out of the Common Core effort because its education leaders feared federal intrusion into what they were doing, and they wanted to maintain their state's independence. State education leaders in Texas and Alaska raised similar concerns in explaining why they weren't signing up for the Common Core effort. Specifically, states' education leaders initially bought into the idea but then began to have concerns about federal intrusiveness and loss of local control.

BETTER STANDARDS

Despite the concerns of a federal takeover of public education that were stoked by the Obama administration's efforts to tie federal dollars to the adoption of common standards, the Common Core deserved support as long as the standards were actually an improvement over current state standards and the states (representatives) themselves continued to lead and own the effort at the state level.

Sheila Byrd Carmichael, W. Stephen Wilson, Gabrielle Martino, Chester E. Finn, Jr., and others (2010) at the Thomas B. Fordham Institute summed up the opportunity cogently:

> The Common Core represents a rare opportunity for American K–12 education to re-boot. A chance to set forth, across state lines, a clear, ambitious, and actionable depiction of the essential skills, competencies, and knowledge that our young people should acquire in school and possess by the time they graduate. Most big modern nations—including our allies and competitors—already have something like this for their education systems. If the U.S. does it well and if—this is a big if—the huge amount of work needed to operationalize these standards is earnestly undertaken in the months and years to follow, this country could find itself with far-better educated citizens than it has today. Many more of them will be "college- and career-ready" and that means the country as a whole will be stronger, safer, and more competitive. (p. 1)

Still, are the Common Core standards better than current state standards? For most states, the answer is yes. According to a review by national experts commissioned by the Fordham Institute in July 2010, the Common Core standards "are clearly superior to those currently in use in 39 states in math and 37 states in English. For 33 states, the Common Core is superior in both math and reading" (Carmichael, Martino, Porter-Magee, & Wilson, 2010, p. 3).

Three jurisdictions had English standards that were superior to the Common Core: California, Washington, D.C., and Indiana. Eleven states had

English standards that were of equal quality to those of the Common Core, and in math, 11 states and the District of Columbia had standards that were "at least as clear and rigorous as the Common Core standards" (p. 3).

The Common Core standards as promulgated appear deeper, more specific, and more cogent than most state academic standards. They are well grounded on what students will need in order to be successful in college and in a career. In the language of current reform efforts, the new K–12 common core standards will better ensure that students are college and career ready. This is good for both young people and their futures and for the health of our nation over-all as shared higher standards will surely make our citizens more competitive in the global economy in years and decades to come.

CONCLUSION

For millions of children across the United States, the Common Core standards set the stage for improved educational opportunities. Even high achieving states like Massachusetts are apt to benefit from the Common Core. David P. Driscoll, former Massachusetts commissioner of education and a key player behind that state's education miracle, sensibly penned for *The Boston Globe,* "Massachusetts will benefit from these common standards, and their rollout will end the injustice some children face in schools that follow standards that are much lower and less challenging. Their adoption will set the basis for a strong common assessment that will allow us to compare our progress against other states and learn—state by state, city by city, and school by school—those areas in which we need to improve."

High academic standards do not automatically translate into stronger student performance. These higher standards must be matched with aligned and well designed assessments, rigorous accountability systems, aligned curricula, and a serious commitment on the part of states to ultimately hold their schools, teachers, and students accountable for mastering these higher standards. For example, education leaders of the states have to have the political wherewithal to actually hold back students that don't meet the standards, and such political fortitude has been lacking in most states in recent years.

At the same time, states need to build the support systems required to help schools, teachers, and students meet these higher standards. The process for developing the Common Core was driven by the states, and in going forward, strong state ownership and investment will be necessary for the effort to lead to shared assessments and even common curricula, textbooks, professional development opportunities, and software programs. If these important pieces can be brought together around the Common Core standards, then there is little doubt that individual students and our nation as a whole will benefit from these more demanding expectations.

COUNTERPOINT: John White
University of Dayton

Will Common Core academic standards make the United States more competitive? Theoretically, one would like to hope so, but when the human and political elements are taken into account, the likelihood of success is slim. While the idea of having a common set of standards makes sense on some level, too many factors militate against the success of Common Core standards, not the least of which is the notion held by proponents of common standards and expressed by Terry Ryan (Thomas B. Fordham Institute) in the previous essay that at the very "heart" of education one finds an academic standard. The Common Core is based on a federal end run around the U.S. Constitution, and it has little research to support the absolute certainty with which its proponents promise its success.

The U.S. Constitution makes no mention of education. The Tenth Amendment implies that this silence means that education is to be regulated either by the individual states or by the people. American public education was founded on the principle of subsidiarity; that is, the most efficient way to manage affairs is at the most local level. This has made public schools a central feature of local American life; schools have historically been central to communities and to their identities as they have come to reflect the culture and ethos of their communities. Throughout American history, this fact has been recognized; safeguards designed to ensure local control are always a part of federal education legislation; the No Child Left Behind Act of 2001 (NCLB) specifically stated that the federal government cannot and will not create curriculum for America's schools.

PREVIOUS ATTEMPTS AT NATIONALIZATION

The Common Core State Standards Initiative is hardly a new concept; in fact, there have been many attempts at moving toward a national curriculum geared to prepare students for college. As early as 1892, the Committee of Ten, chaired by Harvard President Charles Eliot, recommended a series of secondary school content area "studies" appropriate for student admission to college. In 1895, the National Education Association created the Committee on College Entrance Requirements, or the "Committee of Twelve." As American public schools have historically enjoyed wide curricular independence and as colleges and universities each had their own admission standards, this committee's 1899 report sought to bring order to what appeared to be a chaotic and inefficient system.

For much of the 20th century, the College Board exercised considerable sway over what should be taught in the schools. Since the establishment of the U.S. Department of Education as a cabinet level office in 1980, each presidential administration has attempted to expand federal influence on local education.

A carrot-and-stick approach to federal involvement in local education began with the NCLB in 2001; the Bush administration connected federal education funding to a requirement that the states develop assessments in basic skills. Standardized examinations were to be given to all students in grades 3 through 8. Yet the NCLB act did not mandate national standards, leaving that function to the states. The states then developed their own standards and their own definitions of what constituted proficiency that were uneven in quality from state to state.

Ten years later, virtually everyone agrees that the NCLB program was seriously flawed. Many states, dependent on high test scores to receive the federal funding that the NCLB act provided, designed standards and set passing scores that were low so that passage rates would remain high enough to continue to qualify for funding. In essence, a proficient student in one state could, conceivably, be lacking proficiency in another state.

The NCLB act also led to a narrowing of the curriculum as school boards anxious for continued funding instructed teachers to concentrate on subjects that were to be tested, which also led to an emphasis on test preparation. The growing frustration with the NCLB act led to the call for national standards, as though nationalizing the curriculum and giving the federal government broad authority over what wasn't working at the state level would equal success.

DOES THE RESEARCH SUPPORT THE CLAIMS ABOUT THE COMMON CORE?

One argument used in favor of common standards is that the United States needs common standards to compete internationally. Proponents compare the United States with other industrialized nations, concluding that the success of those countries coupled with the relative lack of success in the United States are attributed to those nations having a common national curriculum. Alfie Kohn (2010), William Mathis (2010), and Neal McCluskey (2010) each pointed out the fallacy of this argument. While 8 out of the top 10 nations scoring on the latest Trends in International Mathematics and Science Study (TIMSS) exam have centralized curricula, 9 out of 10 of the lowest performing countries have them as well. In the 1995 TIMSS, the United States was 4th from the bottom in math and science. The 3 nations below the United States had national standards, while 3 of the top 5 countries, including the Netherlands, which was the highest scoring country, did not have national standards or curricula (McCluskey, 2010).

McCluskey (2010) claimed that proponents of national standards must resort to the use of "factoids" about the success of nations with national standards to support their position because of the paucity of empirical research connecting national standards with student achievement. The data simply do not support the assertion that common standards will lead to global competitiveness. Even at the state level, the connection between standards and student achievement is inconclusive. Little empirical, peer-reviewed research has been conducted on the effectiveness of standards having a direct causal effect on student achievement. Mathis (2010) maintained that with nearly 20 years of experience with standards-based accountability systems, we still have no clear evidence that they are particularly effective. He quoted Grover Whitehurst, Director of the Brown Center on Educational Policy at the Brookings Institute, who compared states' math proficiency using National Assessment of Educational Progress (NAEP) scores. Using the definitions of *high* and *low* standards as defined by the Fordham Foundation, Whitehurst found no relationship between the rigor of a state's standards and its NAEP scores.

Christopher Tieken (2011) examined all of the background materials used by the National Governors Association (NGA) and the Council of Chief State School Officers (CCSSO) in endorsing the standards, and he too found the evidence lacking, as the NGA and CCSSO primarily based their "large and growing body of knowledge" in support of common standards on a single report that they produced themselves, a report that makes little use of scientific or empirical research to support its conclusions. He also faulted those supporting the standards for limiting themselves by looking only at what happens in classrooms, thereby, failing to account for differences in health care, housing, and child mortality rates between the United States and those countries that regularly outscore the United States on these exams. While Tieken does not claim to have done sufficient research to fully support this theory, he does say that the data points in that direction and that a comprehensive social system provides a "quality safety net for children and mothers that has the greatest influence on ultimate educational outcomes" (p. 10).

Even those who most strongly support common standards admit that the evidence of a connection between them and high student achievement is weak.

William Schmidt, Richard Houang, and Sharif Shakrani's 2009 report published by the Fordham Foundation, *International Lessons About National Standards,* maintained that despite the lack of empirical evidence, the United States would benefit from national standards like those in Germany. Yet when challenged at a conference to provide empirical evidence to demonstrate the beneficial effect of national standards, Schmidt admitted, "It is very difficult to establish that, because virtually everybody in the world has national standards" (quoted in McCluskey, 2010, pp. 10–11).

WHERE DID THE COMMON CORE STANDARDS COME FROM?

In a masterful display of casuistry, President Obama has managed to oversee the creation of national standards in math, English, and history while maintaining the illusion of detachment from the process. Meanwhile, Obama creates the sense that these standards represent a consensus among educators and administrators, government officials, and academics. In a speech at TechBoston Academy in Dorchester, Massachusetts, in March 2011, Obama distilled his education plan for his young audience. He described Race to the Top as a federal challenge to the states:

> If you show us the most innovative plans for improving teacher quality and improving student achievement, then we'll show you the money. And for less than 1 percent of what America spends on education each year, Race to the Top has led over 40 states to raise their standards for teaching and learning—standards, by the way, that were developed not in Washington but by Republican and Democratic governors all across the country. (http://www.whitehouse.gov/the-press-office/2011/03/08/remarks-president-winning-future-education-boston-massachusetts)

This is not exactly true. The standards were not developed by governors but by testing companies and proaccountability groups, largely out of the public eye. Politically, it is important for the federal government to be able to claim that the standards are creatures of the individual states, thereby deflecting any criticism that the standards represent federal intrusion into the local curriculum. Despite being technically voluntary, the connection between state adoption of the standards and Race to the Top and Title I funds will mean that they are de facto federal standards, and as McCluskey (2010) pointed out, it is difficult to foresee a revised NCLB that does not mandate adoption of the standards.

While the NGA and CCSSO endorsed the standards in April 2009, they were not immediately involved in the drafting of the standards, which was done by Achieve, Inc, a bipartisan education reform organization in Washington, D.C. Mathis (2010) estimated that there were only 65 people involved in the creation of the standards, with Achieve being assisted by representatives of the College Board, the American College Testing (ACT), the Gates Foundation, and a few proaccountability groups. Mathis noted that only one teacher and no school administrators were involved in the process.

The standards were written in less than a year, and the states were given a very short time to accept the standards, with acceptance a prerequisite for applying for Race to the Top funds. Far from being the result of consensus, Gerald Bracey (2009–2010) even suggested that Achieve designed the standards prior to there being a proposal or even a call for common standards. Like a politician who holds off on releasing controversial or embarrassing news until late Saturday afternoon, when there is little time for attention or debate, the NGA and CCSSO released the "final recommendations" of the standards in June 2010, with a 60-day deadline for comments or revisions. This, of course, is when school is out and teachers and administrators are the least likely to pay attention to new or controversial initiatives. The Common Core standards are the very definition of a heavy-handed, top-down reform.

Why would something this seemingly wonderful be shrouded in secrecy and produced by a small, tight, homogeneous group? Why was the process not transparent and inclusive of all those with a stake in American education? It is because the Common Core State Standards Initiative is essentially an attempt by a small number of conservative think tanks and testing companies to control the academic content taught in our schools, couched in language designed to frighten the public into believing that we need these standards to compete internationally and to make all students "college and career ready," with political acquiescence purchased from cash strapped, desperate state governments by connecting adoption for the standards with access to Race to the Top and Title I funds.

To understand the secrecy and closed atmosphere surrounding the new standards, one should look at what happened when national history standards were proposed and federally funded in the early 1990s. The standards were funded and drawn up, but they were killed in 1995 when the U.S. Senate voted 99 to 1 against them in a "sense of the Senate" vote.

Education historian Linda Symcox maintains that the movement for common standards has its origins in a 1980s neoconservative attempt to control American curriculum and to purge it of elements of "political correctness." In her 2002 book, *Whose History?*, Symcox traces the development of the quest for national content standards, which began with the publication of *A Nation at Risk* in 1983. Many of the characters who most loudly call for the Common

Core standards today are the very same people who sought common standards in the 1980s and 1990s, men and women who were responsible for the movement to create the national history standards but who quickly turned against them when they did not fit their political worldview.

When national standards for history were being written in the 1990s, education historian Diane Ravitch, conservative education critic Chester E. Finn, Jr., University of Virginia professor and cultural literacy guru E. D. Hirsch, Jr., former Secretary of Education William Bennett, and then president of the American Federation of Teachers Albert Shanker were in the forefront of the movement for common national standards in history. This small and self-appointed group reached their own "consensus" on what comprised American history. The standards were to be designed by academic historians and by K–12 teachers and educationists whose interpretations of American history differed from those of the select group calling for standards.

When the standards were released, the neoconservatives were distressed to see that they no longer told the story of American exceptionalism, but rather, they reflected the state of American social, economic, and political historiography and presented a history that was at odds with the narrative that the Fordham Foundation and Diane Ravitch wished to tell. Immediately, Finn and his allies turned against the standards and successfully saw them defeated and abandoned (Symcox, 2002, pp. 127–156).

It is my contention that those who sought national standards 15 years ago learned their lesson from their defeat, and they have seen to it that the new national standards will be comprehensive and will be as tamperproof as possible, insulated from interests who disagree with the agenda being set by the Gates Foundation, the Fordham Foundation, E. D. Hirsch, Jr., Diane Ravitch, America's Choice, Student Achievement Partners, and the Hoover Institute. This is why the standards were rolled out in their entirety and why there was no public discourse involved in their construction.

If the standards are somehow adjusted so as not to fit the agenda of these groups, then we should expect them to turn on these standards just as they turned on the history standards when other American voices demanded to be heard. As Finn himself stated in an interview with Garry Boulard and the National Council of State Legislatures in September 2010, "they [the Common Core standards] would not be a good thing if the standards were sleazy or low or weak or politically correct or in other ways inferior" (http://www.ncsl.org/default.aspx?tabid=21085).

In 2006, Finn, along with Liam Julian and Michael Petrilli, wrote *The State of State Standards 2006* in which they warned that "if written by committee, or turned over to K–12 interest groups, they [common standards] could turn out to be vague, politically correct, encyclopedic, and/or fuzzy" (p. 16). It is logical to conclude that the secrecy surrounding the Common Core standards was intended to preserve the new standards from any input from those "K–12 interest groups," that is, unions, parents, liberal university professors, or the liberal media who might bring dissenting ideas to the table.

There are already cracks in Finn's vision for the standards, however. The winter 2010/2011 edition of *American Educator,* the official journal of the American Federation of Teachers (AFT), is entirely devoted to the Common Core standards and to the contribution that the union will make to those standards as specific content and assessments are plugged in to the standards. It will be as decisions are made about the specific content that will flesh out the standards that trouble will occur. While one suspects that Finn and Ravitch will not object to the sentiments in Hirsch's article in that issue in which he offers to bring the content resources of his core knowledge philosophy to the Common Core, there are other voices in the AFT who will most certainly bring ideas about specific content to the conversation that the Common Core cabal will try to dismiss as political correctness. If their history is a barometer, as soon as the Common Core State Standards Initiative begins to reflect the principles and traditions of broad American democratic discourse, then those who are currently its loudest proponents will again turn out to be its loudest critics.

Finally, even if the Common Core standards somehow survive the gauntlet of a messy democracy, there is little to suggest that the standards will eliminate the state of hyperaccountability that currently plagues American education. Rather, Common Core and the standardized testing that will surely follow it will be added to the long list of accountability structures already in place. Value-added formulas will be determined for the new assessments to please Bill Gates and the other business interests whose ideas and dollars currently exert an undue influence on education. Those responsible for the business mind-set in today's public schools will not relinquish control so that students might be assessed via portfolios or performance assessments.

CONCLUSION

Kohn (2010) pointed out that words such as *exploration, intrinsic motivation, developmentally appropriate,* or *democracy* do not appear on the Common Core website. Rather, education is defined by "success in the global economy" and "America's competitive edge." He also wrote that buzzwords such as *rigorous, measurable, accountable, competitive, world-class, high expectations,* or *raising the bar* are not meaningless. They reflect a philosophy that is more economic than educational and serves those whose goals are to train a new generation of employees who will ensure that we dominate the world economy. This type of education does have an academic standard "at the heart of just about every-thing that matters in K–12 education" as Ryan asserts in his point essay. The corollary to that belief is that one wastes his time looking there either for a child or for a beating heart.

As with every other top-down reform in the history of American education, the Common Core State Standards Initiative will ultimately fail. Governors and state education officials, desperate for federal funding in the worst eco-nomic crisis since the Great Depression, agreed to the carrot of Common Core's money despite the knowledge that they would most certainly have to deal with the stick later. Without seeking input or buy-in from teachers and administrators at the local level, the Common Core will be yet another aloof and invasive program forced on the schools that will be cleverly circumvented and short circuited, which will lead to a further demonization of classroom teachers and their collective organizations.

In spite of the centralizing and unconstitutional wishes of reformers whose ultimate goal is to control the information to which children have access, those in schools still think in local, human terms. The danger is that prior to being pronounced a failure, the Common Core standards will destroy the last vestiges of local control in American education. At the very best, the Common Core will ensure that the American K–12 curriculum will be forever politicized, subject to the whims and ideologies of successive federal administrations.

FURTHER READINGS AND RESOURCES

American Educator, Winter, 2010–2011.

Bracey, G. (2009–2010, December/January). Our eternal (and futile?) quest for high standards. *Phi Delta Kappan*, pp. 75–76.

Branchero, S. (2010, June 3). Governors' group seeks national education standards. *The Wall Street Journal*. Retrieved from http://online.wsj.com/article/NA_WSJ_PUB :SB10001424052748704515704575282920918415774.html

Carmichael, S. B., Martino, G., Porter-Magee, K., & Wilson, W. S. (2010). *The state of state standards—and the Common Core—in 2010*. Washington, DC: Thomas B. Fordham Institute.

Carmichael, S. B., Wilson, W. S., Martino, G., Finn, C. E., Jr., Porter-Magee, K., & Winkler, A. M. (2010). *Review of the draft K–12 Common Core standards*. Retrieved July 25, 2010, from http://www.edexcellence.net/index.cfm/newsreviews-of-the-draft-k-12-common-core-standards

Driscoll, D. P. (2010, April 18). They're good for the state. *The Boston Globe*. Retrieved from http://www.boston.com/bostonglobe/editorial_opinion/oped/articles/2010/04/18/theyre_good_for_the_state

Duncan, A. (2009, January 14). *Address by the secretary of education at the 2009 Governors Education Symposium.* Washington, DC: U.S. Department of Education.

Editors. (2010, March 17). Standard bearer (Editorial). *The New Republic* (New York City). Retrieved from http://www.tnr.com/article/politics/standard-bearer

Feinberg, M., & Levin, D. (2009, January 9). What "Yes, we can" should mean for our schools. *The Washington Post.* Retrieved from http://www.washingtonpost.com/wp-dyn/content/article/2009/01/08/AR2009010803262.html

Finn, C. E., Jr., Julian, L., & Petrilli, M. (2006a). *The state of state standards 2006.* Washington, DC: Thomas B. Fordham Foundation.

Finn, C. E., Jr., Julian, L., & Petrilli, M. (Eds.). (2006b). *To dream the impossible dream: Four approaches to national standards and tests for America's schools.* Washington, DC: Thomas B. Fordham Institute.

Isaacson, W. (2009, April 15). How to raise the standard in America's schools. *Time.* Retrieved from http://www.time.com/time/nation/article/0,8599,1891468,00.html

Kohn, A. (2010, January 14). Debunking the case for national standards: One-size-fits-all mandates and their dangers. *Education Week.* Retrieved April 9, 2011, from http://www.alfiekohn.org/teaching/edweek/national.htm

Mathis, W. (2010, July 21). *The "Common Core" Standards Initiative: An effective reform tool?* Boulder, CO, and Tempe, AZ: Education and the Public Interest Center & Education Policy Research Unit. Retrieved April 10, 2011, from http://epicpolicy.org/publication/common-core-standards

McCluskey, N. (2010, February 17). Behind the curtain: Assessing the case for national curriculum standards. *Policy Analysis,* No. 661. Washington, DC: Cato Institute. Retrieved April 9, 2011, from http://www.cato.org/pubs/pas/pa661.pdf

Schmidt, W., Houang, R., & Shakrani, S. (2009). *International lessons about national standards.* Washington, DC: Thomas B. Fordham Institute.

Symcox, L. (2002). *Whose history? The struggle for national standards in America's class-rooms.* New York: Teachers College Press.

Tieken, C. (2011). Common Core standards: An example of data-less decision making. *Journal of Scholarship and Practice, 7*(4), 3–18.

Will standards and accountability enhance innovation and change?

POINT: Joel Vargas and Janet Santos, *Jobs for the Future*
COUNTERPOINT: Philip Smith, *The Ohio State University*

OVERVIEW

The push for standards and accountability has focused primarily on ensuring the academic competitiveness of students in the United States. Some reformers argue that the United States is simply losing its competitive edge in an array of activities ranging from business and industry to education because no common academic standards exist in this country. These reformers also argue that for far too long, officials in poorly performing schools and districts have not been held accountable for the weak academic performance of assigned students. Other reformers assert that the academic achievement gaps now evidenced in the United States between racial and ethnic groups is attributable, in part, to the inability of educational (and political) leaders in school systems to offer rigorous curricula to all students and to hold teachers responsible for delivering that curriculum.

Embedded within the policy debate is the whole notion of how to create schools that foster value-added learning environments for all students regardless of race, ethnicity, or the socioeconomic status of their families. The challenge of creating such school learning environments will require more than an embrace of the status quo. Succeeding in this challenge will necessitate having educational leaders focus on meaningful and thoughtful innovation in delivery systems. The question then arises: Will the push for rigorous standards and accountability enhance or mitigate efforts to innovate school structures and classroom practices?

In this chapter, the contributors examine this question from very different perspectives. Joel Vargas and Janet Santos (Jobs for the Future) are with an organization with a national reach that focuses on promoting education and workforce strategies that will help the United States to compete in a global economy. Philip Smith (The Ohio State University) is an academic who brings a more philosophically grounded view to his analysis of the relationship between more accountability and enhanced educational innovation. Taken together, the pieces offer a view of the inherent complexity associated with examining the connections between accountability and innovation.

Vargas and Santos describe with historical context how standards and accountability have been powerful forces in focusing attention on the inequities endemic to educational practices and outcomes in American public schools. These authors also cogently capture some of the emerging successes in terms of creating "schools that work," that is, schools that reduce academic achievement gaps and enhance educational opportunities for students with the greatest needs. Vargas and Santos place particular attention on some of the recent program successes, such as early colleges, that have emerged in recent years as a result of frustrations with traditional urban schools that have failed to be accountable to the various publics they putatively serve.

Smith takes a very different and more philosophical view. For Smith, the standards and accountability movement is about control and power. Smith explains that schools at their best help young people think critically and problem solve effectively. Achieving this "end," or outcome, Smith posits, is not something that will emerge from more top-down oversight, and to expect innovation in such an environment is even more fatuous to consider. The accountability movement will not, according to Smith, push educators toward innovation and excellence; rather, it will mitigate opportunities for enlightened action and foster professional behaviors that are more "rote" and less critically informed.

As you read these two essays, consider two key questions: First, would innovation be more likely to flourish in an environment where top-down accountability did not exist? Second, can school systems and educators be truly innovative if they are constantly being evaluated relative to a set of defined outcomes, particularly if they have no input in the process by which their performance is measured?

Thomas J. Lasley, II
University of Dayton

POINT: Joel Vargas and Janet Santos
Jobs for the Future

For more than 25 years, standards-based accountability—the idea that what students should learn ought to be consistently defined and that they and their schools should be evaluated based on measures of that learning—has been the nation's core strategy for improving educational outcomes. Today, the consensus behind the concept is more widespread than ever: All but two states plan to adopt Common Core State Standards that are designed to ensure all high school graduates are prepared for college, careers, and citizenship.

Standards and accountability have been powerful forces for focusing attention on inequities in academic achievement between low income students and racial minorities. Yet the nation's schools, especially our high schools, have by and large struggled to help these, namely, "all," students meet common standards. There are states, schools, and systems that represent notable exceptions, in many cases spurred by private and public initiatives to encourage innovation in the redesign of the high school experience. As states adopt policies to implement higher and shared standards, they will need to promote the growth of innovative schools and programs that succeed in helping struggling students achieve these standards and spread proven practices from those schools to others.

STANDARDS: COMMON EXPECTATIONS FOR ALL

In 1983, *A Nation at Risk,* a report by the National Commission on Excellence in Education, raised the urgency of the need for educational reform and made the quality of American high schools a central concern. The report noted the weakness of the nation's public secondary school system as judged by the skills of its graduates. Subsequent examinations of high schools documented the various practices and policies contributing to the problems, including weak curricula, disparate standards and curricula for different students, and promotion based on age rather than level of learning. A push began to establish state-wide academic standards to drive changes in local education systems, and that strategy has been a key feature of educational reform ever since. The trend was encouraged in the 1990s by federal initiatives, such as Goals 2000.

As more states developed higher standards, they also turned their attention to the development of assessment and accountability systems. These were designed to evaluate student learning against standards, base promotion on that learning, and evaluate the quality of schools by how well their students performed. The No Child Left Behind Act of 2001, the reauthorization of the

Elementary and Secondary Education Act, made federal funding for states dependent on the development of such systems and required those systems to evaluate schools based on how well subgroups of students—particularly those with traditionally low educational attainment (e.g., racial and ethnic minorities, low income, and special needs)—performed on state assessments. By 2010, all states had established mathematics and English standards or assessment-based accountability systems. The latest and boldest development in standards-based reform is the Common Core State Standards Initiative. In 2010, all but two states signed on to adopt common standards calibrated to the skills needed for college and career success. Alaska and Texas are states that have not adopted standards-based reform. There is evidence that in Texas—a state long considered a trailblazer in standards-based reform—standards are consistent with college-ready standards, as benchmarked against two previous national sets of college-ready standards in English language arts (Rolfhus, Cook, Brite, & Hartman, 2010).

With federal funding of over $300 million, a large group of states is collaborating on the development of assessments aligned to those standards. The Common Core represents a departure from the custom of states setting and implementing their own accountability systems, which had resulted in state standards and assessments that varied widely in content and level of expectations for students. In contrast, the Common Core standards assume that

- all students should possess a common set of knowledge and skills by the time they complete high school to ensure a successful transition to higher education,

- a postsecondary credential is a prerequisite for the economic well-being of individuals and society, and

- high school standards and state assessments must be aligned to and benchmarked against these goals.

THE PROBLEM OF THE HIGH SCHOOL

In many ways, the progress and prospects for education's improvement and equity have never been greater. The assumptions and expectations of recent standards-based reforms represent a complete turnaround of the purposes of the American high school. Less than 30 years ago, in *A Nation at Risk*, the authors lamented the impact of a high school experience designed around different curricular tracks—reflecting the assumption that only a select group of students needed preparation for college. Another seminal analysis of the traditional high school criticized its evolution into a "shopping mall" of course and program options instituted to accommodate the diverse interests and abilities of a heterogeneous group of students (Powell, Farrar, & Cohen, 1985). In expecting that all students should learn a common set of competencies and content, standards and accountability are disruptive forces for equity by declaring a more rigorous path for all students through high school. But setting all students successfully on that path is a very real challenge.

Standards and accountability systems have quantified gaps in achievement for low income students, students of color, and other underserved groups. Moreover, pressure has increased on schools to improve outcomes for each group or face consequences. Yet thus far, despite the increased attention, the educational attainment and achievement of these groups have remained stubbornly low—especially so at the high school level. Although the average reading and mathematics scores for Black and Hispanic students on the National Assessment of Educational Progress (NAEP) have improved significantly since the early 1970s, they still lag behind the average scores of White students. This pattern is prevalent across all grade levels and ages tested. And it is pronounced for high school students for whom NAEP performance has remained stagnant during the same time period (*The Nation's Report Card*). This should come as no surprise; new reform policies are asking high schools to do things that they were not designed to do.

Continued accountability for getting all students to achieve at higher standards is essential, along with better strategies for helping schools improve. At the same time, raising standards and accountability and attaching high-stakes consequences for students and teachers—in the face of persistent evidence that high schools have little capacity for the dramatic change needed to meet new expectations—runs the risk of subverting or distorting reform goals. For example, some argue that the current high-stakes environment created under NCLB has resulted in a number of unintended negative consequences: lowered standards to improve the chances of student success and graduation, incentives to "teach to the test" at the expense of engaging pedagogy and well-rounded curricula, and "gaming" in reporting to make student retention, promotion, and dropout rates look better (Ravitch, 2010). Further, a formerly staunch advocate of standards-based reform, educational historian Diane Ravitch has recently echoed and lamented these shortcomings.

A COMPLEMENTARY STRATEGY: INNOVATION

Concurrent with the rise of standards-based reform, many new and redesigned high schools have been created that are demonstrating success in supporting underserved students to succeed in high school and get ready for college. Some have started at the initiative of school districts themselves, such as the University Park Campus School, a partnership between Worcester Public Schools and Clark University. And others have been initiated and supported by special-purpose school development organizations—some as charter schools, others in partnership with states and local districts. The Coalition of Essential Schools, founded in 1984, focused on reenvisioning the structure of high schools. More recently, the Knowledge Is Power Program (KIPP), the North Carolina New Schools Project, the Texas High School Project, New Visions in Public Schools, and the organizations composing the Early College High School Initiative (ECHSI) have helped start hundreds of innovative high schools—designed to help more struggling students meet high standards and graduate prepared for college entry and success.

In general, the successful innovations share common ideals. These include, to name a few, support for strong, differentiated instruction focused on meeting common standards in a college-ready course of study; a commitment to personalization where every student is known by adults; and a college-going-for-all ethos that permeates the school culture, including the curriculum, instruction, and guidance counseling. These features appear to be essential to a supportive school environment fostering student engagement and achievement.

Indicative of the progress that is possible when strong standards gain traction on the ground is the North Carolina New Schools Project, an innovative high school design effort that has helped districts to start over 100 new or redesigned high schools since 2004. Twenty-seven of these are redesigned comprehensive high schools, with high student poverty rates, converted into small schools with a focus on college readiness and often with a special thematic focus such as health and life sciences or STEM (science, technology, engineering, and mathematics). In 2009–2010, these schools on average outpaced statewide results on the 1-year improvement on tests passed by students under the state's ABC accountability system: 13.5% improvement for students in redesigned schools versus 9.5% statewide. Graduation rates for the first wave of all new and redesigned high schools supported by the New Schools Project are 84% compared to statewide rates of 74% (North Carolina New Schools Project, 2010).

The North Carolina New Schools Project has also initiated over 70 early college high schools, part of a national network of over 200 early college schools nationally. These are schools designed so that underserved youth graduate high school with one to 2 years of transferable college credit or an associate's degree within 5 years. Preliminary findings from a federally funded random assignment study of North Carolina's early college schools indicate that their students take and pass college preparatory courses in mathematics at significantly higher rates than do students who attended other high schools. The schools are also closing racial gaps in enrollment and success in college prep curricula, according to Julie Edmunds and colleagues (2010). These successes are echoed in data about early college schools nationally: Students are graduating high school at higher rates and with an average of over 20 college credits, a strong indication of their readiness for college, according to Clifford Adelman (2004). Data are from a national annual survey of schools in the ECHSI program administered by the evaluation firm American Institutes for Research (AIR)/SRI International and stored in a Student Information System maintained by the organization Jobs for the Future.

The results from innovative schools are not always consistent; we should not expect all innovations to succeed. Many charter schools and other schools of choice have started under a banner of innovation, but their success in improving student outcomes is mixed (Center for Research on Education Outcomes, 2009; Hassel & Terrell, 2006). However, a critical mass of innovations has succeeded, particularly those with well-defined design principles and those that have paid attention to supporting improved classroom instruction. They provide examples of practices and design that can potentially be refined and replicated to reach many more young people and help them meet college-ready standards.

STANDARDS AND INNOVATION: FUTURE DIRECTIONS

If the promise of better and more consistent standards and accountability systems is to be realized for all students, scaling up successful innovation will have an important role to play in helping high schools make the massive shifts in organization and practice that will be demanded of them. Although many efforts at innovation have been successful, they have had limited systemic influence and certainly not at a level needed in this critical moment in standards-based reform as Common Core standards are implemented (Mead & Rotherham, 2008). The success of many innovations in modeling what high schools can do differently to help all students—including those who have traditionally struggled most—reach college-ready standards is too notable to be left untapped. It is important, if not imperative, for policymakers to develop better ways for successful innovation to become more systemic.

Although proinnovation, we do not pretend to have answers for how to do this, but we close with three observations that suggest directions to take and avoid.

1. Scaling up promising innovation beyond islands of excellence is a challenge, but there are examples of promising approaches

Building on the success of their early college high schools, some districts and states have developed strategies to test replicable practices for adoption and adaptation in other high schools and in entire districts. If successful, these school- and districtwide approaches would enable many more students to benefit from schools with an early college design even if they do not attend a small, stand-alone early college high school. We suggest that innovation policies and initiatives be built on a strategy that consciously plans for using schools that show success to positively affect others. By the same token, an ongoing problem is that unsuccessful innovations are sometimes not abandoned. For example, many charter laws were passed with the premise that new schools would be sanctioned only as long as their results justified their autonomy. Yet not all charter laws were written this way, and those that were have not always been followed when new schools underperform.

2. States that have implemented innovations with a consistent level of quality have created entities to own and manage the innovation process

This process involves such functions as managing the financial and other resources for planning and start-up, ensuring the consistency of school design and implementation, and educating key stakeholders about the role of innovation in statewide education reform. It requires nimbleness and flexibility to secure staff with appropriate expertise, attract private resources leveraged by public support, and broker local partnerships to support innovation efforts.

The Texas High School Project and the North Carolina New Schools Project are two examples. Both are partnerships and alliances between the state and private funders. The organizational structure that these partnerships take is not as important as the functions they carry out. Also important is the recognition that government acting alone will probably be unable to execute all of the aforementioned necessary tasks; these partnerships will need an external spur and guidance about innovative practices.

3. Policies that create space for spurring innovation with accountability can be a strategy that complements efforts to raise standards

In one noteworthy example, North Carolina's Innovative Education Initiatives Act of 2003 established cooperative education programs between local school boards and community colleges for students who would benefit from accelerated instruction or were at risk of dropping out. The legislation facilitated a fast-tracked process for such schools to seek and receive waivers from policies—such as restrictions tied to high school seat time rules—that would have stood in the way of early colleges and other innovations seeking to accelerate the movement of prepared students into college courses. The North Carolina Board of Education annually reviews the progress of innovative schools and regularly reviews waivers for continuation. The technical issues that the waivers solve for innovators are important, but just as important in this kind of policy is the strong signal sent to local school leaders about the state's support for specific types of innovation.

Short of instituting bold new policies and initiatives to stimulate innovation, states should take care that policies to implement higher standards—including assessment, graduation requirements, and accountability—do not inadvertently quash school innovations that are succeeding. Policymakers should engage with leaders of innovative schools to understand the flexibility they and other innovators need to continue practices that do, in fact, prepare all students for college and careers.

COUNTERPOINT: Philip Smith
The Ohio State University

I magine that we all lived in a nation of several hundred million people where there were huge variations of individual talents, attitudes, beliefs, and behavior. Imagine, too, that we professed to value these differences, not to merely tolerate them but to actually encourage and celebrate them to a large and generous extent. Moreover, our reason for this stance was not simply because it showed a healthy respect for individuals, who might otherwise be constrained to their detriment or who might become targets of unwarranted ridicule, exclusion, exploitation, or even persecution, but because we were convinced that encouraging and celebrating individual differences would also benefit us and our society as a whole. We figured there would be less waste of human resources, fewer unrepairable conflicts, and fewer social pathologies. As far as we were concerned, human differences strengthen and enrich our national culture similar to the way biological diversity engineers a dynamic robust ecology.

For most Americans, and those sympathetic with America's self-image, grasping this idea is hardly a stretch. However much everyday life diverts from this ideal, it pretty much represents what the culture embraces and encourages. From its beginning, the rallying cry has been *e pluribus unum* ("one out of many"). The founders of our nation saw themselves working to create a "new race," one that defined itself by its commitment to the values of a modern enlightened democracy, not by blood or tradition. They were convinced that diversity, along with the right kind of socialization, would produce a national culture that lived out its respect for all persons regardless of their origins (Schlesinger, 1998, p. 17). Our social nature as human beings requires that we live together not merely out of practical necessity but to find personal fulfillment. Rather than imply a loss of personal freedom, however, our social relationships provide the grounds for our autonomy. When they fail in this regard, they must be rethought and reformed. Here is the point where education begins to show its mettle.

This sounds nice in theory. But how are things working out? What are the risks and costs of living this way (i.e., as if our social relationships were liberating as well as bonding, as paradoxical as that sounds)? What happens when our efforts fall short of our expectations, where our differences appear to divide us rather than bring us together? Smart people, such as John Winthrop, William James, and John Dewey, were convinced we could do this in the United States. But how should we respond when the very thing that is supposed to be our strength begins to look more like a threat?

Constructive replies to this question are hard to find. Many people prefer simply to ignore it, insisting the problem is exaggerated or overblown. Others regard it as ill conceived or impossible to deal with, except competitively where there are clear winners and losers. The first attitude ignores reality. The second is a repudiation of the American sense of a new race. For anyone who believes that the American promise of a modern enlightened democracy is not a delusion, it is preposterous to suggest that success for some can come only at the expense of others. If our world is not exactly "one for all and all for one," then the life they seek still requires the melding of human variations within a meaningful framework of fraternity and solidarity.

Be this as it may, we cannot rely solely on the authority of our culture to direct us. First of all, we want to keep our culture as open-ended and flexible as possible. In addition, we want a culture we can control rather than one that controls us. So the idea of looking for precise guidance from on high, from the culture itself, is pretty much out of the question. Our only choice is to work out the details ourselves, "on the fly," so to speak, without being told exactly what to do by some higher authority. We need to be good fabricators, good pragmatists who can figure things out as we go along. If we cannot know *a priori* what a modern democratic culture should look like and cannot specify in advance what behavior is called for in public and private life, except in the most vague and general fashion, then we have no choice but to trust our wits. Our fate is in our hands. Our official position is that there is no aspect of life, no field of endeavor—from law to business to politics to religion to education—where this is not true. On what grounds then should we operate?

However seriously we ask this question about ourselves, we usually ask it with greater urgency about others, perhaps for good reason. We want to know what others know, and we want to know if they know what they are supposed to know. We expect them to be able to communicate with us, to talk things over and to work cooperatively with us when necessary. We get upset if we think other people cannot, or will not, do what we think they should. When this happens, one option is to seek a legal remedy, to go to civil court, for instance, and sue the offending parties for damages, for *misfeasance* (incompetence) or *malfeasance* (bad intentions). Our legal system sets relatively clear standards for holding people accountable. But notice, legal remedies are always "after-the-fact" actions. Even if justice is served, the damage has already been done. The promise of preventing problems from occurring in the first place is a huge factor in explaining our interest in education. But what should we do when we believe that education has failed to deliver on its promise?

To begin with, there are probably as many motives behind complaints about American education as there are people who gripe about it. Should we really be surprised? We have deliberately dimmed the lights of our culture and given as much discretion as possible to individuals. Then we say to people, qua individuals or as members of functional groups, "OK, now take care of these problems." And so they do, more or less, as best they can, or as well as they want, with whatever motives they possess, good or bad. Is it any wonder that things do not always turn out as well as we hope or as we expect? It is a great deal to ask of people; and it requires considerable faith in their abilities, talents, and good will.

The risks of operating this way can seem too great, the costs too high, to move ahead with this American experiment. Yet what choice do we have? It is naive to believe we could ever find a single source of meaning and value that we would agree on, even if we tried, or thought we should. We are left to figure out how to live and work together without much help from a centralized authority. Clearly, this is easier said than done. It is especially obvious in professional fields, where certain individuals possess, or lay claim to, expertise that others must depend on. The rest of us can only hope that those who assert this expertise will behave responsibly. Yet even the most casual observer would have to admit that "unprofessional" conduct is everywhere these days and that the problem is getting worse. In part, this stems from uncertainty within the professions themselves as to what responsibility consists of. Now, more than ever, questions about one's professional duty are answered with minimal assurance and even less consensus.

There are two ways to approach this problem. The first is to look at the context and figure out in sufficient detail how professionals should behave and what nonprofessionals can rightfully expect. Judgments are involved here on all fronts. In the end, professionals are held responsible for the consequences of what happens on their watch. The second approach is modeled on the legal liability example cited above. It grows out of dissatisfaction with the discretion given to professionals to establish their own goals and standards; and it limits the extent to which their specialized knowledge can be used to privilege their judgments. It also looks for ways to drop the moralizing language of responsibility in favor of a more straightforward matter of fact vocabulary of the sort found in law and business. In this view, the moralizing language of responsibility was adopted out of a naive belief that it would prevent problems from happening in the first place rather than merely redress them ex post facto. But in the modern secular world this approach will not work. Remedies for failure in law and business may come too late for many, but they look to be our best and only option. To the surprise of many, they have proven to be remarkably effective.

This latter approach to achieving goals and objectives and solving problems along the way has come to be known as *accountability*. This raises a number of significant questions. Is it really different from the first approach that features responsibility? Does the vocabulary of accountability fundamentally change the nature of our concerns? What are the risks and costs of each approach, assuming they are different? Do we lose anything important when moral sensitivity disappears as a motive force behind professional conduct? Or would we gain more than we lose? Why have so many people, inside and outside of professional life, come to prefer accountability to responsibility as a mode of professional assessment?

Accountability in the arena of public education grew markedly in importance over the last 30 years as a way out of a long-term dilemma. As seen by one critic, it

> began in the 1980s at the urging of leaders of business and industry and was quickly picked up by politicians and a large segment of the voting, tax-payer public. The reform message preached by Democrats, Republicans, and the mainstream media is simple: One: America's schools are, at best, mediocre. Two: Teachers deserve most of the blame. Three: As a corrective, rigorous subject-matter standards and tests are essential. Four: Bringing market force to bear will pressure teachers to meet the standards or choose some other line of work. Competition—students against student, teacher against teacher, school against school, state against state, nation against nation—will yield the improvement necessary for the United States to finish in first place internationally. (Brady, 2009)

If some of those who support this type of reform have smaller ambitions, they nevertheless embrace this approach and accept its basic assumptions.

While most people would see *accountability* as synonymous with *responsibility*, as meaning more or less the same thing, or at least as not in conflict with it, the logic and attitudes of ordinary language show this not to be the case (Craig, 1982, pp. 133–140). Accountability implies having a duty or expectation to act in a manner that has been specified in advance. The idea embodies the logic of contracts, wherein nothing important is left to the discretion of those who carry them out. The terms and conditions are settled prior to their execution. By contrast, if one is *responsible*, it means that one is morally answerable as a cause of what occurs. It implies an agent who can initiate behavior and reflect on the "why" of the "what," and the "what" of the "how."

Accountability involves *external* sanctions and controls. With responsibility, sanctions and controls are *internal*. A person could behave mindlessly and still be accountable, so long as the presumed standards were met. Responsibility makes this impossible as a matter of logic. It is silly to say that a person is responsible for prespecified behavior, unless that individual has the authority to do otherwise. To be held responsible for behaving as directed, in any coherent sense of the term, one would need to qualify as an agent who consciously endorsed the intent of what was done. In contrast, a person who worked to implement prespecified behavior, or carry out orders, could be held accountable, even without qualifying as an agent who acted approvingly.

As seen by its advocates, accountability filters out bias, avoids the fog of human perception, and renders judgment unnecessary. This is accomplished by limiting the focus of evaluation to what is quantifiable or countable. But precisely for this reason, it works better in some areas than others. There is an old saying in statistics: "to be is to be the value of a variable, that whatever exists exists in some amount, and whatever exists in some amount can be quantified." In some worlds, this may be true; in others just as real, it most decidedly is not, or it is true only in certain aspects. The point here is to ask about the motivation for this attitude. Why would anyone believe it? "Because it is true" is one possible response. "Because it is useful to assume" is another. Under given conditions, either response could have considerable merit. But if we are asking about the motivation for this attitude, apart from its justification, there is something else we might say: "because it is comforting to know things for sure." How much merit does this response have?

Removing any doubt about what is purportedly known eliminates any responsibility for the consequence of believing it. After all, it is "the truth," and the truth speaks for itself. Telling other people what to do based on purportedly certain knowledge may not eliminate altogether our responsibility for imposing it on others in the form of expectations, but it surely lessens it. Similarly, when people are told exactly what is expected of them, that too pretty much relieves them of any responsibility for what they do. The loss of authority that is associated with being held accountable is seen by many as an easy trade-off. They regard it as a license to do only what is required, especially when doing more might actually get them into trouble. Responsibility always adds to our burdens, sometimes excessively so. Second-guessing ourselves can feel like a curse. But avoiding responsibility oftentimes comes at a cost. It lowers our expectations and moves us in the direction of being merely functional operators, who eventually will be replaced by other more functional units.

Accountability applied to education cannot avoid fossilizing the already formalized structures of schooling. Schooling picks out specific aspects of education and standardizes them for general inculcation. The full richness of educational experience is rarely, if ever, captured. This is not automatically a bad thing. But even this can be done badly. Mark Twain apparently knew it and is purported to have responded accordingly: "I have never let my schooling interfere with my education." Whether or not Twain actually uttered these words, this sentiment was expressed by his alter ego, Huckleberry Finn, who just prior to his big adventure down the Mississippi River could hardly wait to finish his schooling, so he could commence what he believed would be his real education. While schools can do certain things extremely well and while they play a critical role in education for modern life, they cannot do everything; and they can easily make matters worse, as Huck's case illustrates. Everyone would agree that schools should not be allowed to flounder. Yet it is easily forgotten in the hustle and bustle of everyday life that their primary mission in a society like ours is to cultivate independent-minded, responsible democratic citizens. Other things matter, too, of course. Yet if they do not hook up with this prime directive, they will fail in their most important charge. If accountability makes it harder for the schools to succeed in their primary mission by downplaying the importance of responsibility, especially in regard to the teachers themselves, it will be worse than wasted effort. It will cause school experience to be more dreadful and demeaning than it is already.

Accountability makes more sense for some professions than others. Where the best practices of a profession are generalizable and not in dispute, accountability makes a lot of sense. Still, where professional decisions about what to do, how, when, where, and why are not generalizable or obvious, where they require agents who are well prepared and trustable, who always keep in mind their highest professional aspirations, then, in that case, accountability is likely to be an impediment to good practice. Soldiers, surgeons, factory managers, accountants, engineers, police officers, and professional athletes are examples of professionals who probably could be assessed largely on accountability standards—with politicians, lawyers, family physicians, and scientists perhaps less so and preachers, counselors, and therapists maybe less yet. What about teachers? Where do they fit? To what extent would they be helped or hindered by working under the specter of prespecified expectations? Granted that teachers, like all professionals, need a certain level of freedom, the question is, how much? This is where the rubber hits the road as far as accountability is concerned.

A system of external sanctions and controls is never limited to the specification of outcomes. One way or another, it prescribes the procedures to be used for securing these results. It is interesting to note that modern life has elevated procedure to a place once held by morality. The reason is not hard to find. The modern mind views morality with suspicion. Concerned as it is with personal freedom, dignity, and practical results, it perceives morality as having done considerable harm in the world when imposed unintelligently without mercy. Determined to do better, modern people like to separate the content of morality from its mode of implementation. If moral content does not calibrate with the methods used for putting it into practice, then it is reformulated to fit those methods rather than the other way around. This would be nothing to complain about if the influence went both ways. But the process is not transactional. Moral content becomes something different without consideration of its integrity, or else it disappears altogether, as utility trumps substance and thought.

In the final analysis, the appeal of accountability has little to do with faith in human potential. It comes more from the promise to control the educational process from top to bottom. There is a widespread belief among Americans today that their schools need to be better managed. Americans feel these institutions have fallen below acceptable performance levels. This applies especially to the public schools. There is a lot at stake, nothing less than our future as an experiment in democratic living. We have little time to waste. Improvements have to be qualitative as well as quantitative. But lest we forget, there is a reason why responsibility has played such a prominent role in education for so long in our educational institutions. It treats individuals as ends-in-themselves, as persons, never solely as means. It assumes they have a disposition to think, and when this inclination is properly developed, it becomes both a cause and effect of our success. No one should be misled about accountability in this regard. Thinking well is not its top priority. The British philosopher Bertrand Russell, in *The ABC of Relativity* (1925), reminded us why it should be: "Most people would sooner die than think. In fact they do so."

The appeal of responsibility in education, such as it is, remains the same as always. It promises to help us think and act better than we would otherwise. This benefits everyone and our society as a whole. If our educational institutions are not paying enough attention these days to the cultivation and exercise of good thinking, or if we fear that our schools might actually be hindering its development, then the remedy is not to adopt a reform technology that skirts any need for deliberation, judgment, and choice. If, for any reason, we believe it is important to hold professional educators more accountable than we do already, we need to recognize the cost. People will do what they are told, or they will not. Accountability assumes there are no other options. Responsibility challenges us to see the world in a more rich and nuanced way, to envision other possibilities, better and worse, that require insight and reflection to appreciate.

Do computers think? Most philosophers today would say no. Their reason is that computers are not conscious, and without consciousness, thinking is impossible. This presumes, of course, the kind of thinking that human beings engage in. But this is what gives the question its force. Processing huge amounts of data with lightning speed is not thinking of the relevant kind. Imagine a person, alone in a room, who has been given a stack of cards on which are printed single Chinese characters. Imagine, too, that the person has been given a sheet of instructions about how to arrange these cards, some to the left, others to the right, of a midline, with each card having a prescribed position. When the cards have been arranged as instructed, that person will still have no idea what they mean without understanding Chinese (Searle, 2002, pp. 51–69).

A computer is like that person, performing flawlessly as instructed but without getting the gist of anything. How could it, not being conscious? No matter how much the computer's performance improves, how good it gets at playing chess, for example, it will never be enlightened. A computer does not reflect on anything, has no feelings or emotions of any kind, never gets depressed or angry, and cannot experience euphoria or amazement. All that a computer does is function, albeit impressively, like the machine that it is. Since a computer could never be a good citizen or a fabulous lover, it makes no sense to hold it responsible for anything—or accountable, for that matter. Accountability pushes people in the direction of a computer by treating them too much like mindless automatons. It retards their development as thoughtful human beings. For that, someone will be responsible.

FURTHER READINGS AND RESOURCES

Adelman, C. (2004). *Principal indicators of student academic histories in postsecondary education, 1972–2000.* Washington, DC: U.S. Department of Education, Institute of Education Sciences.

Brady, M. (2009). *Educational reform: An ignored problem, and a proposal* (E-mail received Aug. 25, 2009: mbrady22@cfl.rr.com). Available from http://www.marion brady.com

Carmichael, S. B., Martino, G., Porter-Magee, K., & Wilson, W. S. (with Fairchild, D., Haydel, E., Senechal, D., & Winkler, A. M.). (2010). *The state of state standards and the Common Core in 2010.* Washington, DC: Thomas B. Fordham Institute.

Center for Research on Education Outcomes. (2009). *Multiple choice: Charter school performance in 16 states.* Stanford, CA: Stanford University.

Craig, R. P. (1982). Some fundamental differences. In M. C. Smith & J. Williams (Eds.), *Proceedings of the Annual Conference of the Midwest Philosophy of Education Society* (pp. 133–140).

Edmunds, J. A., Bernstein, L. Unlu, F., Glennie, E., Willse, J., Arshavsky, N., et al. (2010). *Expanding the college pipeline: Early results from an experimental study of the impact of the Early College High School model.* Paper presented at the American Educational Research Association Annual Meeting in Denver, CO.

Hassel, B., & Terrell, M. G. (2006). *Charter school achievement: What we know.* Washington, DC: National Alliance for Public Charter Schools.

Mead, S., & Rotherham, A. (2008). *Changing the game: The federal role in supporting 21st century educational innovation.* Washington, DC: Brookings Institution.

The Nation's Report Card: http://nationsreportcard.gov/ltt_2008

North Carolina New Schools Project. (2010, August 16). *Innovator: News about high school innovation.* Retrieved August 29, 2011, from http://newschoolsproject.org/uploads/resources/innovator-archive-innovator--aug-16-2010-.pdf

Powell, A. G., Farrar, E., & Cohen, D. K. (1985). *The shopping mall high school: Winners and losers in the educational marketplace.* Boston: Houghton Mifflin.

Ravitch, D. (2010). *The death and life of the great American school system: How testing and choice are undermining education.* New York: Basic Books.

Rolfhus, E., Cook, H. G., Brite, J. L., & Hartman, J. (2010). *Are Texas' English language arts and reading standards college ready?* (Issues & Answers Report, REL 2010–No. 091). Washington, DC: U.S. Department of Education, Institute of Education Sciences, National Center for Education Evaluation and Regional Assistance, Regional Educational Laboratory Southwest. Retrieved from http://ies.ed.gov/ncee/edlabs

Schlesinger, A. M., Jr. (1998). *The disuniting of America: Reflections on a multicultural society* (Rev. & enlarged ed.). New York: W. W. Norton.

Searle, J. (2002). Twenty-one years in the Chinese room. In J. Preston & M. Bishop (Eds.), *Views into the Chinese room: New essays on Searle and artificial intelligence* (pp. 51–69). New York: Clarendon Press.

Will increased federal and state intervention and funding create better schools?

POINT: Susan Tave Zelman, *Houghton Mifflin Harcourt*
COUNTERPOINT: Daniel Fallon, *University of Maryland*

OVERVIEW

Local control has always been a fundamental principle in American education. Insofar as the U.S. Constitution does not specifically outline federal responsibilities for education, pursuant to the Tenth Amendment, decisions about what students should learn and how they should learn it have always been vested with the states. The states, in turn, until very recently, have largely allowed local school boards to determine the academic content that students are expected to learn.

Starting in the middle of the 20th century, the federal government began to put more money into education and as its dollar investment grew so too did its intrusion into the functioning of schools. States became active even before the middle of the 20th century. States were involved in a wide range of efforts including fostering the consolidation of school districts across the United States. In the 1920s, there were almost 120,000 school districts across the United States; by the late 1990s, there were only about 15,000; this number continues to decline annually. The efforts to consolidate to create efficiencies are not unique to education. A similar phenomenon could be seen in a large number of industries across the United States.

The one-room schoolhouse or the small mom-and-pop grocery store may have romantic appeal, but they often are compromised in terms of their ability to deliver high quality products at lower prices for consumers. Of course, there is still debate about whether all of the consolidations have created enhanced student performance and better schools even though the clear intention of much of the consolidation work that was encouraged by states related to a need to enhance educational delivery systems.

In the late 1970s, President Carter created the U.S. Department of Education (USDE). With the creation of the USDE, the federal role in dictating what would occur in public schools became more pronounced. As the federal and state governments also began to infuse more dollars into the educational enterprise, these monies carried with them opportunities for federal and state officials to be more directed about what content should be taught and who should be responsible for teaching these materials.

Looking back over the history of American education, one can see a wide variety of pieces of legislation have influenced policy and practice in American schools. A sample of these laws include the Land Ordinance Act and Northwest Ordinance (1785 and 1787), the Morrill Land Grant Colleges Acts (1862 and 1890), the National Defense Education Act (1958), the Elementary and Secondary Education Act (1965), the Individuals with Disabilities Education Act (1975), and most recently, No Child Left Behind Act (2001; law 2002). Each of these laws brought the federal and state governments more directly into the educational operations of local schools and school districts.

The question is whether such intervention has been good for children. In addition, it appears as though the federal and state governments are becoming even more intrusive. Will such "involvement" create better schools and better educational environments for teachers and students? Susan Tave Zelman (Houghton Mifflin Harcourt and former State Superintendent of Public Instruction, Ohio) takes the perspective that state and federal intervention is both essential and necessary. Daniel Fallon (University of Maryland), on the other hand, asserts that philanthropic investment and focus offers more potential for fostering and sustaining change in educational policy and practice.

Zelman argues for the importance of a national agenda. To this end, she maintains that there is a place for strong federal and state involvements especially as uniform standards are established for students to achieve by the time they complete their schooling, and uniform expectations are established in terms of what students are expected to know and demonstrate as they evidence their college and career readiness. In this regard, Zelman recognizes the limits of state control while strongly urging the involvement of states as they help align curricula and assessments as they help to work with educators to ensure that highly qualified and high quality teachers are in every American classroom.

Fallon describes the way in which philanthropic investment in education has begun to change the landscape of educational policy and practice. He notes that over the past decade, the Gates Foundation and a myriad of smaller but equally significant philanthropic entities have influenced the practices of educators and the direction of policy at the state and national levels. Fallon acknowledges that these philanthropies use dollars and considerable intellectual talent to direct educators into new PreK–12 initiatives and innovations, which can be seen through everything from charter schools to the Harlem Children's Zone to the small schools movement at the high school level.

As you read this chapter, consider these two questions: First, what are the opportunities that are created as a result of increased state and federal intervention in education? Second, what problems are engendered as a result of those federal and state involvements in schooling?

Thomas J. Lasley, II
University of Dayton

POINT: Susan Tave Zelman
Houghton Mifflin Harcourt

The world is full of problems such as the global economic crisis, climate changes, energy shortages, unequal distribution of wealth, extreme poverty, and disease. The United States must educate its next generation to be creative problem solvers who can clean up the crises that they will soon inherit. Americans have a moral responsibility to provide students with the knowledge, skills, and dispositions needed to create a better humanity than they have been given. The problems facing the United States are complex and in some ways interconnected. As such, these challenges transcend the efforts of local communities, states, and nations to solve them because they are global in nature.

American education has developed a strong tradition of local control such that many policymakers and citizens believe that education is more effective when left to local communities and the state. The result of local control is that where one lives dictates what one gets. As such, there is tremendous variability in classrooms within schools, in schools within districts, and in districts within states.

The National Assessment of Educational Progress (NAEP) data demonstrate the incredible variability in achievement among states. For example, just compare results from Massachusetts and Mississippi. Many states have experienced the recession differently as some states are in more dire need than others. Regardless, all states are feeling the tight squeeze of state and district budgets. Policymakers, such as Jacob E. Adams, Jr., noted in a recent *Education Week* article that they cannot postpone education as they can postpone building maintenance. This point essay argues that federal and state interventions, funding, and agendas will help create better schools that will help American students succeed and thrive in a new global economy. The United States is facing an international crisis; our world as we know or knew it is changing. Therefore, while Americans honor the tradition of local control, we need effective and efficient federal and state policies to ensure that our schools will better educate our students for the new millennium.

Local school boards and states alone cannot ensure that American students will meet international standards. International assessments such those by Trends in International Mathematics and Science Study (TIMMS) and Programme for International Student Assessment (PISA) have shown that American students are scoring much lower than their counterparts in other industrialized countries. Moreover, graduation rates in American high schools, colleges, and universities are lower than those in other industrialized nations.

At the same time, competition for high paying technical jobs is now global as will be competition for future jobs that we cannot now imagine. As discussed in the report *Rising Above the Gathering Storm,* American students are seen by multinational corporations as losing their competitive edge; corporations are going overseas to find needed technological talent in the fields of science, technology, engineering, and mathematics (STEM).

There are vast opportunity and achievement gaps in this country. In the 1960s, the federal government enacted the Elementary and Secondary Education Act (ESEA) to provide assistance to states with disproportionate numbers of minority and low income children. After years of failure by the federal government to hold states accountable for demonstrating improvement in student achievement, in 2002 President George W. Bush signed into law the bipartisan No Child Left Behind Act (NCLB), which required states to hold schools accountable for academic achievement of all children in language arts, mathematics, and science. The requirement for states, boards, and individual schools to disaggregate achievement data by race, ethnicity, income, English language learners, and special needs shined a light on the horrendous achievement gaps among various groups of students.

NCLB has become even more important because the face of the United States has been changing. American students are now more racially and ethnically diverse than at any other time in our history. In some states such as California, minority students are becoming the majority. By 2050, more than half the country will be Hispanic. Educators need support on how to teach to the strengths of this diversity. In the current economic condition, one in every four babies in the United States is being born into poverty. Parents who are faced with problems resulting from economic stress have a difficult time in providing supportive learning environments for their children. The achievement gap begins to present itself when these students are born and becomes obvious in kindergarten readiness assessments. States and local districts vary in the policies and programs that support high quality interventions for the children and families who need them the most. This is a national problem that requires federal and state resources.

This essay evaluates how policy improvements to the reauthorization of ESEA and additional funding at federal and state levels will improve schools. The essay also sets forth a national and state agenda around increased expectations arising from improved system performance, high capacity of the system to meet the increased expectations, and aligned incentives to improve our schools.

First, this point essay addresses the roles of the federal government and states in meeting the need to increase expectations. Here, a review of management literature suggests that people respond positively when there are clear and high goals. Being clear about what Americans want our students and our educators to know and be able to do is extremely important to school success. To address the variability of 50 different quality state academic standards, the National Governors Association (NGA) and the Council of the Chief State School Officers (CCSSO) led a state driven initiative that set up common core state standards. These standards currently cover English language arts and mathematics even as states are working on science standards. Secretary of Education Arne Duncan has pledged to support the standards by recommending federal funds for high quality assessments, high quality professional development for teachers, and research to support continual improvement of the standards and assessments. Still missing from this national education agenda is the need for states and their governors to articulate standards for educators.

The standards movement must clearly articulate what good teaching of the standards looks like. The promise of federal dollars for this initiative is missing from Duncan's endorsement. Effective policy supports the alignment of expectations, assessments, curriculum, and teaching strategies. Unlike the centralized education policy of other high performing nations, American federal and state policies have for the most part shied away from mandating national and/or statewide curricula and have left these decisions to local school districts. However, the variability in the capacity and wealth of districts and the absence of clear, evidence-based curricula truly aligned to the standards has led to inconsistent and harmful implementation of practices in American schools. In some schools, the curriculum has been reduced to teaching to the test, and the curriculum becomes the test items released by state assessment directors. In other places, where there is high quality teaching, the curriculum can be rich and engaging, but these practices are developed by individual teachers, schools, or districts.

The U.S. Department of Education recently granted approximately $350 million to two state consortia to produce a new set of assessments that will go beyond paper-and-pencil tests and will align to the new Common Core standards. In addition, student e-portfolios or project-based rubrics would be an improvement over what is currently used to measure student achievement and teacher effectiveness. The absence of evidence-based curricula aligned to the new assessments reduces credibility and fairness in evaluating both students and teachers.

The lack of alignment of the Common Core standards and new assessments with curricula leads to less clarity in the teaching practices that are keys to student achievement. Aligned curricula would make our investments in teacher training and professional development more cost effective and efficient. Duncan should require the two assessment consortia to address curriculum issues while providing federal resources, perhaps from Title II funding. Given that local school boards adopt curricula that may not be aligned to standards and state assessments, the colleges, universities, and local educational leaders are at a loss to prepare their aspiring and seasoned teachers properly with high quality instructional practices that are needed to implement the Common Core standards.

Of course, not everyone at the federal and state levels endorses the Common Core. This controversy will be an important issue in the reauthorization debates of ESEA/NCLB. The United States is a nation of individualists. Many Americans see common standards as an example of the "government" coming in and telling localities what to teach.

Government can, though, reduce the disparity in educational opportunity among and within states by ensuring that high quality curriculum and instruction are aligned to common standards and assessments. The quality of student work should be the same regardless of the zip code of the student. Clear, high expectations for students are particularly important for bilingual, poor, racially and ethnically diverse, and special needs students. Insofar as teachers have not been given needed tools on individualizing and customizing curricula to these special populations, many educators as well as the general public do not believe that all children can learn. President George W. Bush described this phenomenon as the "soft bigotry of low expectations."

To the extent that the Common Core standards are more rigorous than past state standards and will be aligned to new assessments, governors and chief state school officers will have to admit to the public that prior policies gave the appearance that students were college and career ready when they were not prepared. The public may find the results of the new common assessments disappointing, and the role of the federal and state governments in adopting the new standards may encourage advocates of nongovernmental interference in local decisions and result in barring our students from successful competition in a new global economy.

When the federal and state governments demand major changes and higher expectations, they have moral and political obligations to provide support to the education system. At a time of economic crisis, the reality is that support must come in the form of more federal and state funding of local school districts to implement the new policies to ensure that teachers are not laid off, art and music programs are not eliminated, and curricular and technology purchases are not deferred. If federal and state funds are not available, students' learning will suffer, and the United States will not recover its level of high educational attainment.

In addition, federal and state governments should invest in data systems that are able to connect with one another. These systems should be able to provide data about student achievement, educators, financial factors, and family and community demographics. The data systems should also house digital learning libraries to help educators individualize and customize instruction. Data can inform educator decision making as well as provide information for research and evaluation to promote shared best practices and innovations. Preparing educators on how to use these databases can result in more efficient and effective use of resources and save taxpayer dollars by aligning fiscal and instructional information.

The federal and state governments must also support a human resource system for the profession by helping districts develop policies on recruitment, induction, retention, professional development, leadership, and retirement of educators. A national consensus on the standards of teacher quality is needed. States and professional organizations should come together to define common pedagogical knowledge and specific content pedagogical techniques. While the CCSSO recently released Common Core standards on a coherent set of expectations describing professional practices for teachers throughout their careers, the standards do not spell out specific subject matter teaching competencies aligned to subject-specific content standards. States should unite to define and adopt teacher effectiveness and to develop multiple measures for certification and educator evaluations that are evidence based.

An effective teacher in Mississippi should be judged similarly to an effective teacher in Massachusetts. There should be a system of national portability of pensions. The federal government should help states provide incentives to ensure that publicly supported preschools, Head Starts, and hard-to-staff urban and rural schools have effective teachers. Incentives such as bonuses for high performance, loan forgiveness, and tax credits can ensure that underrepresented and underserved students are served by the best teachers. These initiatives would help to reduce the costs of remediation programs. As an example of one such program, the federal Teacher Incentive Fund has helped states create differentiated roles for the profession, evaluation systems, reorganization of classrooms, and pay for performance. Properly designed federal and state programs and aligned incentives will make teaching a more valued and honored profession.

For years prior to the enactment of the NCLB, states and local school boards ignored failing, dysfunctional schools. The NCLB now requires states to take specific actions to turn around failing schools as a condition for receiving school improvement dollars. Unfortunately, the federal government mandated specific actions based on the number of years during which schools did not show Adequate Yearly Progress (AYP). The federal government can be helpful to states and school boards by providing funds for them to come together to develop diagnostic tools and technical assistance strategies to identify and address specific problems that low-performing schools face. School improvement and Title II (Teacher Quality provision of the ESEA) dollars can help fund activities that can result in more effective evidence-based school improvement practices.

The reality is that educators need help and support from the community to educate all children in the 21st century. Students are rooted in families and communities and have difficulty learning when they lack good physical and mental health and are not nurtured or supported by their families or communities. Coordinated investments are needed for federal and state agencies to provide local community development dollars to at-risk neighborhoods and to support full-service schools from preschools to high schools. Geoffrey Canada's Harlem Children's Zone is an example of how health, human services, and economic development agencies can work together to promote human development in low income neighborhoods. The Obama administration modeled its Promise Neighborhood Initiative after the Harlem Children's Zone with an investment of $200 million. A more substantial investment in this program is needed.

A perfect example of aligned incentives is the Obama administration's tying of the Race to the Top (RTT) proposals to states' adoption of Common Core standards, support of charter schools, and the use of test scores as one measure of teacher effectiveness. Forty states quickly adopted the Common Core standards, and state legislatures changed laws that barred states and districts from using test data to measure teacher quality and lifted caps on the number of charter schools in their states. Over the past year, the allure of federal dollars in tight economic times has produced a substantial amount of cooperation among states to develop common educational policies. The California State Board of Education, which has traditionally focused on monitoring and compliance issues and does not weigh in on district decision making, is now calling for a countrywide online database to measure teacher effectiveness. Working with philanthropies, such as the Gates Foundation, the federal government can use the results of their research on teacher effectiveness to guide national and state policy. Particularly in tight economic times, money and incentives matter and can drive policy changes. However, encouraging states to publicize value-added teachers' scores on student achievement tests as one measure of teacher effectiveness without dealing with conditions such as classroom assignment of students is unfair, unjust, and hurtful to the profession.

Defining effective education incentives to advance a national agenda will be a major issue in the reauthorization of ESEA/NCLB. This point essay has thus argued for a strong federal and state role while providing examples of how the federal and state governments can act in concert with local school boards in responding to high expectations, capacity building to support these high expectations, and properly aligned incentives to drive the changes that are sorely needed in our nation's schools.

COUNTERPOINT: Daniel Fallon
University of Maryland

As a person with experience in educational philanthropy, my counterpoint to the idea of state and federal intervention on behalf of teaching and learning is somewhat oblique. This is because, in fact, most philanthropy encourages federal and state support for sound educational policy. Since in a democracy the government is the people, long-term change usually depends on explicit or implicit support by government, and government thus becomes a favored objective of philanthropy. Nonetheless, government often acts impulsively, driven by momentary strong political currents, and can promote public policy in a poorly informed way. Once laws are on the books, they are difficult to retract or alter, and the schools, along with the teachers and pupils in them, can find their mission hampered rather than helped by government intervention.

Philanthropic organizations cherish their independence, which is their strongest comparative advantage, even if in the long run they aim for substantive social and political change to improve public welfare and contribute to the improvement of human society. Insofar as philanthropy is agile, it can quickly test ideas that emerge from laboratory investigation, scholarly review, or keen analytical reasoning. Some tested methods or systems prove to be durable and productive whereas others are shown to be weak or ineffective. Once philanthropy has given a venture secure footing and shown it to be successful, it can become a candidate for broad implementation through state or federal political support. Sometimes, successful ideas do not need further state or federal intervention, instead becoming widely adopted simply by the demonstration of their value. In this counterpoint essay, I focus on the role of philanthropy in promoting educational progress.

CHANGING DEFINITION

Of course, *philanthropy* aims to do good in the world. That is, after all, the meaning of the word from its Greek etymology: "love of people" (*philia*, love + *anthropos*, human being). In the English-speaking world, philanthropy is an example of a word that changed its meaning dramatically in the space of less than 100 years. In the 18th century, it meant literally love of people, but by the end of the 19th century, it was used to characterize the donation of money for public purposes, either by individuals or by businesses or foundations. This change in the meaning of the word *philanthropy* occurred during the lifetime of a remarkable person, Andrew Carnegie. A strong case can be made that Carnegie's philosophy and his actions were the cause of this change.

When we consider the historic meaning of philanthropy in the English language, even animals that were friendly to people were once considered philanthropic. For example, here is a definition from a Zoology text published in 1769: "The dolphin was celebrated in the earliest time for its fondness for the human race . . . and distinguished [from other fishes as] . . . boy loving and philanthropist." A more common use is illustrated by this sentence by the English novelist Henry Fielding, from his book, *Tom Jones,* published in 1749, "In friendship, in parental and filial affection, and indeed in general philanthropy, there is a great and exquisite delight."

The first mention I have found of the word in the universal way it is used in English today was a notice in the Society Press of London in 1875 where it was reported that "a great philanthropist has astonished the world by giving it large sums of money during his lifetime." This was Carnegie's practice. Carnegie championed the use of the word *philanthropy,* around which he built his life's philosophy, and he painstakingly distinguished philanthropy from charity, a practice he found abominable and unethical. Giving a coin to a homeless person on the street, he felt, only trained the person to beg. Instead, as he put it, the purpose of philanthropy should be "to assist, but rarely or never to do all" and to build "ladders upon which the aspiring can rise" (Carnegie, 2006, pp. 11–12). As Carnegie began to develop his ideas about philanthropy, he first championed the view that he alone, who had earned the greatest personal fortune in the world, should be the sole determiner of how that fortune should be distributed. It was his goal initially to give away his entire fortune before he died, claiming that the rich who hoard their assets deserve only scorn. He stressed this point in the stirring conclusion to his essay on wealth, writing, "The man who dies thus rich, dies disgraced" (Carnegie, 2006, p. 12).

STRATEGIC PHILANTHROPY

Strategic philanthropy, of the kind developed and championed by Carnegie, seeks to use its treasure as a stimulus or lever for positive change. The ultimate change that occurs could be state or federal policy or the behavior of individuals, groups, or organizations in society. In my view, the most dramatic example of this kind of philanthropic influence on education was Carnegie's establishment of a pension plan for college and university teachers.

On joining the board of trustees of Cornell University in 1890 at the request of his friend Ezra Cornell, Carnegie was surprised and dismayed to learn that university faculty, whose profession he admired as among the most noble and valuable, had no means of support for their retirement and were thus obliged to teach until infirmity or death overtook them. In Carnegie's view, establishing pensions for persons who pursued virtuous careers was a prime example of proper application of philanthropy. Therefore, in 1905 Carnegie created the Carnegie Teachers' Pension Fund, but within a year, changed its name to reflect a broader mission, receiving a charter from the U.S. Congress to establish the Carnegie Foundation for the Advancement of Teaching.

Carnegie appointed Henry S. Pritchett, then President of the Massachusetts Institute of Technology, as the Foundation's first president and then appointed as trustees an extraordinary collection of intellectual leaders including the president of Harvard, C. W. Eliot, the president of Yale, A. T. Hadley, the president of Columbia, Nicholas Murray Butler, the president of Stanford, David Starr Jordan, along with the presidents of many leading liberal arts colleges and of the premier institution of higher learning in Canada, McGill.

With Carnegie's approval, the trustees sent a letter of invitation, in the form of a survey, to 627 postsecondary institutions in the United States and Canada, from which 421 replies were received. Initially, the survey went to only private institutions because Carnegie was concerned that state governments might consider his initiative awkwardly unwelcome for state funded colleges and universities. However, on receiving numerous entreaties from state funded institutions, from legislatures, and officially from what was then called the National Association of State Universities, Carnegie in 1908 enthusiastically endorsed the inclusion of state funded colleges and universities in the pension program and increased the size of the Foundation's endowment accordingly.

The survey conducted by the trustees asked for information about the size of the institution's endowment, ties to religious sects, admissions standards, qualifications for faculty, and many other defining characteristics. At Carnegie's insistence, the trustees excluded any institution with clear ties to a religious denomination from participation in the pension fund. Carnegie insisted that postsecondary institutions should be secular, since, in his opinion, "what denominationalism really meant—several sects each claiming to proclaim the truth and by inference condemning the others as imperfect" (Carnegie letter to Abram W. Harris, March 16, 1909, qtd. in Wall, 1989, p. 876) was contrary to any spirit of true higher learning. Among other requirements, the trustees insisted that applicant institutions have a minimum endowment of $200,000 and set admission standards for entering students at a minimum of 15 completed units of college preparatory instruction. Of the 421 initial applicants, only 52 institutions were admitted to the pension fund.

Since in its original form, the pension fund required no financial contribution either from the institution or from individual faculty, it was an important perquisite for a postsecondary institution to join. The most qualified faculty and the most qualified students wanted to teach and study only at institutions that offered Carnegie pensions, thus, creating immense pressure for aspiring postsecondary institutions to meet the standards set by the trustees for membership. This act of philanthropy, for example, led institutions to change charters linking them to religious denomination, the most famous and contentious cases being Northwestern, which ultimately broke its ties to the Methodists, and Brown, similarly with the Baptists. The University of Virginia was at first excluded because of weak admissions standards, since it required less than 7 units of college preparatory instruction of its beginning students. When it moved quickly and forcefully to raise its admissions standards to 15 units, Virginia immediately set a pattern for institutions throughout the South, both at the secondary and at the postsecondary level.

Ultimately, so many institutions joined the pension fund and so many postsecondary employees became eligible that the original endowment, although substantial, was unable to accommodate the burden. This led to the first formal demographic analysis of potential pensioners conducted in the United States, undertaken by the Carnegie Foundation for the Advancement of Teaching in 1915, which later served as the foundation for legislation in the 1930s creating the U.S. Social Security System. The analysis also then led to a rewriting of the rules for eligibility for pensions, now requiring contributions from individual faculty members and from institutions. A new organization was created by the Foundation to administer this new system, the Teachers Insurance Annuity Association or TIAA.

IMPACT OF PHILANTHROPY ON EDUCATION

For education, the impact of Carnegie's philanthropy in the first 2 decades of the 20th century was profound beyond measure. By its incentives, it moved high schools throughout the United States to create curricula that would allow their graduates to qualify for admission to the most recognized colleges and universities. These requirements, naturally enough, began to be called *Carnegie Units*, since they constituted the standards for admission to postsecondary institutions that qualified for Carnegie pensions. The incentives similarly moved postsecondary institutions toward a common set of basic standards: to secularize, to raise admissions standards, to set themselves on sound financial footing, and to improve the qualifications of their faculty.

Without intending to do so, the Carnegie Foundation for the Advancement of Teaching became, in the 2nd decade of the 20th century, a de facto national accreditation agency for higher education. A reasonable conclusion from this history is that the establishment of the Carnegie Teachers Pension Fund was the single most important catalytic agent imposing order on postsecondary education in the United States at a critical moment of development. By its impact on higher education, it also raised standards and regularized high school education throughout the nation. These effects were accomplished not by law, but by the power of philanthropy. Today, the Carnegie Teachers Pension Fund has become Teachers Insurance and Annuity Association–College Retirement Equities Fund, or TIAA/CREF, is fully independent of any connection to its founding philanthropy, and is regulated like all other such organizations by appropriate federal and state laws and regulations.

Of course, one can argue that philanthropy is not an unadorned blessing. It is certainly open to the charge that it proceeds arrogantly, bullying its recipients into compliance with the lure of riches. The Carnegie pension fund became controversial in the progressive era of which it was a part for precisely this reason. The most public example at the time was William Jennings Bryan, a graduate and trustee of Illinois College, who railed against the pension fund and Carnegie with one of his characteristic phrases, declaring that the college could not simultaneously serve "God and Mammon!" (qtd. in Wall, 1989, p. 874). When the college nonetheless proceeded to apply for pensions for its faculty, Bryan resigned from his position as trustee in a furious letter to the president.

Bryan's anger at Carnegie's pension fund was driven in part by the perception if not the reality that a single wealthy person, a *robber baron*, to use a term popular at the time, was dictating the rules of the game for the entire society. Yet Carnegie was about to take steps that would institutionalize philanthropy, making it less a personal enterprise than a public trust. In 1909, Carnegie's financial secretary informed him that his fortune was earning money faster than he could give it away. Despairing of his inability to give away his entire fortune during his own lifetime, Carnegie hit upon the idea of establishing a long lasting permanent trust, and he went about securing specific legislation from the federal and state governments to make this possible. The result was the creation of Carnegie Corporation of New York (CCNY), the first major national philanthropic foundation. Carnegie then transferred virtually all of his remaining assets to this new organization, ensuring their ongoing use in perpetuity, and making it at the time by far the largest philanthropy the nation had ever seen. He entrusted the purposes of this philanthropy to a self-perpetuating board of trustees, which he declined to constrain, asking them only to ensure that funds be spent "to promote the advancement and diffusion of knowledge and understanding among the people of the United States" (qtd. in Wall, 1989, p. 883).

PHILANTHROPY TODAY

Philanthropy today operates differently than in Carnegie's era. It was then a novelty; it is now a fixture of American life. Philanthropy in the contemporary world is embedded in a variety of state and federal laws and regulations that serve as checks and balances on its action. It is common practice for philanthropic organizations to be governed by boards of trustees and to select operating officers on the basis of specific expertise and qualifications. Some philanthropy is local, limited to giving to interests in a particular state or community, and some philanthropy is private, controlled exclusively by personal or family interests. The major national philanthropic organizations, however, such as the Gates Foundation or CCNY, are defined by law as public charities and regulated accordingly.

Interventions in education by philanthropy do not follow a uniform pattern. In some cases, philanthropy will reach out proactively to enable what in its judgment is a good idea. That was the posture of CCNY in the early months and years of Teach For America, when external support proved vital to the founding of what has become a robust presence in the arena of teacher supply, now supported by federal and state funds as well as contract income and donor contributions. In other cases, it will respond to proposals to intervene at a propitious moment in an effort to influence public policy, as CCNY provided resources to establish the National Commission on Teaching and America's Future (NCTAF). NCTAF had a significant impact on teacher education policies in many states and provided much of the framework for the most recent, to date, reauthorization of the Elementary and Secondary Education Act in 2001, called by its authors No Child Left Behind.

More common approaches include responding to proposals received unexpectedly from persons in the field or inviting proposals for funds in support of some major initiative. An example of an idea presented by hopeful applicants that arrived in the offices of CCNY entirely on its own is what has become the Collegiate Learning Assessment (CLA), currently the leading instrument for measuring growth in student learning during the student's matriculation at an institution of higher learning. The proponents, who had been unsuccessful in persuading other foundations or donors of the value of their project, insisted that they could develop high quality, authentic assessments that would measure the value-added of liberal education. With support from CCNY, instruments were developed that resulted in the CLA, which was endorsed by a presidential commission, received the support of several state governments, has been used by more than 200,000 students across hundreds of colleges and universities, and is now serving as a prototype for an international assessment to be conducted through the Organisation for Economic Co-operation and Development in Paris.

An example of invited proposals is the major teacher education reform initiative called Teachers for a New Era (TNE). CCNY prepared a detailed prospectus describing the initiative in detail and indicating what would be expected of participating institutions including, in this case, a significant matching funds requirement. CCNY then assembled a panel of experts in the area of teacher education to assist in the selection of a small group of institutions considered representative of teacher education in the nation at large and that, in the judgment of CCNY, possessed the capacity to carry out the reforms. These institutions were then invited to participate by submitting a plan of action over 5 years to accomplish what the prospectus called radical change.

It is too early to evaluate the success of TNE, but it did require the institutions, beginning long before such ideas became more common, for example, (a) to find ways to evaluate the success of their program in terms of the growth in learning by pupils being taught by graduates of the program and (b) to include mechanisms to ensure clinical induction to the profession through mentoring and support by the program of the program's recently certified novice teachers. Now that such measures are increasingly being required by the states and by the federal government, the TNE institutions have experimented with a variety of models that are available to the profession for adoption and adjustment.

Many other examples of the influence of philanthropy on educational innovation and reform could be cited. These include advances in adolescent literacy, Early College High Schools, value-added modeling of student learning, development of observation protocols, and Common Core standards. Although officers at foundations provide leadership and administrative support, no philanthropy can be successful without heavy and critical reliance on guidance and counsel from experts and practitioners in the field.

Philanthropy assists in turning promising ideas into practice, in supporting successes that emerge from the field, in generating the research base that will make evidence the determining guide for decision making, and in helping to point the way toward a better more effective future for schools and our nation's children. Some ideas and initiatives will not prove useful. The more successful programs will ultimately achieve long-term support from the public, through state and federal government policy, or from donors or from other forms of revenue generation. As Carnegie put it, philanthropy can attempt "to assist, but rarely or never to do all" and to build "ladders upon which the aspiring can rise" (Carnegie, 2006, pp. 11–12). In the end, philanthropy depends on dedicated and knowledgeable professionals in the field to bring forward promising ideas, methods, and systems. Officers in philanthropic organizations work together with individual entrepreneurs, citizens groups, and knowledge professionals to serve those beneficial goals on which we commonly agree.

FURTHER READINGS AND RESOURCES

Carnegie, A. (2006). *The "Gospel of Wealth" essays and other writings* (D. Nasaw, Ed.). New York: Penguin.

Committee on Prospering in the Global Economy of the 21st Century: An Agenda for American Science and Technology Committee on Science, Engineering, and Public Policy. (2008). *Rising above the gathering storm: Energizing and employing America for a brighter economic future* (July 2008 revisions). Washington, DC: The National Academies Press. Retrieved August 29, 2011, from http://www.nap.edu/catalog.php?record_id=11463

Common Core State Standards Initiative. (2010). *Common Core State Standards.* Available from http://corestandards.org

Finn, C. E. J., & Petrilli, M. J. (2010). *Now what? Imperatives and options for Common Core implementation and governance.* Washington, DC: Thomas B. Fordham Institute.

Krass, P. (2002). *Carnegie.* Hoboken, NJ: Wiley & Sons.

Lagemann, E. C. (1989). *The politics of knowledge: The Carnegie Corporation, philanthropy, and public policy.* Middletown, CT: Wesleyan University Press.

Nasaw, D. (2006). *Andrew Carnegie.* New York: Penguin.

Wall, J. F. (1989). *Andrew Carnegie* (Rev. ed.). Pittsburgh, PA: University of Pittsburgh Press.

Should more rigorous teacher education standards be instituted to ensure teacher quality?

POINT: Kate Walsh, *National Council on Teacher Quality*
COUNTERPOINT: Mary E. Diez, *Alverno College*

OVERVIEW

One of the most important issues confronting administrators is ensuring that all classrooms in school buildings are staffed by qualified and effective teachers. For years, the emphasis in the United States has been on teacher qualifications. Specifically, the issue is whether all teachers are appropriately credentialed. More recently, attention has been given to the teacher's effectiveness and to ensuring that all students have the opportunity to be taught by effective teachers. A wide variety of educational researchers have now documented that having effective teachers makes a difference in terms of student academic growth. All parents intuitively understood this to be the case, but there is now substantial psychometric documentation to indicate just how important it is for students to have multiple effective teachers as opposed to even one ineffective one.

Much of the policy debate is about how to ensure the presence of qualified and effective teachers for all classrooms. As noted in other parts of this book, some would argue for deregulating the teacher and principal licensure process. For the deregulationists, the emphasis is on attracting human capital to the educational enterprise, and many in the deregulation camp do not perceive that traditional university-based teacher education programs have the ability or capacity to ensure that an effective teacher is in every classroom. For deregulationists, the teacher education monopoly, regardless of how it is regulated or accredited, is simply unable to provide the professional talent that schools require.

In this chapter, Kate Walsh from the National Council on Teacher Quality (NCTQ) and Mary Diez from Alverno College approach the teacher quality issue from the perspective of teacher education standards and the accreditation process. For years, traditional teacher education programs have been accredited by either the National Council for the Accreditation of Teacher Education (NCATE) or, more recently, the Teacher Education Accreditation Council (TEAC). NCATE has specific accreditation standards, and TEAC has defined protocols for assessing whether teacher education programs have in place the structures and systems needed to produce quality teachers. Some states mandate NCATE/TEAC accreditation and other states rely on state-defined approval procedures for determining whether institutions have the legal right to license teachers for classroom practice. NCATE continues to update its standards to make them more outcomes-based and less "inputs" oriented. The issue is whether this approach is sufficient for ensuring teacher quality.

Walsh argues that even more rigorous teacher education standards are required to ensure that the United States has the teachers that it needs. She asserts, for example, that traditional teacher education programs still rely too heavily on students who enter programs with weak academic credentials. Traditionally, accredited programs (NCATE or TEAC) have "approved" structures in place, but if they have academically weak students, their best effort will be compromised in terms of the quality of the teachers they prepare and graduate. Walsh argues that standards need to be in place that limit who is admitted into teacher education programs and more rigorous standards need to be in place to control and dictate what happens to students as they move through their preparation programs.

Diez takes a different view in asserting that NCATE (and TEAC) have evolved in very positive and professionally responsible ways. They have, for example, placed much more emphasis on candidate learning outcomes and, as a consequence, the public should be more assured that it is getting high quality, not just highly qualified, teachers. More significantly, contends Diez, teacher education institutions operating under NCATE and TEAC accreditation are placing more emphasis on performance assessments that will capture real evidence of a prospective teacher's effectiveness. For Diez, the current standards work, especially given the emergent work on preservice teacher performance assessment.

As you read this chapter, focus on three issues. First, are more rigorous accreditation standards needed? Second, are these standards the answer to the teacher quality issue? Third, what preparation policies need to be in place to ensure that every young person has the opportunity to be taught by a highly effective teacher?

Thomas J. Lasley, II
University of Dayton

POINT: Kate Walsh
National Council on Teacher Quality

This essay uses examples from our experiences at the National Council on Teacher Quality analyzing teacher preparation programs to identify weaknesses in current approaches to program accountability, including problems with the design and application of national accreditation policies. We propose changing an outmoded and ineffective approach by creating policies that will accelerate program reform, close down the programs unable or unwilling to change, and produce highly effective teachers.

Years ago, the National Council on Teacher Quality began studying the quality of U.S. teacher preparation programs. Our first task was to figure out the number of U.S. campus-based teacher preparation programs. No federal agency knew. Accrediting groups could only tell us how many institutions they had accredited or turned down—hundreds less than our working estimate. Associations could only tell us how many institutions were members, again hundreds short. The number of programs with state approval remained a mystery.[1]

It was our first indication of chaos in the system for preparing teachers. From the federal government to the deans and department heads of approximately 1,400 education schools, there is no responsible party for ensuring the quality of teacher preparation.

We review attempts by various authorities to bring order and accountability to teacher preparation programs. These include federal and state governments, accrediting bodies, and colleges and universities. Our conclusion is fourfold:

1. Neither the federal government nor states have been able to establish a meaningful threshold of quality.

2. The national accreditation movement of the past 20 years has failed to establish such a threshold.

3. With a century under its belt, teacher education has yet to agree upon a standard program of study.

4. Too many programs will deprive aspiring teachers of quality preparation unless the field commits to two things: an accountability system premised on graduates' performance data and standards that define a high-caliber program of study.

FORAYS BY THE FEDS

In recent years, the federal government has examined regulation of teacher preparation. In 1998, Congress instructed states to require programs to report the percentage of candidates who passed licensing exams, a move that had potential to nudge states to close programs with low rates. Shortly after the report card structure was established, institutions joined professional associations including American Association of Colleges for Teacher Education, or AACTE, and NCATE to defeat the goal of the reporting system. Even state agencies were complicit. The strategy used required teacher candidates to pass all required teacher tests *before* graduating. It gave a pass on accountability because schools could report 100% pass rates among graduates without disclosing the percentage of candidates who failed one or more tests.

Since 1998, less than 2% of all teacher education programs in the United States were flagged as low-performing, but they all are judged to have improved enough to be taken off these lists. Nationwide, 31 programs were labeled "at-risk or low-performing" in 2006, up from 17 programs in 2005 and 11 in 2002.

These are *programs* being identified, not institutions. There can be as many as 8 programs at a single institution, preparing all types of teachers for certification. We estimate that there are about 7,000 such programs in the country, meaning that the *identification* rate of troubled schools amounts to no more than half of 1 percent (0.5%). In the past 5 years, we found no evidence that a state shut down a single program for non-performance.

Subsequent federal efforts have also been mixed—such as the provision in No Child Left Behind that the credentials needed by middle school teachers had to mirror those of high school teachers and not those of more broadly educated elementary teachers. Nearly 10 years after the law's passage, a third of states have not complied.

The latest federal effort to foster teacher quality and preparation program accountability is embedded in the Race to the Top (RTT) initiatives of 2009. States had to agree to link teachers to their preparation programs and report publicly on graduates. Systems to collect and manage these data, for most states, are still years away. In the few states that have this capacity, there are still many questions about controlling for the impact of districts on teacher performance. One could argue that lackluster efforts to raise teacher quality are a manifestation of states' resistance to federal interference. But constitutional principles do not justify repeated failure to bring order to the process.

Figure 5.1

States still out of compliance on No Child Left Behind regulations

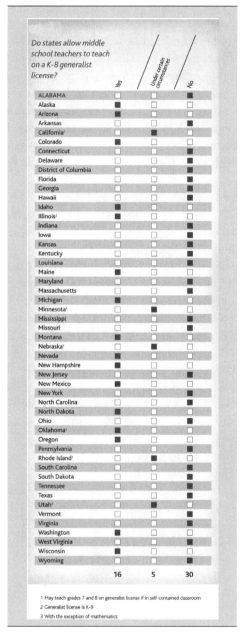

Source: National Council on Teacher Quality, State Teacher Policy Yearbook, 2009.

Note: There are still 21 states permitting middle school teachers to teach with only elementary teacher qualifications, certainly meaning they are out of compliance with federal law.

STATES: WHO'S ON FIRST?

To oversee teacher preparation programs, states have departments of education, higher education boards, and professional standards boards. State legislatures also weigh in. It's tempting to liken the process to Abbott and Costello's "Who's on first?" Here, we'll look at three states: Texas, Maryland, and California.

Texas: Aggressive Regulation, Little Enforcement

Policymakers and educators show concern with how U.S. students are faring on international tests of mathematics and science. Our interest is to understand what skills teachers do or do not have to teach these subject areas well. We asked the Texas department of education how many math courses teacher preparation programs in Texas require. The response was three, though the regulation did not stipulate the content. We then learned that a third of the state's programs did not enforce the requirement. When we reported this, the higher education board said it did not require private education schools to comply.

Such deviations make sense if the goal is to protect institutional autonomy and academic freedom. It makes no sense if the policy goal is to uphold uniform standards of teacher quality. If state officials decide that an effective elementary teacher generally needs at least three mathematics courses, the policy should apply for all teachers eligible for Texas licensure. Better yet would have been consensus about the mathematics content. It was clear that the 67 Texas programs had no common understanding of what elementary teachers need. Some institutions required one course, others up to five. The content varied even more.

In a nutshell, core features of Texas's approach to accountability are well-meaning but often flawed, and these flaws are made worse by how universities interpret or ignore state policy. The regulatory system puffs out its chest under various pronouncements, only to release a lot of hot air and then be met with resistance in defense of academic freedom. This disarray and the failure to include content in policy fail to serve the interests of children. A system that permits full institutional autonomy fails to acknowledge that some institutions will perform poorly, and student learning suffers.

Maryland: Compliance Without Consequences

While Texas pursued an activist role (particularly legislatively), Maryland has taken a more laissez-faire approach. The only objective criterion that Maryland uses for program quality is the federal requirement discussed above: The 1998 Higher Education Act required that low-performing programs be identified but let states define low-performing. Setting the bar low ensured that few programs would be identified. Maryland requires its programs to maintain a pass rate of at least 80% of candidates on the state's licensing exam. In the 9 years

Figure 5.2

The field's lack of consensus

There are no fewer than six different models practiced in Texas for preparing elementary teachers in mathematics

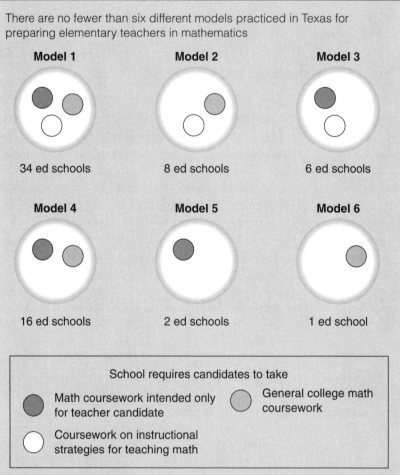

Model 1	Model 2	Model 3
34 ed schools	8 ed schools	6 ed schools

Model 4	Model 5	Model 6
16 ed schools	2 ed schools	1 ed school

School requires candidates to take

Math coursework intended only for teacher candidate

General college math coursework

Coursework on instructional strategies for teaching math

To make matters even more confusing, within each of these models the amount of required courses varies substantially. For example, Southwestern University, The University of Texas at El Paso, and Tarleton State University all use Model 1. However, Southwestern University requires only one math course intended for teacher candidates, The University of Texas at El Paso requires two, and Tarleton State University requires three. Unless elementary teacher candidates at each campus have significantly different needs, there is no good rationale for this variance.

Source: National Council on Teacher Quality, *No Common Denominator*, 2008.

that the requirement has been in place, only one identified program failed to meet Maryland's standard. After setting a remediation plan that was never released to the public, the program regained its standing. At no point was the public informed that a program was in peril. The low standing of this program could be found nowhere on the state website; it was many clicks deep on one site maintained by the federal government.

Obscure standards, weak enforcement, and no public disclosure render accountability meaningless. Other states emulated Maryland's approach to program oversight, tying their preparation programs to Interstate New Teacher Assessment and Support Consortium (INTASC) or NCATE standards that lack teeth; only occasionally does a state bear down on a weak program. These states also protect the weak programs (but not the students who will be academic victims of their graduates) by burying adverse findings or never disclosing them.

California: Confusing Compliance With Quality Control

State authorities seem to confuse compliance, which they are very good at enforcing, and quality control, which they are not. Let's look at California. After we reported that the state did not appear to be measuring the quality of its teacher preparation programs, officials claimed that the National Council on Teacher Quality did not understand the state's role. California's role, they asserted, was to assess whether teacher preparation programs meet certain "preconditions." We asked for the preconditions; their response was, "Preconditions specify requirements for program compliance, not program quality." Clearer words by bureaucrats were never written.

California helps illustrate the futility of some regulations. This should be taken to heart in many other states, where paper reviews and information dumps to state oversight agencies are viewed as ways to foster program quality. In fact, institutions actively seeking ways to get better find these oversight processes beside the point.

The details of policy failure in Texas, Maryland, and California are context-specific, but what we found in these three states reflects how the other states approach, and have failed at, real accountability. Let's look at the role of national program accreditation, which for other professions has been demonstrably effective.

ACCREDITING BODIES: RIGHT IDEA, WRONG IDEOLOGIES

In teacher education, it is often confusing to figure out the roles of accreditors and states. There are two specialized accrediting bodies for education schools,

NCATE and TEAC, but there are also regional accreditors. Regional accreditors accredit the institution at large, not the teacher preparation program. TEAC will soon merge with NCATE, the real powerhouse, having accredited some 600 education schools compared to fewer than 100 for TEAC. NCATE is not a public agency, but many states either require that their education schools earn national accreditation to receive program approval or so closely align their approval process with accreditation that the NCATE imprimatur often substitutes as a regulatory seal of approval (see Figure 5.3).

Figure 5.3

The complex relationship of states with NCATE

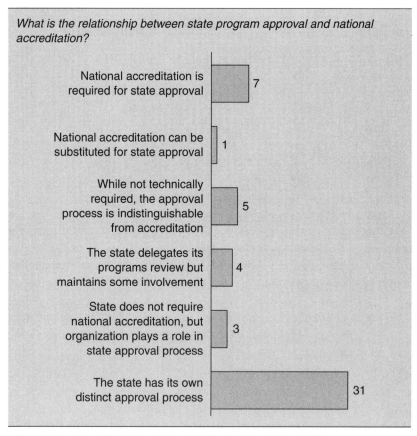

What is the relationship between state program approval and national accreditation?

National accreditation is required for state approval — 7

National accreditation can be substituted for state approval — 1

While not technically required, the approval process is indistinguishable from accreditation — 5

The state delegates its programs review but maintains some involvement — 4

State does not require national accreditation, but organization plays a role in state approval process — 3

The state has its own distinct approval process — 31

Source: National Council on Teacher Quality, *State Teacher Policy Yearbook,* 2009.

While NCATE has been around since the 1950s, for decades it was unable to persuade institutions to earn accreditation. Beginning in the 1980s, NCATE gained traction, not with institutions but with the states charged with conferring program approval. NCATE argued to states that it was in a better position to assess programs than government officials. Over a decade, 40% of states and the District of Columbia ceded some portion of program approval authority to NCATE, though under many manifestations. Almost all states, while not appearing to cede authority, entered into partnership. Within the last 5 years, there has been relatively little additional movement, suggesting that these NCATE-state alliances may have peaked.

While the political success of NCATE has been impressive, its impact on teacher quality is less apparent. For years, many programs have complained that NCATE's reporting requirements do not add value; as such, some programs, including highly regarded ones, have never sought accreditation. About a third of the 25 education schools whose graduate programs are most highly ranked by *U.S. News & World Report* are not accredited by NCATE. Currently, only about half of university-based programs are nationally accredited, compared to other professions, which essentially refuse to license the graduates of non-accredited preparation programs.

The problem for NCATE is lack of credibility: Few believe that all of the 600 programs with its accreditation are better than those without. NCATE was the target of stinging criticism by a former dean at Teachers' College, Arthur Levine, who presented evidence in 2006 that NCATE was more likely to accredit weaker institutions than stronger ones in terms of admission selectivity and rankings by *U.S. News & World Report*. Levine asserted that teachers coming out of NCATE programs were no more effective than those from other programs; though the exercise that produced these results was a bit rudimentary, others have affirmed his assertion in a more scholarly fashion. NCATE rebutted Levine, but it thereafter announced a redesign and a transition to new leadership.

Institutions need to achieve quality control, and national accreditation could provide a means. We contend that accreditation should have a stronger, more assertive role. Other professions figured this out long ago. To be a functioning medical school in the United States, accreditation by the Liaison Committee on Medical Education is an obligation, not an option. In the majority of states (notably not California), a person cannot sit for the bar exam without having attended a law school accredited by the American Bar Association. While specific national accreditation is optional for engineering and architecture schools, it's widely sought.

NCATE'S ACHILLES' HEEL: STANDARDS

At the heart of NCATE's credibility problem are its program quality standards; they lack the coherence and specificity that would distinguish between programs that do a good job and programs that do not. It is at least partially true that the reason NCATE eschews measurable standards is that too many programs would fail. Another reason is that the field has not concluded what elements do make a difference, making consensus problematic.

An obstacle to consensus is the fondness for teacher education's "big tent"—its tolerance of multiple and conflicting views of what it means to prepare a teacher. In particular, NCATE will not impose the most important standard of all—the need for greater selectivity in admissions. NCATE needs to insist that education schools stop accepting every candidate who walks in the door. Yet such a standard is derided as elitist, even though research and practice in other nations indicate that higher academic standards are essential for raising teacher quality.

NCATE's standards for defining high quality preparation are expressed in generalities. No program gets the guidance it needs; strong programs often fail to earn recognition. Because standards are ambiguous, accreditation teams get too much latitude in interpreting whether institutions are meeting them.

Let's look at a standard for which there would be little disagreement: the quality of a cooperating teacher charged with developing the skills of the student teacher. A cooperating teacher's quality will dictate whether the experience is going to add value. Unless a program believes that the best way to train teachers is to have them observe what *not* to do, it would seem as pointless to assign a student teacher to an ineffective teacher as it would to assign a medical resident to the worst doctor in the hospital.

NCATE (2006) agreed. It stated that accredited schools must choose cooperating teachers who are "accomplished professionals . . . prepared for their roles as mentors and supervisors" (Chapter 1, Standard 3). It also said, "Criteria for school faculty are clear and known to all of the involved parties." It viewed as unacceptable when "school faculty do not demonstrate the knowledge and skills expected of accomplished school professionals."

But what is an accomplished professional? Must the cooperating teacher be an effective teacher? By any measure? NCATE never articulates its expectation, an ambiguity hard for accreditation teams to interpret. It also helps explain what we found in a study of 134 student teaching programs: Half the programs in education schools accredited by NCATE failed to impose any criteria on the selection of cooperating teachers having to do with effectiveness or ability to mentor. We were unable to find any common thread defining "accomplished professional."

Let's look at a more controversial standard: reading instruction. NCATE insists that as part of a balanced literacy approach, its institutions must teach scientifically based reading instruction. But its approach, we argue, is tepid at best. NCATE should embrace the incontrovertible research on early reading and then influence, reeducate, and, yes, require the integration of that research into instruction. Caught up in the politics of the reading wars, NCATE squandered this opportunity.

The proof is in the pudding. Of the 103 institutions accredited by NCATE that we have reviewed over the past 6 years on the quality of their reading preparation, we found that only 38 *expose* their candidates to the scientific findings. How well these 38 institutions teach these principles we could not discern.

OVERSIGHT OF PROGRAMS BY THEIR OWN INSTITUTIONS

We've started at the top, demonstrating the ineffectiveness of the federal government at improving teacher preparation programs, states' unwillingness or inability to do so, and the disappointing results delivered by NCATE. What's left to bring some order?

Do not look to the universities and colleges, where there is the most resistance, due, we postulate, to their conviction that there really is no such thing as high quality teacher preparation, that the knowledge and skills teachers need to be effective remains an unknown or is a subjective question. Colleges and universities contend that the decision about what gets taught should be left not only to the schools of education but also to the individual professors. Many postulate that the reason academia exerts so little control is that they don't want to mess with a "cash cow," a theory that doesn't quite explain why universities wouldn't want a high quality cash cow, since most of what brings higher quality is not necessarily costly.

Again, look to the evidence. Often, there is not even consensus within the same state or university system. In Texas, the University of Texas at Austin requires 12 biology courses of its middle school science teacher candidates; the University of Texas–Pan American, in the same university system, requires 3. In the state university system in Illinois, two institutions do not require any course in elementary mathematics content of elementary teacher candidates; six others require 2.

Stranger still is the field's tolerance for delivering conflicting content to teacher candidates within the same institution. The field appears comfortable with discordant practices that tolerate one professor teaching that the scientific findings on reading are bunk and another faithfully teaching the science.

No medical school in the United States would tolerate a professor extolling the virtues of bleeding patients, but that is what teacher preparation allows when teacher candidates aren't taught that if they take a "whole-language" approach to reading instruction, they will successfully teach 60% of a class to read (on average), while they could successfully teach 95% with a more systematic and explicit approach.

Make no mistake: Higher education is much more willing to fall upon its sword defending academic freedom than for what is best for the nation's public school students.

Self-regulation is problematic in light of the general failure of specialized and regional accreditation. To the extent that accreditation functions as a mutual protection society through the involvement of many agencies and individuals unwilling to set and enforce high standards, devolving this responsibility to individual institutions would not solve the problem. Neither institutions nor accrediting bodies have shown interest in concentrating accountability on measurable, meaningful outcomes for student learning (including achievement, retention rates, graduation rates, and employment outcomes).

THE FIX WE PROPOSE

The good news is that all of this disarray is fixable—though not easily and not without breaking some eggs. As we have shown, legislative and regulatory responses and self-policing have been inadequate. The most promising solution, we contend, is to compel teacher preparation programs to produce the teachers that school districts need. The only way is to use the pressure of the marketplace—where boards choose to hire their teachers—to reinforce successful programs and shut down those that remain impervious to demand.

A variety of factors must be in place. First, the public needs the ability to compare programs. Second, the comparisons must be trustworthy, ideally based on objective measures and not individual judgments.

There are two possible sources of these data. The first is state longitudinal data systems, which hold promise. These systems, though in their infancy, are quickly being developed, many through RTT grants. Once completed, they will allow us to measure the performance of graduate students, learning which teacher preparation programs produce graduates capable of raising student achievement in mathematics and reading. But even though these data will move us ahead, they also have limitations:

- Until new tests are adopted, they will only tell us about the performance of teachers' students in grades 3 through 8, only in reading and mathematics, and only on states' standardized tests. In the discussion of how to hold PreK–12 teachers accountable, using this lone measure to decide if a teacher is effective has proven untenable; this may also be the case for teacher preparation programs.

- The findings resulting from value-added measures tend to be very "noisy"—meaning it is difficult to distinguish the impact of the district where the teacher is employed from the impact of the preparation program. Researchers can control for the district's influence but not always. Most challenging are those programs that send small numbers of teachers to many different districts or if a program tends to be the sole supplier for a district's teachers.

- A value-added tool alone runs the risk of identifying a mediocre program as a model, simply because it is the highest performing. Many districts using value-added data are seeing only small differences between the top-performing schools and the bottom, which suggests this could be an issue.

- No matter how good states get at applying the value-added measure, the results will never tell us why one institution is better than another.

Performance assessments are a second possible source of data that allow objective program comparison. These are observational rubrics used by trained observers. California has included a performance assessment (Performance Assessment for California Teachers, or PACT) in its licensing exams. As part of the Measures of Effective Teaching Study funded by the Gates Foundation, Harvard researcher Thomas Kane is investigating the correlation between the scores teachers receive on six performance assessments and the academic growth of students. The results could be a boon.

Nonetheless, it's hard to see how this sort of "outcome" assessment could be an effective and efficient measure of determining teacher quality. By their very nature, these assessments can only take a snapshot of teacher performances, most of which are "content-free." Mathematics teachers might score highly on some of these rubrics even if they were not teaching correct content. One could make the rubrics more subject-specific and observe teachers more frequently, but doing so would increase the demand for trained observers so much that the system would become prohibitively expensive.

The limitations of "output" data can be ameliorated by factoring in another source of data on teacher preparation programs, that is, their performance against a set of meaningful standards that capture the knowledge and skills that schools need to raise student achievement.

Despite resistance from many education schools, NCTQ has been working on such standards for more than 5 years, consulting with districts and field-testing these standards across the country (view the standards at www.nctq .org). These standards measure the capacity of education schools to attract talented individuals and prepare them in the *specific* ways that will make teachers more effective.

In our discussions, superintendents are clear that they want smarter teachers, teachers who know their subjects, how best to teach those subjects, how to assess their students, and how to manage classrooms, among other competencies. In our field studies, we find little relationship between the qualities superintendents identify and what education schools think are important.

The complaints from education schools about these standards are directed at both the content of our standards and our methodology of relying on syllabi and textbooks to determine the content of a course. Rarely do these criticisms get more specific, but when they do, they reveal the disconnect between what schools seek in future teachers (the basis for our standards) and how education schools prepare them.

For example, we hear many criticisms of our standards for lacking a research basis, but when pressed, the primary target is the standard with the most research behind it (scientifically based reading instruction). We believe that the furor of education schools over the standards stems from the fact that so many institutions fail to meet them, an outcome that NCATE has pointedly avoided (and in our view the wrong decision).

CONCLUSION

Efforts to put education schools on the same page, or even in the same book, failed because they do not capture what PreK–12 schools need. High quality teacher preparation can improve student outcomes. We are neither willing to work around education schools by relying only on alternative means of preparation nor willing to tolerate underperforming schools producing teachers unable to add value to a child's education.

Attracting more elite students cannot be the sole strategy. Nor can "alternative certification" be a panacea. We advocate for greater selectivity, but teacher preparation still holds potential because people become better teachers, particularly of younger students, if they have purposeful and systematic preparation. Achieving that goal will require rigorous demands and metrics for teacher education programs.

COUNTERPOINT: Mary E. Diez
Alverno College

As a high school debater, I learned well that the definition of terms in an argument is a critical first step in preparing a case. The question, Should more rigorous teacher education standards be instituted? needs a lot of unpacking if we are to have a clear argument. So let me begin by defining the terms *rigor, teacher education standards,* and *instituted.*

One can, for example, define rigor in terms of inputs—the strictness of adherence to a set of specific requirements in a teacher education program. Or one can define rigor in terms of outputs—the depth of the knowledge and skill teacher education candidates have mastered as a result of the program. This essay argues that the outputs are far more important for ensuring quality and propose that *more* rigorous means *deeper* and *stronger* development rather than more *specified* requirements.

The notion of standards also requires some attention. There are three kinds of standards: content standards, performance standards, and opportunity to learn standards, all of which apply to teacher education. *Content standards* identify the key areas of knowledge that teacher education candidates should master. There is increasing agreement about what those areas of knowledge are, tied to standards for K–12 student learning and to standards for teachers in the discipline areas. *Performance standards* set the bar for how candidates demonstrate their skill in applying their knowledge in context. *Opportunity to learn standards* call for assurance that, before candidates are held accountable for their knowledge and skill, the program provides them with suitable curriculum and field experiences, along with formative feedback to support their development. This essay argues that effective standards need to address all three: content, performance, and opportunity to learn standards.

Asked in passive voice, the question, Should more rigorous teacher education standards be instituted? leaves unaddressed the subject of the action, namely, who should institute teacher education standards. The authority to institute standards is found in three groups—government agencies, accreditation bodies, and teacher education programs themselves. When teacher education standards are imposed on a program from outside, either by an agency with legal responsibility for teacher education at the state level or by the profession through an accreditation agency, we might call them extrinsic standards.

When standards are internalized and owned by a teacher education program, we might call them intrinsic standards. In teacher education, standards are ideally both extrinsic and intrinsic. States and accreditation agencies identify teacher education standards that provide public assurance through a common set of expectations for the profession. But institutions need to go beyond mere compliance with outside requirements; they must "own" their moral purpose in preparing teachers. This essay argues that if standards are to be meaningful, teacher education programs must make standards their own, with state agencies and accreditation bodies providing structures to support that ownership.

Now, let's move on to the full arguments. This essay begins with a brief recent history of standards in teacher education, examines the current expectations for programs preparing teachers, and concludes with reasons for my overall position against the proposition.

A BRIEF HISTORY OF STANDARDS IN TEACHER EDUCATION

Looking back to the late 1980s and early 1990s as one who was involved in the development of the original model standards of the Interstate New Teacher Assessment and Support Consortium, or INTASC (1992), I would say that the standards and assessment reform effort in teacher education was intended to achieve three things:

1. To move teacher education from a focus on inputs to a focus on outcomes

2. To provide clarity about expectations for beginning teachers

3. To provide an assessment system that would fulfill three purposes—to support candidate growth, to document candidate development, and to contribute to ongoing program improvement

INTASC took the lead in helping states and accreditation agencies examine these three purposes.

From a Focus on Inputs to a Focus on Outcomes

The highly bureaucratized teacher education of the late 1980s was marked by a focus on requirements: required numbers of credit hours, specific content in courses—sometimes with mandated titles, and other details spelled out by state agencies and departments of education. In Wisconsin, there still are vestiges of this system in state code; for example, social studies teacher education candidates are required to have coursework in the economics of dairy cooperatives.

While many prior requirements were replaced by expectations for outcomes, other requirements have been added, particularly around candidate testing. Most states mandate that candidates pass both an entry test and an exit test, with passing scores determined by the states. The unintended consequence of this requirement has been a reduction in the diversity of candidates nationwide—in terms of racial and ethnic minorities as well as persons from varied socioeconomic backgrounds. There is concern among teacher educators that many diverse candidates who are capable of learning and demonstrating the program outcomes have been excluded by this type of narrow measure. In the early application of testing in Wisconsin, programs were allowed to use varied sources of evidence for competence in reading, writing, and mathematics; the local measures used in the program at Alverno College, for example, were strongly correlated with applications of these skills in teaching practice. Yet some teacher educators such as Linda Darling-Hammond have complained that current basic skills tests used by states have not been shown to correlate with effective teaching performance (Darling-Hammond, 2010).

The National Council for the Accreditation of Teacher Education (NCATE) moved toward a focus on outcomes relatively early, at about the same time that the Teacher Education Accreditation Council (TEAC) came on the scene with a similar agenda. Both accreditation agencies sought to have institutions identify clear candidate learning outcomes, focusing on evidence of candidate demonstration of outcomes and subsequent performance by graduates of the program in K–12 schools (NCATE, 2006; TEAC, 2010). Today, as we discuss the difference between highly qualified teachers and high quality teachers, it is clear that the profession is revisiting the awareness that specifying inputs does not always produce the desired results.

To Provide Clarity About Expectations for Beginning Teachers

INTASC grew out of a set of discussions in the late 1980s. Aligning with the Council of Chief State School Officers, the group developed the 1992 INTASC model standards. These model standards offered an alternative to specified inputs in the description of what beginning teachers needed to know, be able to do, and hold as dispositions. Adopted or adapted by 38 states, the INTASC model standards provided teacher educators with a clear picture of the expectations for beginning teachers.

To Provide a Meaningful Assessment System

The INTASC model standards assumed a strong assessment system, both during teacher education and into the first years of teaching. While it did not specify any one system, projects such as Connecticut's BEST (Beginning Educator Support and Training) program, a portfolio assessment for teachers in their second year, provided one robust model of appropriate assessment focused on teacher performance; it also provided significant support for the teachers as they put together their documentation. NCATE, in incorporating the INTASC standards into its system, addresses two key areas: (1) documentation of candidate development of knowledge, skills, and dispositions and (2) the use of evidence for ongoing program improvement. The NCATE standards also spell out the importance of assessment for candidate growth, particularly through formative feedback. TEAC addresses similar issues in its four principles to guide accreditation—specifically focusing on improvement as a continuous process and on the trustworthiness of evidence of candidate learning and K–12 student learning.

CURRENT EXPECTATIONS IN EMERGING TEACHER EDUCATION STANDARDS

In individual states and nationally, work has been completed or is under way to revise teacher education standards. For example, West Virginia and North Carolina have undertaken major revisions to address the demands of 21st-century education. A similar focus has driven the revision of the INTASC standards, promulgated in summer 2010. The INTASC group was guided by a belief that, while standards must still focus on what teachers need to know, be able to do, and hold as dispositions, they need to be reconceptualized in terms of what learners bring—their backgrounds, interests, needs, strengths, and future goals and opportunities. What backgrounds do our K–12 students bring—from language spoken at home and facility with technology to awareness of global issues? What are their interests, strengths, and needs? What do they need to be prepared for in a global marketplace, with jobs that have not yet been invented?

Amazingly, the group found much of the content of the 1992 standards areas has held up well over 18 years of application; the standards revision group, as in West Virginia and North Carolina, sought wording to capture a deeper awareness of language and cultural diversity, of the power of technology as a learning tool, and of rich opportunities in formative assessment to support student learning. Recognizing that understanding of one's discipline is still key, the group sought to foreground the ability to link that discipline with other fields and with key skills necessary to expand learning. Affirming the need to understand learners, their development, their differences, and their similarities, they expanded the expectation that teachers more effectively address the needs of individuals and groups.

While acknowledging the ongoing need for teachers to be able to plan and deliver instruction, the revision calls for a broader practice of collaboration with learners in the design of learning experiences and the development of the learning environment. Building on the need for reflection and community engagement, the revision also expands the meaning of professional responsibility to include teacher leadership. The goal of the revision was both to capture the research on learning and teaching in the past 20 years and to challenge conventional practice with new awareness of multiple ways, modes, and places for learning. These revised standards are likely to influence the extrinsic forces in teacher education standards—the states and the accreditation agencies—as they did in the 1992 version. But there is already considerable action in states and accreditation bodies. Moreover, NCATE and TEAC are discussing an alliance that would provide teacher education programs with a range of options for accreditation, a policy in keeping with a focus on outcomes rather than inputs.

Current work on performance standards and processes holds the promise of more meaningful assessment for teacher education programs. The recently formed Teacher Performance Assessment Consortium (TPAC) brings together the American Association of Colleges for Teacher Education, the Council of Chief State School Officers, and Stanford University, whose leadership with the Performance Assessment for California Teachers (PACT) provides a base for the development of a nationally available performance assessment for teacher education candidates. Twenty states have signed on to this effort and are participating in pilot studies over the next 3 years.

TPAC is developing a performance assessment to capture evidence of effective teaching practice through documentation of a 3- to 5-day "teaching event," which includes planning, reflection, videotaping, and samples of student work with teacher feedback. The PACT work on this kind of assessment is very promising, having documented strong validity and reliability of the instruments and process (Pecheone & Chung, 2006).

TPAC also affirms the need to address opportunity to learn standards, by combining embedded signature assessments in individual teacher education programs with the capstone teaching event used across the group of institutions. These formative assessments scaffold candidate learning throughout the program and help provide practice in important teacher roles. These assessments also provide formative feedback to candidates on their progress in demonstrating the program outcomes. Examples typically include child case studies, analyses of student learning, development of learning activities and appropriate assessments for pupils, and analyses of curriculum or teaching events. Feedback on performance in the capstone teaching event may suggest areas in the program that need strengthening, sparking the development of additional embedded signature assessments to provide additional learning and practice opportunities for candidates. Taken together, the embedded signature assessments and the common capstone assessment support the kind of rigor that are needed in teacher preparation—rigor that is defined by deeper and stronger development of the knowledge, skills, and dispositions of the teacher.

RESPONDING TO THE PROPOSITION

As we stand at the end of the 1st decade of the new millennium, what should be our direction in teacher education? How should we look at the proposition before us in this question: Should more rigorous teacher education standards be instituted? This section summarizes three arguments against the proposition.

First, given the definition of rigor as the depth of knowledge and skill that teacher education candidates have mastered as a result of the program, the current work with content standards (e.g., INTASC, West Virginia, and North Carolina), coupled with current work on performance standards (i.e., PACT and TPAC), provides the best approach to ensuring that depth of candidate development toward mastery. The bottom line needs to be the evidence we have for teacher education graduates being ready to work effectively in K–12 classrooms—not the test scores they enter with and/or the specification of details of their programs. Because outcomes are far more important than inputs for ensuring quality, returning to the prior focus on specification of inputs would be a serious mistake.

Second, if effective standards need to address content, performance, and opportunity to learn, then current work with content standards, coupled with current work on performance standards, is a key piece already in place. The notion of opportunity to learn standards is a key element of the NCATE assessment system, as well as the embedded signature assessments in TPAC. If we are to have a strong and diverse teaching force, then we ought not to screen candidates at the beginning to include only those who can already pass state program completion tests, as some programs do. Each teacher education program needs to ensure that candidates who have the potential to develop as strong teachers have the opportunity to do so; teacher education programs also need to be able to make decisions about candidate completion based on evidence using TPAC or a similar outcome-focused assessment.

Third is the notion of intrinsic versus extrinsic control. There will always be state and accreditation agency oversight of teacher education; it's a public responsibility. However, I'm reminded of a cheeky commercial that Continental Airlines posted last year in airports around the country: "There are industry standards; fortunately, we have our own." If standards are to be meaningful and effective, teacher education programs must make standards their own, with state agencies and accreditation bodies providing structures to support that ownership. Ultimately, the moral obligation to develop teacher candidates with strong and deep knowledge, skills, and dispositions lies with the teacher education program. We have enough experience to know that compliance with a set of extrinsic specifications does not guarantee quality teacher preparation. But NCATE and TEAC are both good examples of the kinds of structures that allow institutions to make their case for quality and rigor. NCATE currently does so through the design of outcomes and assessment systems; TEAC uses the vehicle of the evidence brief to structure its support. With the addition of instruments like TPAC, teacher educators combine local ownership of programs with a valid and reliable assessment of teacher candidate readiness to take responsibility for a classroom.

NOTE

1. Our latest estimate is 1,408, but we now know that it is a number that will be revised, as we no longer rely on any state counts but are looking at the level of each institution in the country. The level of inconsistency is remarkable: The National Research Council (NRC) produced a report in May 2010 on teacher education, stating on page 13 of that report that there are 1,096 institutions housing education school programs in the nation and on page 161, there are 1,300 institutions (see NRC, 2010).

FURTHER READINGS AND RESOURCES

Crowe, E. (2010). *Measuring what matters: A stronger accountability model for teacher education*. Washington, DC: Center for American Progress.

Darling-Hammond, L. (2010, February). *Teacher performance assessment: Raising the bar for teacher effectiveness*. Panel presentation at the Annual Meeting of the American Association of Colleges for Teacher Education, Atlanta, GA.

Interstate New Teacher Assessment and Support Consortium (INTASC). (1992). *Model standards for beginning teacher licensure and development: A resource for state dialogue*. Washington, DC: Council of Chief State School Officers.

National Council for the Accreditation of Teacher Education (NCATE). (2006). *Professional standards for the accreditation of schools, colleges, and departments of education*. Washington, DC: Author.

National Research Council (NRC). (2010). *Preparing teachers: Building evidence for sound policy.* Washington, DC: National Academy of Sciences.

Pecheone, R. L., & Chung, R. R. (2006). Evidence in teacher education: The Performance Assessment for California Teachers (PACT). *Journal of Teacher Education, 57,* 22–36.

Teacher Education Accreditation Council (TEAC). (2010). *TEAC's philosophy of accreditation.* Retrieved April 9, 2010, from http://www.teac.org/?page_id=168

U.S. Department of Education, Office of Postsecondary Education. (2009). *The secretary's sixth annual report on teacher quality: A highly qualified teacher in every classroom.* Washington, DC: Author.

Wilson, S., & Youngs, P. (2005). Research on accountability processes in teacher education. In M. Cochran-Smith & K. Zeichner (Eds.), *Studying teacher education* (pp. 591–644). Washington, DC: American Educational Research Association.

Will alternative routes to teacher licensure attract stronger teachers to American classrooms?

POINT: Jesse Solomon and Edward Liu, *Boston Teacher Residency Program*

Sarah Kelly, *New Visions for Public Schools*

COUNTERPOINT: Sandra A. Stroot, *The Ohio State University*

OVERVIEW

As can be seen in some of the other chapters in this volume, *Standards and Accountability*, there is real debate about how to solve the human capital problem in terms of the teachers needed for classrooms in the United States. A wide variety of policy solutions exist vis-à-vis ensuring qualified and effective teachers for American classrooms. Some reformers argue for tougher accreditation standards for teacher education institutions. Others suggest that deregulation is the answer, maintaining that by deregulating the teacher licensure process, it becomes possible to attract in the classrooms a wider array, and hopefully more enhanced pool, of teacher talent. Finally, as can be seen in this chapter, there are those who suggest that alternative routes are really the most efficacious way to attract the talent that schools and school districts require.

Some preliminary research suggests that there is a clear relationship between the academic quality of a teacher and the ability of that teacher to foster student learning. If that research proves to be true, then it is clear that one of the central tasks of all those who are invested in recruiting and retaining quality teachers would be the identification of individuals who possess strong academic backgrounds. Indeed, groups such as the National Council on Teacher Quality (NCTQ) are suggesting that all future teachers should be individuals who have graduated from the top half of their high school graduating classes. Implied in this requirement is the imperative of a teacher who personally possesses the academic qualities that subsequently need to be instilled in and fostered with the students they teach.

Two individuals offer arguments in this chapter relative to alternative routes as a mechanism for enhancing teacher quality. Most teachers in the United States are prepared through traditional university-based programs. Recently, policymakers across the United States have argued for alternative routes as a means of enhancing the talent pool in classrooms. Readers will see how this plays out in terms of debating the efficacy of the alternative approach through the work of Jesse Solomon (Boston Teacher Residency), Edward Liu (Boston Teacher Residency), and Sarah Kelly (New Visions for Public Schools) and Sandra A. Stroot (The Ohio State University). Solomon, Kelly, and Liu make the case for alternative routes, while Stroot contends that the talent pool classrooms need to succeed can effectively be secured through traditional programs that are already in place and possess accreditation.

The Boston Teacher Residency program and others that Solomon and his colleagues describe are examples of alternative routes to the classroom. As they point out, these programs do not focus on preservice education but rather endeavor to attract degreed individuals who evidence a strong interest in teaching. Instead, Solomon and his colleagues demonstrate that these programs enable participants to work in situ and to have direct and significant interactions with real students and skilled teachers. The participants in alternative programs are able to see through direct clinical and field placements the connection between theory and practice and to work with teachers who are already successful with the learners for whom they subsequently will have responsibility. The approaches that Solomon, Liu, and Kelly highlight are not the only alternative models in place, but the Boston Program, in particular, has been, most recently, represented as one of the most effective ways of recruiting and placing high quality teachers in the classroom.

Stroot takes a different perspective. She asserts that teacher preparation really matters and that there is research to document the salience of the teacher education process. Stroot acknowledges that the extant system could be improved, but she contends that with extensive preparation experiences in preservice programs and with exposure to classroom assignments that are relevant to future classroom responsibilities, then schools across the United States can and will secure the teacher talent they require. She argues against alternatives that provide limited classroom exposure before classroom assignments are made. In her analysis, Stroot notes that students who are taught by the teachers who exit alternative options are often the ones who most need high levels of teacher expertise. In essence, she maintains that the alternatives put at further risk the very same students who are in the most danger because they are already "at risk."

In reading these two essays, consider the following questions. First, what students are typically most likely to be taught by individuals who have come through alternative teacher preparation programs? Put another way, what category or groups of students tend to be taught by those with alternative teacher licensures? Second, in what ways should traditional teacher preparation programs be modified to ensure that the teachers who do receive licensure are individuals from the academic talent pool that is necessary for schools in the United States to be more competitive internationally?

Thomas J. Lasley, II
University of Dayton

POINT: Jesse Solomon and Edward Liu
Boston Teacher Residency Program

Sarah Kelly
New Visions for Public Schools

The development of alternative routes to teacher licensure undeniably is attracting stronger teachers to American classrooms and infusing teacher education with critical innovations to foster necessary improvement. This said, setting so-called alternative programs against traditional training and asking, which is better? oversimplifies the issue. Questions such as this one focus on adults and focus on inputs, while the ultimate beneficiaries of teacher preparation need to be our nation's children. The question should be, what does teacher preparation need to look like to provide the best outcomes for students? The answer, as this chapter explores, necessarily incorporates both alternative and traditional models—thus supporting the argument that the deregulation of licensure routes has brought us closer to the teacher preparation ideal, providing the field with many of the necessary advances through which to make it a reality.

The consensus from all sectors has long been that we need stronger teachers—and not just because our students consistently trail behind their counterparts in China and elsewhere throughout the world. America's demographics are changing swiftly, while at the same time increasing globalization and technological advances are demanding new skills and resources in the field. To that end, alternative licensure programs have demonstrated clear successes: They target high-need subject areas such as math, science, special education, and English as a second language; they supply candidates for hard-to-staff urban and rural areas, ensuring more even distribution of highly knowledgeable educators; and they respond nimbly to the local context. Research into individual alternative programs has shown that in some cases, their graduates stay in teaching jobs longer and are more effective than graduates of traditional programs.

Arguably, the most important contribution of alternative routes to teacher licensure is the injection of competition and innovation into the teacher preparation field as a whole. Alternative programs, which range from the long-established Teach For America to newer "medical model" teacher residency programs, actually are helping to enhance all types of teacher training. They have brought a sense of urgency, an excitement to experiment, and a wide range of new ideas to education practices that had stayed largely the same for a century or more. Since their inception in the 1980s, alternative preparation approaches have had a profound impact on so many schools of education—and, notably, vice versa—that the distinction between the two has blurred. So, too, have the results; we cannot explicitly say that either route has the market covered on preparing strong teachers.

There is one caveat worth stating before exploring the question further: As a field, educators are not very skilled at measuring the strength of teachers. This question has come to dominate the current education reform landscape—how to define effectiveness, how to measure it, and on what skills and practices and outcomes those measures should be based—but it is still an emerging area of expertise. Researchers know enough to say that "stronger" teachers have the ability to teach to all students' intellectual strengths, moving them forward to proficiency and beyond through a range of research-based, collaborative instructional practices tightly linked with what students need to know and be able to do in a given grade level and subject area. No one would deny that bringing more teachers with these competencies to the classroom is in the best interest of education. Thus, the overall question has to be viewed through the prism of both teacher quality and student outcomes: *What* do teacher preparation programs, both traditional and alternative, *need to do* in order to produce teachers who will have the greatest impact on student learning?

THE ALTERNATIVE CERTIFICATION RATIONALE

The arguments and rationales for alternative route programs have evolved over time. From the 1980s to the early 2000s, alternative certification was largely seen as a mechanism for increasing the supply of teachers. Underlying many of the arguments for these programs was a critique of government regulation and monopoly. Unlike medicine and law, in which professional organizations have a high degree of control over the preparation and entry requirements of candidates, entry into the teaching profession is controlled by state governments. Teacher preparation programs must be approved by the state in which they operate, and individuals must complete an approved program in order to be licensed to teach.

In the 1980s and 1990s, some policy analysts argued that this arrangement in essence granted a monopoly to universities, which, in turn, gave them little incentive to respond to market conditions or the changing needs of schools and districts (Thomas B. Fordham Foundation, 1999). At the same time, they argued, certification requirements constituted a barrier that prevented many able candidates from entering teaching. Studies in the 1980s and early 1990s found that the Scholastic Aptitude Test (SAT) scores of students entering schools of education had been declining (Hawley, 1990), and some argued that deregulating entry would naturally increase supply and attract individuals with stronger academic backgrounds. Implied in this argument (or sometimes stated outright) was a view that much of the coursework in traditional teacher preparation programs was unnecessary. Indeed, some researchers provided evidence of a weak relationship between teacher certification and student performance to buttress this perspective (Ballou & Podgursky, 1994, 1998).

These policy arguments provided a more explicit and coherent rationale for the existence of the alternate route programs that had emerged in the 1980s in states such as New Jersey, Texas, and California. In 1984, New Jersey passed legislation creating a statewide alternate route for certification and became "the first state to grant permanent licenses to prospective teachers who had earned degrees in other fields, bypassed colleges of education, and received on-the-job training in the classroom" (Barclay et al., 2007, p. 6). Thus, the mission of the original alternative licensure movement was to remove barriers to entry for good candidates who were unable or unwilling to go the traditional route. It was based on the belief that traditional programs presented two major obstacles: Their length and expense deterred top candidates, while much of the coursework was not practical and therefore not relevant to developing good teachers.

The first alternative programs attempted to address these problems head on. Their goal, essentially, was to go out and find good people and get them into the classroom as fast as possible. Much of the training was on the job, maximizing "real world" teaching experiences and minimizing the amount of time candidates had to spend without a salary. The initial purpose and design of many alternative route programs made them controversial from the start. Since they tended to bypass much of the coursework and preservice preparation of traditional programs, these programs were and continue to be criticized for placing teachers into classrooms before they are ready to teach. At worst, such programs are said to be exposing the very children who need the best teachers—those in underperforming, hard-to-staff schools—to teachers without the skills or knowledge they need. While there is some truth to that claim, proponents of alternative routes point to the fact that these classrooms were often being led by unlicensed teachers or even a string of substitutes. The alternative to an alternatively certified teacher is often not a fully prepared teacher but rather a minimally prepared teacher operating under an emergency waiver.

In more recent years, the rationale of alternative certification has shifted to include a greater emphasis on quality and addressing the needs of schools and districts. While there is still an emphasis on reducing barriers to entry and getting candidates into schools earlier, proponents of alternative certification have increasingly argued for the benefits of the school site as a context for training. They have argued that school-based clinical preparation has the potential to equip candidates with more real-world skills and understanding of students. Indeed, one could argue that elements of high quality alternative certification programs are similar to those of professional development schools, which have long been advocated by those who have sought to increase the quality of teacher preparation. Moreover, alternative certification programs can customize their training to meet local needs. Rather than offer generic training, they can prepare candidates for a particular district's curriculum, policies, and student population (Johnson, Birkeland, & Peske, 2005).

THE CURRENT LANDSCAPE

Alternative certification programs have proliferated since the 1980s. Today, about one in five—20%—of the 210,000 new teachers of record hired each year in the United States receives licensure by "alternative" means. Still, the vast majority—about 80%—of new hires learn the profession in university-based graduate and undergraduate teacher education programs. Typically, these "traditional" programs have required 30 to 36 credit hours of coursework and a prepracticum experience in one or more schools then student teaching of 6 to 16 weeks.

Schools of education have come under a great deal of scrutiny of late as the debate over their quality has been highly politicized for years. While some of the attacks tend to the vitriolic, many teacher educators acknowledge that some concerns have had merit, from low academic standards for admission to the overly theoretical coursework required. Secretary of Education Arne Duncan summed up the critique in a major speech at Columbia's Teachers College in 2009: "By almost any standard, many if not most of the nation's 1,450 schools, colleges, and departments of education are doing a mediocre job of preparing teachers for the realities of the 21st century classroom."

As will be argued below, however, too much can be made of the distinction between traditional and alternative routes to teaching. The lines between the two are blurring, and each route includes programs of varying quality and a diversity of designs. Developing the organizational capacity to deliver a strong program and consistently produce highly effective teachers is something that all teacher preparation programs, regardless of type, struggle with (Johnson et al., 2005).

In addition, given certain changes in society and the economy, the education field may need to provide multiple routes into the profession to attract the high quality candidates it needs (Johnson & The Project on the Next Generation of Teachers, 2004). The generation of teachers retiring in the early 21st century is an unusual one in that a large proportion of its members stayed in the profession for most of their entire working lives. For most of U.S. history up to the 1950s, teaching was more of a short-term occupation (Lortie, 1975). In addition, women and people of color, who were largely excluded from other professions up through the 1970s, provided a steady supply of highly educated and talented teachers.

In the decades since, the career context in the United States has changed radically. Opportunities have opened up for women and people of color, and the competition that schools and districts face for talent has increased as well. Moreover, it has become common for individuals to try multiple lines of work before settling on a career and for people to have multiple careers over the course of a lifetime. Alternative routes to education provide a way for the field to adapt to this changed career context by reducing the barriers to trying out teaching before making a longer term commitment and making it easier for individuals to enter teaching in mid career (Peske, Liu, Johnson, Kauffman, & Kardos, 2001).

ALTERNATIVE MODELS

The number of alternative programs has grown rapidly over the past 2 decades, primarily to help urban and rural districts facing difficulty attracting sufficient numbers of highly qualified teachers. Dozens of different types of "alternative" models across the 50 states have brought about 500,000 new teachers to the profession since the mid-1980s.

Though they differ in many respects, programs considered alternative today generally are market driven and most place candidates as teachers of record very early on. They prepare teachers in specific content areas to fulfill distinct gaps, providing a significant increase in teachers for high-need subjects and high turnover schools and geographic areas. The formal training often centers more heavily on skills perceived as immediately applicable to the classroom, such as class management.

This section describes three well-known approaches: Teach For America (TFA), The New Teacher Project (TNTP), and teacher residency programs.

Teach For America

Probably the best-known "alternative" program, Teach For America technically is not an alternative route to certification. Rather, TFA is a recruitment and placement program—with a short, but intensive, preparation period, aimed at high poverty, low-achieving districts. Though the exact arrangements differ from state to state, TFA participants, called corps members, receive some sort of licensure (often on an emergency basis), which allows them to start teaching right away. They then enroll in a local program, with which TFA has partnered, to earn state licensure and a master's degree, if they choose. Corps members receive 5 weeks of summer training and then commit to teach for 2 years in a high-need school. TFA employs local program managers to support the development of their corps members for these 2 years. Created in 1989, the program was the first large-scale attempt to confront the growing problem of uncertified, unqualified teachers serving our nation's neediest students. It is perhaps best known for its success in attracting a large group of recent graduates from prestigious colleges, which has allowed it to be very selective in its admissions process. It has placed 28,000 teachers in 20 years, and it opened the door for other, more intensive preparation programs.

The New Teacher Project

The New Teacher Project (TNTP), which started in 2001, has started a series of alternative route programs across the country. Its flagship program, the New York City Teaching Fellows (NYC Teaching Fellows), was created in conjunction with the New York City Department of Education to address the most severe teacher shortage in the city in decades. The lowest performing schools were filling up with staff teaching high-need subjects beyond their expertise; approximately 20% of teachers in failing schools were not certified. The Fellows program provided a faster track to licensure with ongoing training: 6 weeks of intensive content-based preparation prior to classroom placement, with continued coursework toward certification concurrent with the first 2 years of teaching. Highly competitive, the program accepts fewer than 10% of applicants each year, following the selective TFA model but targeting mid-career professionals with strong academic backgrounds who are intent on making a change to do more meaningful work. As of the 2010–2011 school year, more than 9,000 fellows are teaching in New York City, accounting for one in five science teachers and one in four math and special education teachers. This has coincided with a dramatic decrease in the percentage of teachers in the highest poverty schools who fail New York's standard teaching exam. TNTP works in a set of underserved, high poverty school districts across the country; currently, more than 37,000 TNTP teachers are teaching in classrooms nationwide.

The Residency Model

As teaching fellows programs were growing over the past decade, the broader market for nontraditional certification routes was expanding and shifting. By

2004, three new urban teacher residency programs, based on the medical model of training alongside an expert practitioner, had been created in Boston, Chicago, and Denver. Responding both to the need for highly effective teachers in hard-to-staff areas and the rising influence of fast-track programs, the Boston Teacher Residency (BTR) and its partners built a new, intensive apprenticeship approach. Rather than quickly training new teachers and putting them immediately in charge of classrooms, teacher residents are paired with a highly knowledgeable and skilled mentor in an urban classroom for a full academic year, while taking master's degree coursework tightly connected to their classroom experience. The residency programs have made it their mission to attract, prepare, and retain effective teachers in high-needs areas; these areas vary slightly by region and district but generally include teachers of color and teachers of math, science, and special education. Seventeen residency programs now operate across the country.

IMPACT OF ALTERNATIVE CERTIFICATION
Bringing High Quality Teachers to High-Needs Areas

All three alternative models addressed here, and their offshoots, have made significant contributions to increasing teacher quality. They have helped strengthen the overall teacher pool in the nation's neediest cities, while developing innovations with far-reaching implications for improving teacher quality for years to come.

According to the National Center for Education Information, alternate licensure programs are helping fill positions in high-needs geographic, demographic, and content areas. For example, nearly half of all alternative route teachers work in urban areas, and the programs also are attracting a growing number of men and people of color to the field (National Center for Education Information, 2005). Further, 20% of alternate route teachers were teaching mathematics in 2005, whereas 7% of all teachers were teaching mathematics. In the sciences, including biology, geology, physics, and chemistry, 28% of alternate route teachers, compared with 18% of all K–12 teachers, were teaching science subjects. Similarly, 44% of alternate route teachers were teaching special education (Feistritzer, 2009).

Bridging Theory and Practice

In starting the BTR program, the Boston Public Schools were trying to address the problem that far too many teachers, coming largely from traditional education programs, were not prepared for the realities and demands of teaching in the city's schools. Based on the idea that the best way to learn how to teach in an urban district is to do it at the elbow of an experienced mentor, BTR ensures that its residents engage in a year-long reflective, data-based conversation about students, student learning, and effective practice—before they ever become teachers of record. While many university programs require a pre-practicum experience and a 13-week student teaching experience, BTR is based on a full-year practicum—starting the week before school starts and continuing through the last day of school.

During their full-year practicum, BTR participants, called teacher residents, spend all day, 4 days per week, in a Boston school as a member of a team led by an effective and experienced veteran teacher in charge of the classroom. BTR designs and provides all of the accompanying, aligned master's coursework, allowing the program to tailor its offerings to the specific needs of the Boston Public Schools. For example, as part of its elementary math course sequence, BTR includes an emphasis on the curriculum used in Boston. The goal is that all graduates in their 1st year as teachers of record will already be familiar with the curriculum; the learning trajectory of a first-year teacher is steep enough without having to learn a new curriculum at the same time.

In this way, BTR and other residencies provide the link of theory and practice that has been missing from many traditional schools of education, while also responding to the market needs of urban districts for strong teachers in hard-to-fill subjects—who will then stay in their jobs. According to BTR-compiled statistics, BTR has an 80% retention rate as it enters its 8th year, compared with just over 50% in Boston overall for new teachers in their first 3 years. Its founding residency partners, the Academy of Urban School Leadership and the Boettcher Teachers program, have retention rates of 85% and 96%, respectively. Combined with generally accepted data on teacher effectiveness increasing over time, these teachers are not only staying longer, but also they are on average probably more effective; a remarkable 95% of principals surveyed say they would recommend hiring another BTR graduate to a colleague.

Measuring Teacher Quality

Another important contribution of BTR and other alternative licensure programs is the recognition that the field needs more sophisticated measures of teacher effectiveness to make a lasting difference on teacher quality—and they are committed to developing them. For example, BTR has launched a value-added study of its graduates, among other methods, to help refine every area of the program in response to noted gaps.

TNTP is pioneering a program building on research showing the best predictor of a teacher's future impact to be his or her past effectiveness in the classroom. TNTP is developing a system to recommend certification based on a teacher's demonstrated classroom performance. By 2015, all new teachers trained by TNTP will have to show that they can raise student achievement above a target threshold to be recommended for certification and remain in the classroom. TFA has recently published its *Teaching as Leadership* framework. Based on an ongoing analysis of the characteristics of its most effective teachers, this framework has already contributed significantly to the national conversation about what makes a great teacher.

Blurring the Line

Schools of education, seeing the growing appeal of the alternative movement, have begun to develop similar programs of their own—to attract those candidates seeking expedited routes and paid training. Occasionally lost in the rush to build new programs have been the standards that initially defined the movement—particularly high selectivity, theory and practice alignment, and intensive support. However, a number of colleges of education—including the University of Michigan, Stanford, and the University of California, Los Angeles—have evolved programs that appear to meld key characteristics of both alternative and traditional routes and in these hybrid approaches are strengthening the education school model.

While alternative programs were initially created in response to the traditional university-sponsored education programs, this distinction today is almost meaningless. There are alternative route programs sponsored by individual schools (public, private, and charter), school boards, state education agencies, nonprofit organizations, and colleges of education themselves. In fact, it is estimated that 75% of all colleges of education operate or are partners in alternative route programs and that more than half of alternative programs actually are administered by institutions of higher education.

CONCLUSION

It is indisputable that alternative routes to licensure have opened up the field to innovations that will better serve both students and teachers in all areas. By parsing the question further, as done throughout this essay, there is conclusive evidence that these innovations have led to improvements across the field of teacher preparation—and have set the stage for the large-scale educational transformation that is so urgently needed, with groundbreaking approaches to clinically based preparation, continuing skill development, and accountability measures for teachers in all areas.

Today, there is more variation within any particular type of teacher preparation route than there is between traditional and alternative routes. In addition, alternative routes have taken root to the extent that some feel they are no longer, in fact, alternative at all.

Certainly, no one program has the market covered on preparing America's strongest teachers. The highest quality programs, whether traditional or alternative, focus on student needs and develop their mission, recruitment, selection, curriculum, and support structures in response to those needs.

The alternative movement has been essential in pushing traditional programs to innovate, and to ensure the critical shift in attention from inputs to outcomes. Alternative certification programs will continue to pursue the most ambitious methods to ensure academic growth for students, thus, changing the focus from, Which route did you come from? to the most critical question of all, Are your students learning?

COUNTERPOINT: Sandra A. Stroot
The Ohio State University

The purpose of this chapter is to debate the question, Will alternative routes to teacher licensure attract stronger teachers to American classrooms? The answer is no, alternative routes are not the way to attract stronger teachers to American classrooms. The rationale for taking this stance is framed by addressing two primary aspects of teacher preparation: the *quantity* and *quality* of teachers produced through alternative routes. This counterpoint essay addresses additional factors that influence decisions to hire alternatively licensed teachers such as including retention and unnecessary costs to boards hiring alternatively licensed teachers. The essay finishes by stating my perspective on what should be done to attract and retain stronger teachers to American classrooms.

DEFINITION OF ALTERNATIVE ROUTES

Before we get into the details of the debate, it is important to define the term *alternative route* since it can be confusing. The confusion lies in the variety of pathways to teaching that are termed alternative and similar variations found in the historic, well-known pathway labeled as *traditional*. Generally, traditional pathways are housed in colleges or universities, are approved by state and/or national accrediting bodies, and lead to a bachelor's or master's degree. The alternative pathways are those that may not meet the same criteria and act as "alternatives to the traditional state-approved, college-based teacher education program routes for certifying teachers" (National Center for Alternative Certification, n.d., "An Introduction"). Even with this definition, the confusion remains, as experts found that "the distinctions among pathways and programs are not clear-cut, and there is more variation within categories such as 'traditional' and 'alternative'... than there is between categories" (National Research Council [NRC], 2010, p. 174).

The National Center for Alternative Certification (n.d.) claims there are 136 alternate routes to certification in the United States with almost 600 alternate route programs supporting these alternate routes. Some of the well-known alternative pathways are supported through national programs, such as Teach For America (TFA), Troops to Teachers, and the American Board for Certification of Teacher Excellence (NRC, 2010). In addition, most states have their own alternative programs, such as the New York (NYC) Teaching Fellows program or the Alternative Teacher Certification program in Texas.

This essay focuses on two of the more visible national and state programs to illustrate its points, specifically citing one of the larger, well-publicized national programs, TFA, and another well-known state level program, the NYC Teaching Fellows. Again, remember these are only two of many programs, and the variations within the pathways are significant. For example, the NYC Teaching Fellows alternative route to licensure is closely aligned with the traditional teacher preparation program. Thus, teachers licensed through this alternative route may attend the same local institution to receive their master's degree as the preservice teachers moving through a traditional program. In other cases, universities are not involved and there are few criteria required to enter or complete a program. Some alternative programs suggested eliminating coursework for teacher education altogether "in favor of simpler and more flexible rules for entry" into teaching (Walsh, 2001, p. vii). Though there are many variations, the key point focuses on the amount of preparation required for a teacher to have full responsibility for student learning in a classroom, thus, becoming a *teacher of record*.

Historically, prospective teachers were required to complete significant coursework in the relevant subject matter and take a series of education courses focused on teaching methods that enable teachers to individualize instruction and meet the needs of all students. In traditional programs, before teachers become the teacher of record, they have knowledge in areas such as child development, student learning, and teaching methods that include teaching children with special needs and English language learners. They experience integrating technology into the learning process, and they should know culturally relevant pedagogical strategies to engage children from diverse backgrounds. These teachers have had opportunities to develop an understanding of families and communities where their children live as a part of their preservice program. In addition, traditionally prepared teachers have had multiple, highly supervised clinical placements with experienced teachers before becoming a teacher of record in a classroom. In many alternative pathways, teachers become the teacher of record with only a bachelor's degree in their content area and few if any courses on how to be effective teachers.

As mentioned earlier, there are hybrids of the two extremes with a continuum of quality preparation within these pathways that enable teachers to become teachers of record (see Figure 6.1). It can thus be argued that alternative pathways that do not require substantial coursework in these areas are not going to prepare stronger teachers for America's classrooms.

WHY ARE ALTERNATIVE ROUTES TO TEACHING INCREASING?

There are a variety of reasons why alternative pathways to teaching have increased over the last decade. One has been the strong, public criticism of our education system and the lack of respect teachers receive in the United States. Most, if not all, have heard the H. L. Mencken quote, "Those who can—do. Those who can't—teach." This statement clearly implies that the people who are not competent enough to succeed in other professions are the people who become our teachers. Teaching is one of the few professions where those who have never taught in a classroom think they can do better than those who are trained experts. This essay suggests the people who think they can teach with little or no preparation should spend time in one of our urban middle schools, to help them better understand the complexities of teaching. Ironically,

---

Figure 6.1

Continuum of preparation to become a teacher of record

Minimal Coursework in Teacher Preparation	Less ←— Continuum of Preparation to Become a Teacher of Record —→ More	Substantial Coursework in Teacher Preparation

H. L. Mencken also stated, "For every complex problem, there is a solution that is simple, neat, *and wrong*" [emphasis added] (http://www.thinkexist.com/English/Topic/x/Topic_298_1.htm). Criticism of America's education system continues to exist well into the 21st century, and it is increasingly clear that the general public and many of our policymakers share the viewpoint of the critics. There is widespread agreement that we must address the challenges presented in our schools and colleges to improve teacher quality and student achievement. The debate is about *how* we make these improvements.

Another reason that alternative pathways to teaching have been increasing has been the well-publicized need for large numbers of highly qualified teachers. The need for new teachers hired in public schools is on the rise. William J. Hussar (1999) and the National Center for Educational Statistics staff stated that the total number of newly hired public school teachers needed by 2008–2009 ranges from 1.7 million to 2.7 million. As we look further into the future, the need for teachers is confirmed and is still increasing. Daniel Aaronson and Katherine Meckel (2008) projected the need for a total of 3.9 million new hires for school years 2008–2009 through 2020–2021 (pp. 2–3). Hussar and Bailey (2009) found that the total number of elementary and secondary teachers increased 27% between 1993 and 2006, a period of 13 years, and is projected to increase an additional 16% between 2006 and 2018, a period of 12 years. No matter which data set we use, there is no question that we need to prepare more teachers to meet these increasing needs.

WILL THE QUANTITY OF ALTERNATIVELY CERTIFIED TEACHERS RESULT IN STRONGER TEACHERS IN THE CLASSROOM?

To meet the growing need for stronger teachers in the 21st century, officials must recruit, prepare, and retain increasing numbers of effective candidates. However, the number of teachers coming through the alternative pathway is not significant enough to increase the overall quality of teachers in our schools.

According to the National Center for Alternative Certification, it was estimated that 59,000 individuals were issued certificates to teach through alternative routes in 2008–2009. If alternative pathways were providing only 59,000 of the 2,700,000 new teachers needed in 2008–2009, those numbers are not going to provide enough teachers to make a significant difference. With regard to the number of teachers moving through specific programs, the same point can be made. Since the TFA program is one of the largest, its data can be used to illustrate this point. Julian Heilig and Su Jin Jez (2010) stated, "TFA teachers only make up about 0.2% of the US's 3.5 million teachers. Thus, TFA can hardly be considered a panacea, or a major factor in educational reform" (p. 12).

Another challenge is to retain the teachers who move through an alternative pathway, again, using TFA to illustrate the point. The mission of TFA is to "build a diverse, highly selective corps of top recent college graduates and professionals— who commit two years to teach in low-income communities and become lifelong leaders in pursuit of educational excellence and equity" (Teach For America, n.d., "Core Member Impact"). The primary goal of the TFA program is to recruit a pool of strong candidates who have backgrounds in a variety of content areas to teach for 2 years in high poverty urban and rural schools. Basically, this is a service commitment for college graduates from elite universities before they embark on their intended careers, much like the Peace Corps commitment.

Though TFA has successfully recruited a diverse pool of smart, successful students into the program, they do not stay in the schools. Approximately 13% of the TFA teachers leave before completing their initial 2-year commitment (Miner, 2010). After that, over 50% of TFA teachers leave after 2 years, and more than 80% leave after 3 years (Heilig & Jez, 2010). Because of the philanthropic nature of the TFA program and the revolving door of teachers leaving after 2 years, some critics are dubbing TFA as "Teach For Awhile." Due to the recruitment efforts from elite corporate partners of TFA, such as Goldman Sachs, JP Morgan, and Google, others are calling it "Teach for a Resume." In either case, the message is clear: The primary purpose of TFA, and programs like it, is to provide a temporary experience for a bright, diverse cohort of college graduates to teach our most needy students before they move on to pursue their real career in another field.

WILL THE QUALITY OF ALTERNATIVELY CERTIFIED TEACHERS RESULT IN STRONGER TEACHERS IN THE CLASSROOM?

In a time of increased regulation in other areas in the United States, many of the alternative pathways to teaching argue to deregulate teacher education (Cochran-Smith, 2001; Cochran-Smith & Fries, 2001). Those supporting deregulation of teacher education would advocate for easy entry into teacher education, typically requiring only a bachelor's degree in the subject matter and a passing score on a state test. They would argue that the current teacher education programs have unnecessary requirements preventing bright, capable people from entering the teaching profession. Chester Finn (Kanstoroom & Finn, 1999) calls pedagogical courses "hoops and hurdles" that are designed to "limit the potential supply of teachers by narrowing the pipeline" (p. v). They would rather make the entry and hiring process more simple, get rid of the hoops and hurdles, than rely on results of student learning to determine whether teachers should stay in the profession.

Kanstoroom and Finn (1999) also stated in a document published by the Fordham Foundation that, "The surest route to quality is to widen the entryway, deregulate the processes, and hold people accountable for their results—results judged primarily in terms of classroom effectiveness as gauged by the value a teacher adds to pupils' educational experience" (p. 1). Supporters of deregulation argue that it would open the doors to alternative teacher education by giving organizations, other than universities with approved licensure programs, the authority to prepare teachers by providing less rigorous, alternative pathways to teaching.

A growing body of evidence indicates that students taught by teachers who have moved through alternative pathways are not achieving as well as those who have been prepared by university-based programs. In a review of TFA candidates, Linda Darling-Hammond, Holdtzman, Gatlin, and Heilig (2005) found that candidates who moved through a traditional system performed better than those moving through alternative pathways. They stated,

> Although some have suggested that perhaps bright college graduates like those who join TFA may not require professional preparation for teaching, we found no instance where uncertified Teach for America teachers performed as well as standard certified teachers of comparable experience levels teaching in similar settings. . . . Over the course of a year, students taught by uncertified TFA teachers could be expected to achieve at levels that are, in grade equivalent terms, one-half month to 3 months lower than students taught by teachers with standard certification. (p. 20)

In a more recent review of TFA, Heilig and Jez (2010) summarized their findings by stating, "studies indicate that the students of novice TFA teachers perform significantly less well in reading and mathematics than those of credentialed beginning teachers" (p. i).

Darling-Hammond et al. (2005) found that as new teachers gain more experience in their classrooms, differences between teachers who come through various pathways lessen. The differences lessen, because teachers who have minimal preparation before they become the teacher of record, such as the TFA teachers, learn to teach "on the job" by practicing on the children in their classrooms. This point is made in a recent book by a former TFA teacher, *Learning on Other People's Kids: Becoming a Teach For America Teacher* (Veltri, 2010). This problem becomes exacerbated when it becomes evident that teachers from alternative programs, such as TFA, receive as little as 5 weeks of preparation before becoming teachers of record in classrooms, and they are placed in high-need urban or rural schools where they receive "on the job training." This means that the least prepared teachers are sent to work with the students who have the greatest need. One example is from a former TFA teacher, Alex Diamond, who stated,

> I did not leave summer training ready to be a successful teacher. I suspect this is true of nearly all my TFA peers. This was unfair to my first-year students, who spent a large part of the year watching me learn to teach instead of learning world history. . . . As I've progressed as a teacher, my greatest growth has resulted from trial and error—the opportunity to try new things, crash and burn, and then return to the drawing board. ("Do I Really Teach," 2010)

Though all acknowledge the need for more teachers in high-need schools, this on-the-job training solution is not adequate as it will ultimately inhibit the academic growth and achievement of students with the greatest academic need, many of whom are students of color and many of whom live in poverty. We would never consider this option for any other valued profession in our society, so why would we consider this for the teaching profession? Would doctors allow 5 weeks of training for pediatric surgeons and then have them learn on the job by practicing on our children? When acknowledging the fact that the majority of these teachers do not stay past the 2nd year, the cycle just starts over again, and students who have the greatest needs "struggle year after year with a passing parade of inexperienced beginners" (Carroll & Foster, 2010, p. 4).

THE IMPACT OF TEACHER RETENTION ON QUALITY

As noted, there is a revolving door for new teachers from TFA even though it is known that experience does improve teaching performance. Thomas Carroll and Elizabeth Foster (2010) stated, "Research clearly shows that with each year of experience, teachers improve their [teachers'] proficiency and effectiveness during the first seven years" (p. 12). Further, Francis Huang (2009) found that the number of years of teaching experience at a particular grade level was significantly associated with increased student reading achievement. Both works document teacher experience to be an important factor contributing to student learning. However, due to the revolving door of TFA teachers, children who have a TFA teacher never benefit from this continuum of growth.

The issue of teacher turnover is not limited to beginning teachers from TFA programs rotating through the system. Experienced teachers are laid off in cities such as Boston, Charlotte-Mecklenburg, and Washington, D.C. Yet while these experienced teachers are cut from their jobs, positions for TFA teachers are preserved (Miner, 2010). The experience and expertise of the veteran teachers are lost to the children of these districts, and positions for new TFA teachers are retained, even though the majority of the TFA teachers cannot provide the same opportunities for learning as the experienced teachers, and the majority of TFA teachers are not likely to remain in their district after the initial 2-year commitment. It is crucial to keep these experienced teachers in the schools, not replace them with teachers with little or no preparation.

COSTS OF TEACHER TURNOVER

According to Carroll and Foster (2010),

> We now have the oldest teaching workforce in more than half a century. The number of teachers over age 50 has increased from about 530,000 in 1988 to 1.3 million in 2008 . . . the most common age (modal) for teacher retirement is age 59. (p. 6)

As these teachers leave, they must be replaced. It has been well documented that teacher turnover is an expensive endeavor. Irrespective of how they came into districts, when teachers leave, it is costly.

Carroll (2007) discussed the findings of a study of five districts on the cost of teacher turnover, reporting, "It is clear that thousands of dollars walk out the door each time a teacher leaves" (p. 3). He added, "The cost per teacher leaver ranged from $4,366 in rural Jemez Valley to $17,872 in Chicago. The total cost of teacher turnover in the Chicago Public Schools is over $86 million per year" (p. 3). These costs are rising quickly. In 2005, it was estimated that the cost of replacing public school teachers would reach $4.9 billion per year (Alliance for Excellent Education, 2005, "Teacher Attrition"). By 2007, the National Commission on Teaching and America's Future (NCTAF) estimated the cost of teacher turnover to be $7.9 billion per year (Carroll, 2007). Carroll also pointed out that these costs are greater in our urban, poor, largely minority districts because of the high turnover rates in these sites.

Teacher turnover is on the rise, and it is very costly to replace these teachers, particularly those from some of the more well-known alternative pathways. For example, in addition to the regular costs of teacher turnover, TFA adds an additional one-time finder's fee that can run as high as $5,000 per teacher (Heilig & Jez, 2010). If a district hires 50 TFA teachers per year, this cost could be $250,000 per year; as the majority of the teachers do not stay within the district, this one-time cost becomes a recurring expense to the district.

CONCLUSION

Teaching is a complex process, and preparing new teachers to be successful in our schools is an ongoing challenge. Clearly, changes must be made through the entire PreK–20 system of education in the United States, so our children can succeed in this global economy, and we can continue to be academic and economic leaders in the world. Educators have a responsibility for preparing teachers who will be ready to teach 21st-century skills, particularly to children from high-need urban and rural settings. This counterpoint essay expresses the belief that the deregulated agenda, with alternative pathways that encourage teachers to become the teacher of record without substantial preparation, is not the means to create strong teachers for America's schools.

The professionalization agenda discussed by Marilyn Cochran-Smith (2001) and Cochran-Smith and Mary Kim Fries (2001) is the appropriate mechanism for reform as it is the model with the greatest potential to enhance and improve teacher quality in the United States. Darling-Hammond (2010) passionately argued for colleges of education to take responsibility for reform to help teachers prepare children for success as our nation moves from an industrial economy to a knowledge-based economy. Within the professionalization agenda, teacher educators agree to a Common Core set of standards to guide their programs, and common outcome measures that would determine the quality of teacher education programs and of the candidates graduating from these programs. However, this cannot be done in isolation from our schools.

There is need for systemic change that will impact the entire P–20 pipeline of the system of education in the United States, so we must be clear on the relationship among and between our schools and universities. If educators are to prepare teachers to be successful in 21st-century schools, then teacher educators must understand the needs of children within these sites, and candidates must spend time working in high-need schools. Yet researchers are not starting from scratch. University teacher education programs have been in the midst of reform for the past decade, and the results are impressive. Darling-Hammond (2010) discussed the evidence of improvements in teacher education, and she highlighted colleges that redesigned their programs by aligning to quality standards, creating stronger clinical practices, and strengthening coursework around critical areas mentioned earlier, such as student learning, assessment, teaching children with special needs, and English language learners.

Leaders need to strengthen the collaborative partnerships with our schools. Darling-Hammond (2010) suggested creating collaborative school-university partnerships by working closely with strong practitioners to better connect theory with practice. At the same time, a major accrediting body led the Blue Ribbon Panel on Clinical Preparation and Partnerships for Improved Student Learning to enhance and extend the clinical experience for candidates in our university programs (National Commission for Accreditation of Teacher Education [NCATE], 2010). It is imperative to then develop a long-term commitment of continued support by working closely with school partners to develop sustained mentoring and professional development programs for teachers throughout their career. Collaborative partnerships focused on enhancing teacher quality and student learning for all students are crucial for overall success.

Evidence shows quality teacher preparation matters even though there is a great deal of variance in the quality and quantity of teacher preparation. The challenge is to create a system for improving education that will reduce this variance and maintain quality. In a report discussing how to create a better system for better schools, Barnett Berry, A. Daughtrey, and A. Wieder (2010) concluded, "Teachers whose students make the greatest achievement gains have extensive preparation and experience relevant to their current assignment (subject, grade level, and student population taught)" (p. 26).

It is time to take a stand. Would you want your child's teacher to learn to teach in a high quality, university-based program, or would you want your child's teacher to become the teacher of record with little or no training, to learn to teach on the job, and to practice the trial-and-error techniques on your child? It is time to end the debate while focusing energy and resources on developing strong, university-based programs resulting in high levels of student learning for all children in America.

Further Readings and Resources

Aaronson, D., & Meckel, K. (2008). *The impact of baby boomer retirement markets on teacher labor markets* [Chicago Fed Letter]. Retrieved June 20, 2010, from http://www.chicagofed.org/webpages/publications/chicago_fed_letter/2008/september_254.cfm

Alliance for Excellent Education. (2005). *Teacher attrition: A costly loss to the nation and to the states* (p. 1). Retrieved June 20, 2010, from http://www.all4ed.org/files/archive/publications/TeacherAttrition.pdf

Ballou, D., & Podgursky, M. (1994). Recruiting smarter teachers. *Journal of Human Resources, 30*(2), 326–338.

Ballou, D., & Podgursky, M. (1998). The case against teacher certification. *Public Interest, 132*, 17–29.

Barclay, R., Feistritzer, E., Grip, R., Haar, C., Seaton, G., Sherman, S., et al. (2007). *The New Jersey alternate route program: An analysis of the perspectives from alternate route teachers, alternate route instructors, and alternate route mentors.* Retrieved January 24, 2011, from http://www.state.nj.us/education/educators/license/research/alternate.pdf

Berry, B., Daughtrey, A., & Wieder, A. (2010, February). *A better system for schools: Developing, supporting and retaining effective teachers.* New York: Teachers Network and the Center for Teaching Quality. Retrieved June 20, 2010, from http://effectiveteachers .org/research

Carroll, T. (2007). *The high cost of teacher turnover.* Washington, DC: National Commission on Teaching and America's Future.

Carroll, T., & Foster, E. (2010). *Who will teach?* Washington, DC: National Commission on Teaching and America's Future.

Cochran-Smith, M. (2001). Reforming teacher education: Competing agendas. *Journal of Teacher Education, 52*(4), 263–265.

Cochran-Smith, M., & Fries, M. K. (2001). Sticks, stones, and ideology: The discourse of reform in teacher education. *Educational Researcher, 30*(8), 3–15.

Darling-Hammond, L. (2010). Teacher education and the American future. *Journal of Teacher Education, 61*(1–2), 35–47.

Darling-Hammond, L., Holdtzman, D., Gatlin, S., & Heilig, J. (2005). *Does teacher preparation matter? Evidence about teacher certification, Teach for America, and teacher effectiveness* (Education policy analysis archives, North America). Retrieved July 10, 2010, from http://epaa.asu.edu/ojs/article/view/147

Diamond, A. (2010, Spring). Do I really teach for America: Reflections of a Teach for America teacher. *Rethinking Schools Online, 24*(3). Retrieved July 10, 2010, from http://www.rethinkingschools.org/archive/24_03/24_03_tfadiamond.shtml

Feistritzer, C. E. (2009). Teaching while learning: Alternative routes fill the gap. *EDge, 5*(2).

Fordham Foundation. (1999). *The teachers we need and how to get more of them: A manifesto.* Washington, DC: Author. Retrieved June 20, 2010, from http://www.umd .umich.edu/casl/natsci/faculty/zitzewitz/curie/TeacherPrep/107.pdf

Hawley, W. (1990). The theory and practice of alternative certification: Implications for the improvement of teaching. *Peabody Journal of Education, 67*(3), 3–34.

Heilig, J., & Jez, S. J. (2010). *Teach For America: A review of the evidence.* Boulder, CO: Education and the Public Interest Center & Education Policy Research Unit. Retrieved June 20, 2010, from http://epicpolicy.org/publication/teach-for-america

Huang, F. L. (2009, April). *Is experience the best teacher? A multilevel analysis of teacher qualifications and academic achievement in low performing schools.* Paper presented at the Annual Meeting of the American Educational Research Association, San Diego, CA.

Hussar, W. J. (1999). *Predicting the need for newly hired teachers in the United States to 2008–2009.* Washington, DC: National Center for Education Statistics, U.S. Department of Education.

Hussar, W. J., & Bailey, T. M. (2009). *Projections of education statistics to 2018* (NCES 2009-062). Washington, DC: National Center for Education Statistics, Institute of

Education Sciences, U.S. Department of Education. Retrieved from http://nces.ed.gov/pubs2009/2009062.pdf

Johnson, S. M., & The Project on the Next Generation of Teachers. (2004). *Finders and keepers: Helping new teachers survive and thrive in our schools.* San Francisco: Jossey-Bass.

Johnson, S. M., Birkeland, S. E., & Peske, H. G. (2005). *A difficult balance: Incentives and quality control in alternative certification programs.* Cambridge, MA: Project on the Next Generation of Teachers, Harvard Graduate School of Education.

Kanstoroom, M., & Finn, C., Jr. (1999, July). *Better teachers, better schools.* Washington, DC: Fordham Foundation.

Lortie, D. C. (1975). *Schoolteacher: A sociological study.* Chicago: University of Chicago Press.

Miner, B. (2010, Spring). Looking past the spin: Teach for America. *Rethinking Schools Online, 24*(3). Retrieved June 2, 2010, from http://www.rethinkingschools.org/archive/24_03/24_03_TFA.shtml

National Center for Alternative Certification. (n.d.). *An introduction and overview.* Retrieved July 10, 2010, from http://www.teach-now.org/intro.cfm

National Center for Education Information (NCEI). (2005). *Profiles of alternate route teachers.* Washington, DC: Author.

National Commission for Accreditation of Teacher Education (NCATE). (2010). *NCATE Blue Ribbon Panel on Clinical Preparation and Partnerships for Improved Student Learning.* Retrieved from http://www.ncate.org/SearchResults/tabid/37/Default.aspx?Search=blue+ribbon+panel

National Research Council. (2010). *Preparing teachers: Building evidence for sound policy.* Committee on the Study of Teacher Preparation Programs in the United States, Center for Education, Division of Behavioral and Social Sciences and Education. Washington, DC: The National Academies Press.

Peske, H. G., Liu, E., Johnson, S. M., Kauffman, D., & Kardos, S. M. (2001, December). The next generation of teachers: Changing conceptions of a career in teaching. *Phi Delta Kappan,* pp. 304–311. Retrieved from http://blogs.law.harvard.edu/jreyes/files/2006/04/5624599.pdf

Teach For America. (n.d.). *Core member impact.* Retrieved June 2, 2010, from http://www.teachforamerica.org/mission/our_impact/corps_impact.htm

Teach For America. (n.d.). *Our theory of change.* Retrieved June 20, 2010, from http://www.teachforamerica.org/mission/theory_of_change.htm

Veltri, B. T. (2010). *Learning on other people's kids: Becoming a Teach For America teacher.* Charlotte, NC: Information Age.

Walsh, K. (2001). *Teacher certification reconsidered: Stumbling for quality.* Baltimore: Abell Foundation. Retrieved June 20, 2010, from http://www.abell.org/pubsitems/ed_cert_1101.pdf

7

Are alternative school leader preparation programs really needed to prepare next generation school leaders?

POINT: Emmy L. Partin and Jamie Davies O'Leary,
Thomas B. Fordham Institute
COUNTERPOINT: Theodore J. Kowalski, *University of Dayton*

OVERVIEW

The essays in this chapter focus on the issue of how best to recruit the very best administrative talent to leadership positions in schools. For years, the accepted practice has been for school leaders to be prepared through traditional school administration programs with higher education institutions. These programs, almost exclusively housed within colleges and schools of education, consisted of a range of courses from school law to school finance, often with associated and embedded field and clinical components.

The focus on school leader preparation has emerged in partial response to the No Child Left Behind legislation. Clearly, there are expanded expectations regarding what principals can and should be able to do in order to be effective as school leaders. Critics of traditional preparation programs, such as Frederick Hess of the American Enterprise Institute, argue that far too little of the principal preparation curriculum focuses on accountability while far too much deals with issues that simply do not create opportunities for principals to understand how to use data and how to effectively evaluate the personnel who report to them.

Critics such as Hess and others expect principals to be able to use data in ways that will help them manage school programs so that all students are able to achieve to their full potential and so that every teacher can be productive in terms of fostering essential and necessary student academic growth. The critics challenge whether traditional programs have been able to keep pace with the educational demands that are a part of a competitive, globalized economy. Whether such critics "have it right" is debatable, but what both critics and advocates of traditional programs agree on is the fact that the principal is absolutely critical to the success of any school program. Teachers need a school leader who understands how to manage a complex educational environment. The question remains about how best to prepare such school leaders, which serves as the focus for this chapter.

This is not the first time that there have been serious and ongoing efforts to upgrade the quality of administrator preparation, but even with current and previous efforts, serious concerns have surfaced as to whether traditional programs can really deliver to PreK–12 schools the intellectual talent needed to foster educational excellence. Some critics believe that the real solution to the problem is to bring persons with business degrees into schools who understand how to operate, manage, and market businesses. Indeed, some universities around the country are now working through their business schools to prepare individuals who have interests in taking their business degrees into educational environments for the purpose of serving as principals or school leaders.

Emmy L. Partin and Jamie Davies O'Leary, from the Thomas B. Fordham Institute, make the case that more nontraditional, nonuniversity-based options are needed. They argue that programs run by charter management organizations or selected nonprofits, such as New Leaders for New Schools, create new vehicles for attracting talent to school leadership positions that simply are not being evidenced through traditional, university-based programs. In addition, Partin and O'Leary assert that many of the nontraditional options place emphasis on preparing administrators for some of the nation's most poorly performing schools, where the need for quality school leaders is most pronounced.

Theodore J. Kowalski from the University of Dayton takes a different view. Kowalski is one of the nation's thought leaders in terms of school leader preparation practices. He has concerns that the "alternatives" will deprofessionalize school leadership at precisely the time when more professional skills and understandings are required by those assuming the difficult responsibilities associated with school administration. Kowalski perceives that, in general, no shortage of administrative talent exists in the United States and that traditional programs are much better suited to address the preparation demands that are currently found in the educational marketplace.

These two essays capture in a significant way much of the active and substantive debate currently found in the professional literature about how to ensure that the nation secures the school leaders it needs. Everyone agrees that school principals and district superintendents are critical ingredients to educational excellence. What these two essays highlight is the very different approaches that policymakers and practitioners have taken relative to how best to recruit and train the next generation of school leaders.

In reading these two essays, consider the following questions. First, will emerging alternatives really deprofessionalize what it means to be a school leader? Second, if it is really essential to have the right people in a leadership position, how should schools best recruit the talent they need? Finally, is the key to recruiting more professional principals paying them more so that you attract better quality or training them differently so that they are assured of possessing skills they need for success?

Thomas J. Lasley, II
University of Dayton

POINT: Emmy L. Partin and Jamie Davies O'Leary
Thomas B. Fordham Institute

The job of a school leader is dramatically different than it was decades or even a few years ago. To meet the needs of students—especially those in America's most underserved communities—K–12 schooling has rightly taken on a variety of shapes. Today's school leaders oversee not only traditional school buildings but also charter schools, virtual academies, "turnarounds," and district schools that operate within atypical contexts—such as "innovation zones" or portfolio-managed districts. Add to this diversity of settings a sense of urgency around raising student performance and closing achievement gaps and add state and federal accountability systems that require leaders to have expertise in academic content standards, testing, and performance data.

Simply put, a school leader's role today is a very different animal from that of the quintessential red-brick schoolhouse principal of 30 or 40 years ago, whose measure of success has been described thusly: "If the school was tidy and orderly, the staff content, the parents quiescent, and the downtown bureaucracy untroubled, the principal was assumed to be doing his or her job" (Broad Foundation & Thomas B. Fordham Institute, 2003, p. 17).

WHY IS THERE A NEED FOR ALTERNATIVE LEADERSHIP PROGRAMS?

Trends in K–12 education have created new demands and expectations for school leaders and evidence the need for alternative leadership programs. To be clear, "alternative" programs mean those preparing leaders in a different manner and with a different focus than typical schools of education. They include hybrid education–business programs, school-based residency programs, specialty programs specifically designed to meet the needs of charter or turnaround leaders, or any other training option meant to prepare school leaders to be effective in nontraditional settings.

In particular, five trends in education have redesigned the role of school leader.

1. The era of academic accountability is no longer an "era"—it's permanent

Regardless of the type of school they lead, all principals operate within the context of state and federal accountability systems that require expertise in standards, testing, and increasingly sophisticated data. Ushered in even before the No Child Left Behind Act (NLCB), accountability is a hallmark of American schooling. Presuppositions that accountability would be an artifact of Republican leadership have diminished now that the Obama Administration and many other distinguished Democratic leaders have made clear their support for keeping intact large portions of NCLB and have promulgated a Race to the Top initiative that clearly has strong accountability components. States have spent millions establishing academic content standards, assessments, and mechanisms for reporting student performance data. The education community generally recognizes the value of such systems. In other words, accountability in education has gone from being loathed, to somewhat palatable, to now *mainstream.*

At the same time, there is an increasing sense of urgency around lifting the performance of all students while also closing achievement gaps between low income and minority students and their wealthier and White peers. Most educators and reformers realize that accountability—specifically, academic standards, assessments, data-reporting and corrective action—is a vital tool with which to diagnose and address such gaps. School leaders today must be equipped to lead in this high-stakes environment. It is a moral imperative not only to ensure that the gaps are closing but also to ensure that our school leaders are trained to be able to handle this herculean task.

2. Persistent failure is no longer acceptable

NCLB was the original impetus behind turning around low-performing schools, stipulating that schools not meeting student performance targets be identified and corrective action instituted to accelerate student growth. Many such failing schools still languish years later, but recent turnaround policy has put its money where its mouth is. U.S. Secretary of Education Arne Duncan emphasized the need to turn around the nation's lowest performing 5,000 schools in 5 years, and $3.5 billion in Title I money (School Improvement Grants program) has been allocated for states to identify and turnaround chronically underperforming schools. (School turnarounds were also a major pillar of the $4.35 billion federal Race to the Top program and were written into many states' Race to the Top reform plans.) Schools receiving turnaround money had to agree to enact one of four approved turnaround strategies, which include installing a new principal, closing the school, and restarting it—possibly under a charter operator, or requiring the school leader to lead a transformation of the school. And Ohio's recently passed biennial budget, HB 153, stipulates that district schools chronically ranking in the lowest 5% of performance must be overhauled using strategies that are similar to those outlined by the School Improvement Grant program. At minimum, successfully turning around these schools—using any of these methods—will require an equivalent number of school leaders who are trained to take on such a formidable challenge.

3. Charter schools are growing slowly but steadily

More than 5,000 charter schools currently serve 1.8 million children in 40 states and the District of Columbia. In some cities, the market share for charters is very high: 69.5% of New Orleans students attend charters and 39.2% do so in Washington, D.C., according to the latest report on charter market share from the National Alliance for Public Charter Schools (2010–2011 report). In Dayton, 29% of the public school student population attends a charter school. Even a modest rate of growth in the charter sector translates into a need for hundreds, maybe thousands, of school leaders prepared for the unique challenges of charter leadership.

Traditional training programs cannot, and are in fact *not meant to,* prepare charter leaders for responsibilities that their district peers do not normally face. A 2008 report on charter school leader development calls the difference between charter training and traditional programs "striking," and points to coursework in areas vital to charter success that are not covered by the latter in ways that address the unique programming and operating needs of charter schools: labor relations, personnel, charter school law and legal issues, financial management, facilities management, charter renewal, and so on (Campbell & Grubb, 2008). In response to this skill gap, many charter management organizations have developed their own in-house training programs to equip up-and-coming leaders to face the unique challenges of leading a charter school.

4. Decentralization and school level autonomy are increasingly common

School systems are experimenting with alternative ways to manage schools and will continue doing so as more central district offices come under criticism for top-heavy administrative loads and for being out of touch with the needs of individual schools and students. Whether via school-based budgeting—which gives the school leader more control over a building's financial and personnel decisions in exchange for academic performance—or a "portfolio" approach to managing schools as seen in New York City, New Orleans, and Chicago, school leaders may find themselves in situations where expertise beyond that accrued via typical education coursework is essential.

Paul Hill, education researcher and director of the Center on Reinventing Public Education, predicts that by the year 2030, this portfolio-style management will have transformed education broadly, with decentralization and decision making devolved to the school level the new norm (Hill, 2010). School leaders in many urban areas already work in districts experimenting with various forms of decentralized leadership. If Hill's predictions ring true, many more will need to develop the skills necessary to lead in environments similar to what their charter peers face, where decisions over personnel, spending, purchasing services, and so forth, are as frequent as instructional decisions.

5. Job mobility and career-changing is the norm

College graduates today switch careers and have, on average, more and various types of jobs by the end of their working lives than they did a generation ago. To attract the most dynamic leaders capable of leading and transforming our nation's neediest schools, we should recruit leaders from sectors outside of education with proven track records of success and who demonstrate the skills necessary to lead schools in need of turnaround. Talented leaders might be more attracted to working in education if the skill sets they acquired through school leadership training programs were more portable and did not lock them into one career. A hybrid principal preparation program that has coursework in business, for example, may be more attractive to smart candidates who otherwise might be drawn into the private sector.

While the landscape of K–12 education has shifted tremendously—and, by default, what is required of the next generation of school leaders—the vast majority of America's school principals are trained for their jobs in much the same fashion that they were decades ago. This training is often insufficient for those hoping to take the reins of a charter school, district turnaround school, other nontraditional education setting, or even those leading traditional schools facing sizable achievement gaps.

Traditional programs—generally graduate programs offered by colleges of education—simply do not offer adequate and appropriate training for leaders of such schools. And much of the typical principal preparation hasn't adapted sufficiently to train regular school leaders for what they need to know, to say nothing of the next generation. Take academic accountability and school improvement, for example.

NCLB was signed into law in 2002, establishing a system of academic accountability that applied to every public school in the country. Schools were required to meet performance expectations and continually improve or face major overhaul. Yet 3 years later, a study by the American Enterprise Institute

(AEI) found that just 2% of traditional principal training coursework "addressed accountability in the context of school management or school improvement and less than five percent included instruction on managing school improvement via data, technology, or empirical research" (Hess & Kelly, 2005b, p. 37).

That same study found that traditional principal preparation programs spent little time on the use of data or teaching important personnel management topics, such as recruitment, selection, and hiring of teachers; teacher dismissal; or teacher compensation. This is occurring even as education becomes more data driven and results oriented and as more authority over personnel decisions is being devolved to building leaders in districts. It is also evidenced in the charter sector, where school leaders function as small-business CEOs.

What's more, the training that traditional programs do offer may not be useful to prospective school leaders. In his 4-year examination of colleges of education, Arthur Levine, then president of Columbia University's Teachers College, found that administrator-training coursework is "a nearly random collection of courses" disconnected from the realities of principals' jobs (Levine, 2005).

There is also a misalignment between the expertise and perspectives in traditional training programs and what many future school leaders, especially those in niches like charter schools and school turnarounds, need to know.

Scan the websites of any college of education administrator-training program. You will find a faculty comprising brilliant men and women with robust curricula vitae touting interest and research in a wide range of education topic areas. A standard principal licensure program covers areas such as instructional leadership and school culture and may include vague course descriptions of topics such as "educational change" or "political leadership." This is not to say such subjects are not useful to some traditional school leaders, like the lucky ones not facing the sorts of organizational or achievement programs described earlier, but you will find few, if any, professors in traditional schools of education with experience starting up a new school or running one or with expertise in school finance, facilities acquisition, or school funding beyond theories presented in textbooks.

If professors have never developed a 5-year budget for a school, done a market analysis to gauge future enrollment, or used student level academic performance data to make personnel decisions—nor spent time studying those who have—should they really be expected to teach someone else how to do that work?

In the halls of education schools, you will also find few supporters of major education reform ideas, from school choice and charter schools to weighted student funding and pay-for-performance for teachers. A 1997 survey by Public Agenda found this to be the case, and newer research holds it true. AEI's *Learning to Lead* found a strong left-leaning bias in the topic descriptions and assigned readings of traditional principal training programs (and in 2005, when the study was conducted, charter schools, merit pay, etc., could be firmly characterized as "right-leaning") (see Hess & Kelly, 2005b).

When principals-in-training at traditional preparation programs do receive clinical instruction through an internship or practicum, it is often insufficient—whether because of the length of the experience, its content, or other factors. For example, Levine found that it is not standard practice to pair principals-in-training with proven or successful current principals for their internships. Rather, trainees are placed by convenience.

To ensure that school leaders—especially those who will lead our neediest schools—are equipped to effectively manage in a variety of high-stakes and diverse school environments, it is critical to support and grow alternative training programs designed to deliver the training they need.

WHAT DO THESE ALTERNATIVE OPTIONS LOOK LIKE?

Alternative school leadership training programs have cropped up to equip leaders with skill sets they would otherwise not get from a traditional preparation program. By definition, alternative programs are as varied as the needs faced by various schools and student populations.

A chronically underperforming school facing replacement of half its staff, for example, needs a leader who can oversee the immediate and probably chaotic transition and transformation of the school's culture. This type of leader must know how to deliver results quickly and dramatically lift student performance, while also navigating a tumultuous day-to-day environment. A leader of a new start-up charter school might need to handle leasing a school building and developing a school budget, as well as recruiting and hiring new staff and selecting curriculum. Further, charter start-up leaders must understand how to navigate state and federal laws around school funding and spending, maintain student records, and handle students' individualized education programs (IEPs), to name a few.

A traditional school leader whose district has just been named part of an innovation zone, wherein some of the typical regulations imposed by state law and/or collective bargaining agreements are lifted, must be able to think outside the box about how to redesign the school to meet the needs of students. He or she must be self-directed and have business acumen if budgetary decision making is devolved to the school level.

Many training programs already exist to prepare school leaders for these nontraditional settings, and most of them have impressive—and measurable—results when it comes to the performance of students led by their alumni. These programs are housed within universities or run via nonprofits or charter management organizations, and they may be geared toward leaders of a variety of school types. Here are just a few such programs:

Rice Education Entrepreneurship Program

Housed in the Jones Graduate School of Business at Houston's Rice University, Rice Education Entrepreneurship Program (REEP) offers two pathways for the alternative principal license. The master of business administration (MBA) pathway takes 2 years and equips candidates with core business skills as well as courses in leadership, management, organizational behavior, accounting, and data analysis. The business certificate pathway takes 15 months to complete and is highly selective (just 15 students are admitted per year); students enroll in the innovative Rice Advanced Management Program, and they take a variety of courses in business and education. Both pathways require school-based training and previous teaching experience (2 years of experience for the MBA pathway and 4 to 7 for the business certificate). Leaders are equipped to lead a variety of types of schools.

New Leaders for New Schools

New Leaders for New Schools (NLNS) is a yearlong, paid residency that trains principals and places them in 11 urban districts across the United States. Candidates spend 1 year alongside a mentor principal working in an urban public school, while also working with coaches and specialists to fulfill their own individualized "leadership development plan." Since 2001, NLNS has placed 640 leaders in schools across 12 urban areas. The program places principals across all grades in both district and charter schools.

Building Excellent Schools

Building Excellent Schools (BES) is a yearlong, paid fellowship that trains leaders to start and lead their own charter schools in strategically chosen sites across the country. Fellows complete a residency in a high performing charter school as well as a year of planning time in the community where they are founding a school. The program consists of rigorous site-based training, coaching, and advising and prepares leaders to write and submit their own charter application, secure a facility, recruit and enroll students, hire teachers, and build their curriculum. The program is highly selective (4% of applicants are accepted) and by 2011–2012 will grow to 48 schools in 20 cities and will serve 19,500 students.

University of Virginia School Turnaround Specialist Program

Started in 2004 and commissioned by the Virginia Department of Education, this program is geared toward principals and district and school level leadership teams at schools in need of overhaul. The University of Virginia calls the program the kind of executive education that typically is received only by high level business leaders. Specifically geared toward district personnel tasked with turning around the lowest performing schools, it includes coursework ranging from data analysis to case studies on renewing troubled organizations. Results from 43 school turnaround specialists from the program are positive, with school leaders achieving reduced academic failure rates or meeting Adequate Yearly Progress and other benchmarks.

Notre Dame's Educational Leadership Program

A joint program in which candidates receive an executive MBA from the college of business, as well as training from the Institute for Educational Initiatives, Notre Dame's Educational Leadership Program (NDELP) calls itself a "results-driven principal preparation pathway" that is more concerned with teaching leaders to lead successful schools than with "teaching theories about schools and leadership." The program, which began in 2009, requires candidates to have 2 years of teaching experience and like many other alternative training programs, covers a mix of business and education-specific training.

Opponents of alternative preparation programs typically root their arguments in *theories* concerning the overall profession—namely, that alternative preparation "deprofessionalizes" the job, undermines the role of school leadership, or leads to deregulation and a dangerous sort of "anything goes" mentality over who leads our nation's children. In reality, the alternative programs for which we advocate do none of these things. Examine the efficacy of any of the actual programs listed, the student demographics they serve, and the highly selective nature of their admissions processes, and such claims quickly dissolve. If anything, alternative training programs bolster the too often denigrated profession—such programs are highly competitive and attract distinguished leaders who might not otherwise enroll in a school leadership program.

Moreover, the assertion that alternative programs deprofessionalize the role of school leader should be a secondary concern in light of glaring achievement gaps and chronic underperformance in many of America's poorest communities. Existing principal training programs have had decades to adapt and better prepare school leaders to lead chronically dysfunctional schools, and thus far—using stagnant student achievement, graduation rates, or gaps between various groups as metrics—they haven't succeeded. Alternative programs, many of which select the best and the brightest leaders through rigorous admissions processes (thereby adding prestige to the profession rather than detracting it), should be judged by their efficacy, not by abstract ideas about deregulating the profession and protecting adult interests over that of students.

Finally, it is important to note that while all of these programs aim to provide candidates with skills and knowledge they wouldn't otherwise gain in a traditional principal training program, they adhere to a fundament of traditional pathways by requiring that candidates have experience teaching before becoming a school leader. Opponents of alternative training programs often rely on the myth that such programs are somehow antiteacher or antieducation—that "outsiders" who think they know better than traditionally trained educators wish to run our schools—but such arguments simply aren't accurate. Most alternative training programs do not divorce the school leader from the teaching and learning happening in the school and require prior significant teaching experience.

Realizing the need for more training programs capable of preparing principals to work in our nation's toughest schools, Senator Michael Bennet (D–Colorado)—also former superintendent of Denver Public Schools—proposed legislation in June 2010 to create a School Leadership Academy that would train principals to intervene effectively in failing schools. The bill envisions a network of training centers run jointly by nonprofit organizations, universities, and state education agencies or districts—with one specializing in rural turnaround schools. Beyond the trends reshaping the educational landscape in the United States, this demand for alternative training programs—and the political support it is able to muster—is evidence of the need to foster such programs into the future.

More important, such programs aim to get effective leaders into many of our nation's worst-performing schools; candidates enrolling in alternative programs often must demonstrate a strong commitment to improving educational outcomes for low income children. To inhibit alternative programs that are successfully fulfilling this mission is asinine; indeed, to do anything less than fully support their sustenance and growth is doing a disservice to children and families in America's neediest communities.

COUNTERPOINT: Theodore J. Kowalski
University of Dayton

In their article about the politics of principal preparation, Frederick Hess and Andrew Kelly (2005a) described me as a "long-time advocate of traditional preparation" who has "heralded the emergence of a new group of reformers from within the education schools" (p. 157). To be precise, I believe that the tradition of preparing principals in schools of education should be sustained; but I also believe that the nature and number of those programs should be altered. Most notably, preparation programs need to become homogeneous, rigorous, practice-based, and professionally accredited (as they are in other professions). And if this occurs, I predict many of the poorest university-based programs will close because they will be unable or unwilling to meet accreditation standards. Conversely, I believe that the creation of alternative preparation programs is a myopic and even reckless decision, primarily because it exacerbates rather than attenuates several problems that have and continue to diminish the effectiveness of traditional programs.

The term *alternative preparation* has been used in various ways, and therefore, it needs to be defined. This essay describes alternative preparation as including programs that possess one or more of the following characteristics: They are not sponsored or operated by an accredited school of education; they are not based on standards embraced by the education profession (e.g., Educational Leadership Constituent Council Standards); they allow noneducators to enroll. Defined in this manner, alternative preparation almost always challenges common criteria for state administrator licensing, norms such as having a valid teacher's license, having experience as a classroom teacher, and completing a state-approved and professionally accredited preparation program. As a matter of public policy, alternative preparation should be evaluated on the basis of social consequences. Specifically, the process should be sanctioned if there is compelling evidence that it will ultimately improve schools or at least the practice of school administration.

The intent of this essay is to refute four contentions commonly made by those who advocate alternative preparation programs. These assertions relate to the status of school administration as a profession, the shortage of qualified administrators, the effectiveness of university-based preparation, and the social benefit of having nontraditional administrators.

STATUS OF SCHOOL ADMINISTRATION

Alternative preparation is more likely to become public policy if school administration is cast as a managerial role rather than a profession. In most professions, practitioners, possessing an esoteric body of knowledge, essential skills, and appropriate dispositions, are licensed and granted autonomy and prestige in return for their services. This arrangement, intended to protect society from incompetent practitioners and quackery, has been periodically questioned when applied to educators. In large part, challenges have stemmed from inevitable conflict between democracy and professionalism (Levin, 1999). Over time, states legitimized a fragile compromise. Expressly, educators were licensed by states and permitted to call themselves professionals; concurrently, they were denied the status and autonomy accorded to practitioners in most other professions (Kowalski, 2009).

The notion that superintendents and principals should be professionals who recommend and carry out public policy has existed for more than a century. As far back as 1895, for example, Andrew Draper, president of the University of Illinois and later commissioner of education in New York, wrote a national report detailing the merits of professionalism. Explicitly, he urged school boards to give superintendents the authority to employ teachers, supervise instruction, and manage finances (Callahan, 1962). Giving school administrators more autonomy and power remains controversial to this very day, in part because some citizens believe that professionalism diminishes their power and in part because some citizens do not believe that administrators possess an esoteric body of knowledge. For those who harbor these beliefs, alternative preparation is a gateway to deprofessionalization.

If school administration is reduced to a managerial role, then there is no need for principals to understand pedagogy, no justification for them recommending instructional policies, and no need for them to be licensed. Those who seek to institutionalize this change, however, conveniently ignore possible consequences. In the realm of representative democracy, school administrators are expected to forge recommendations based on expert knowledge, and school boards, acting on behalf of their constituents, decide whether to accept the recommendation. Both administrators and school board members are then held accountable to the community (Shedd & Bacharach, 1991). This arrangement always placed public school administrators in the difficult position of forging policy, while remaining subservient to the will of the people (Wirt & Kirst, 2009).

Indirectly if not directly, the concept of alternative preparation casts administrators as only managers, and it removes the need to balance democracy and professionalism. As a result, future policy decisions will be made without the benefit of professional wisdom. We must ask ourselves if this arrangement will help or hinder school improvement.

SHORTAGE OF QUALIFIED ADMINISTRATORS

A second excuse for alternative preparation is that it is essential to ameliorate a critical shortage of qualified administrators. The application of the concept in relation to labor shortages has precedent. During World War II, for example, a dearth of health care providers was addressed by creating fast tracks to physician and dentist licensing. Specifically, academic study in these professions was made continuous (including summers), the curricula were condensed, and the length of medical or dental school was reduced to 2 years. Although this alternative form of preparation apparently served its purpose, three facts need to be weighed, especially by those who believe the same changes should be made for preparing school administrators. First, the shortage of physicians and dentists was validated and accepted not only by policymakers but also by the respective professions. Second, the accelerated education programs were conducted by accredited medical and dental schools and not independent agencies. Third, after the war ended and the shortage subsided, the alternative programs were eliminated because they were an acceptable temporary substitute for traditional preparation. No one considered them to be an equal or superior option.

In the case of school administration, claims of labor shortages have been widely accepted. In truth, the average size of an applicant pool for an administrative vacancy is around 15 to 20 licensed applicants. In what other profession would we declare a labor shortage given these statistics? Recognizing this fact, antiprofessionists have purposefully distinguished between a "licensed" administrator and a "qualified" administrator. The quintessential example is found in *Better Leaders for America's Schools: A Manifesto* (Broad Foundation & Thomas B. Fordham Institute, 2003). The anonymous authors admitted that the shortage problem in school administration "is not one of quantity: Most states have plenty of people licensed as school administrators, often more than they have positions to fill. The urgent problem is quality" (p. 16). Yet the authors neither provided evidence to support this generalization nor defined being qualified.

If quantity and quality issues are considered collectively, then logic suggests that alternative preparation will not eradicate the shortage of qualified school administrators. The few corporate executives and retired generals who have become nontraditional education administrators have been employed as superintendents of large schools systems where they receive high salaries and dozens if not hundreds of administrative assistants. The typical superintendent and principal, however, practice under very different circumstances; for instance, they must directly deal with both leadership and management issues, they have little or no administrative support staff, and they have modest salaries. The contention that there is a cadre of highly competent managers champing at the bit to be school administrators is simply a myth. Consequently, alternative programs are likely to train a combination of educators who want to bypass several years of graduate school and noneducators who have difficulty getting attractive positions in the private sector (Kowalski, 2004). In summary, the purported shortage of administrators is questionable, and even if it were not, providing aspiring administrators with less and more narrow training will lower rather than raise qualifications.

INEFFECTIVENESS OF ALL TRADITIONAL PREPARATION

University-based academic preparation has been disparaged by critics from outside and inside the education profession. Although the nature of the criticisms has often been the same such as citing such claims as irrelevant courses or a lack of practice-based experiences, the two groups have differed in their conceptualizations of traditional preparation and in their proposed solutions. Those from outside the school administration profession (e.g., Hess, 2003; Mazzeo, 2003) have had a proclivity to discuss university-based preparation as a homogeneous process; those from inside the profession have not. Actually, there are vast differences among the approximately 550 institutions preparing school administrators in this country, and because they vary in curriculum, instructional quality, and resources, they are not equally effective.

As a result of their conceptualizations of traditional preparation, external critics see deregulation generally and alternative preparation specifically as beneficial public policy. Many internal critics (e.g., Björk, Kowalski, & Young, 2005; Elmore, 2007; Murphy, 2002) propose an opposite solution; they seek to reform university-based preparation, specifically by making it more practice-based and rigorous.

As a form of deregulation, giving preparation programs a free hand to determine curriculum and standards also is a tested idea. Circa 1830, for example, many states amended physician licensing laws so that medical schools were given autonomy, especially by making a medical school diploma the equivalent of a state license to practice medicine. This myopic policy essentially deregulated state control over physicians. Rather than improving medical schools and producing more qualified physicians, it produced an entrepreneurial environment in which many students of limited ability or academic interest paid high tuition costs for degrees from sham institutions. The United States soon had a glut of physicians, many unqualified to perform services entrusted to them—some were actually illiterate (Numbers, 1988).

As a former teacher, superintendent, and college of education dean, my work has criticized deficiencies in academic preparation for decades. Although I believe that drastic changes to the status quo are warranted, I believe that creating shortcuts, adding more programs, and permitting diverse and unregulated programs will only make things worse. In his study of administrator preparation, Arthur Levine (2005), former president of Teachers College, Columbia University, found that many new programs he analyzed were neither innovative nor more effective than the traditional programs they sought to replace. In some cases, they were worse.

SOCIAL BENEFIT OF ALTERNATIVE PREPARATION

Promoters of alternative programs often suggest that graduates of these programs will outperform traditional school administrators. In large measure, this promise apparently is nested in the perception of administration as solely a managerial role. This supposition like those already addressed needs to be scrutinized. In the first decades of the 20th century, for instance, leading superintendents, prompted by captains of industry, attempted to dissociate themselves from the teaching and the education profession, predominantly by emulating corporate managers.

After studying this period, noted historian Raymond Callahan (1962) concluded that rather than professional leaders, these superintendents were dupes who mindlessly imposed a corporate mentality and efficiency-based culture into their systems. As such, they subordinated educational questions to business considerations, put a scientific label on some very unscientific and dubious methods and practices, and constructed an anti-intellectual climate. Callahan contended that they "did not understand education or scholarship. Thus, they could and did approach education in a businesslike, mechanical, organizational way" (p. 247).

More recently, Diane Ravitch (2010) echoed concerns about promoting a corporate mentality in public education. She offered compelling evidence that reforms such as vouchers, deprofessionalization, and alternative preparation have actually been counterproductive with respect to improving underperforming schools. This conclusion is not surprising for experienced administrators. They recognize that transforming ineffective schools is an exceedingly difficult and complex assignment, one that extends well beyond competent management. Therefore, alternative preparation in the absence of empirical evidence that it is a social benefit is precarious public policy.

Research conducted with alternative preparation of teachers also is insightful because it is indicative of efforts to deprofessionalize education. Richard A. Neumann (1994), for instance, found that teachers from alternative programs were not as well prepared as their peers. Notably, they also were disproportionately employed by inner-city, low income schools—institutions where student needs were the highest. And in their study, Lora Cohen-Vogel and Thomas M. Smith (2007) found that contrary to proponent claims, alternative programs did not increase the quality of applicant pools by attracting large numbers of experienced individuals from other disciplines.

FINAL THOUGHTS

This essay has challenged four of the common reasons espoused by proponents of alternative preparation. The intent was to explain opposition to the concept and to show that the suppositions underlying it are flawed. Past experiments with deregulation and alternative preparation apparently have not convinced antiprofessionists to heed George Santayana's (1980) warning that those who cannot remember the past are condemned to repeat it.

From this opposing viewpoint, alternative preparation programs for school administrators are a manifestation of deregulation, a broader objective intended to deconstruct this nation's public education system (Ravitch, 2010). Specifically, a corporate mentality moves public education from the public marketplace to private marketplace—a move that would allow individuals rather than society to determine the quantity and quality of education provided. Recasting administration as solely a managerial role and preparing future administrators accordingly is one strategy related to this mission. And if it succeeds, it will be detrimental, especially to the schools that most need improvement.

For schools to improve, their principals and superintendents must acquire a level of social authority that permits them to work collaboratively with teachers and other stakeholders to enact necessary changes. Clearly, they will not be able to achieve this lofty goal by simply managing human and material resources. Specifically, their academic preparation needs to be rigorous and based on a core set of validated practices related to leading and managing (Elmore, 2007). It is unimaginable how these improvements will be delivered by programs detached from academe and professionalism. In closing, it is worth noting that alternative preparation programs arguably move in the opposite direction, and they present the possibility that future principals will be merely managers and political operatives.

FURTHER READINGS AND RESOURCES

Björk, L. G., Kowalski, T. J., & Young, M. (2005). National education reform reports: Implications for professional preparation and development. In L. G. Björk & T. J. Kowalski (Eds.), *The contemporary superintendent: Preparation, practice, and development* (pp. 45–70). Thousand Oaks, CA: Corwin.

Bliss, J. R. (1988). Public school administrators in the United States: Analysis of supply and demand. In D. Griffiths, R. Stout, & P. Forsyth (Eds.), *Leaders for America's schools: The report and papers of the National Commission on Excellence in Educational Administration* (pp. 193–206). Berkeley, CA: McCutchan.

Broad Foundation, & Thomas B. Fordham Institute. (2003). *Better leaders for America's schools: A manifesto.* Los Angeles: Authors.

Callahan, R. E. (1962). *Education and the cult of efficiency.* Chicago: University of Chicago Press.

Campbell, C., & Grubb, B. J. (2008). *Closing the skill gap: New options for charter school leadership development.* Seattle, WA: Center on Reinventing Public Education.

Cohen-Vogel, L., & Smith, T. M. (2007). Qualifications and assignments of alternatively certified teachers: Testing core assumptions. *American Educational Research Journal, 44*(3), 732–753.

Elmore, R. F. (2007). Education: A "profession" in search of practice. *Teaching in Educational Administration, 15*(1), 1–4.

Hess, F. M. (2003). *A license to lead? A new leadership agenda for America's schools.* Washington, DC: Progressive Policy Institute.

Hess, F. M., & Kelly, A. P. (2005a). An innovative look, a recalcitrant reality: The politics of principal preparation reform. *Educational Policy, 19*(1), 155–180.

Hess, F. M., & Kelly, A. P. (2005b). *Learning to lead: What gets taught in principal preparation programs?* Retrieved from http://www.aei.org/docLib/20050517_Learning_to_Lead.pdf

Hill, P. T. (2010). Reinvented school districts. In C. E. Finn, Jr. (Ed.), *American education in 2030: An assessment by Hoover Institution's Koret Task Force on K-12 education.* Available from http://www.americaneducation2030.com

Kowalski, T. J. (2004). The ongoing war for the soul of school administration. In T. J. Lasley (Ed.), *Better leaders for America's schools: Perspectives on the Manifesto* (pp. 92–114). Columbia, MO: University Council for Educational Administration.

Kowalski, T. J. (2006). *The school superintendent: Theory, practice, and cases* (2nd ed.). Thousand Oaks, CA: Sage.

Kowalski, T. J. (2009). Need to address evidence-based practice in educational administration. *Educational Administration Quarterly, 45,* 375–423.

Levin, H. M. (1999). The public-private nexus in education. *American Behavioral Scientist, 43*(1), 124–137.

Levine, A. (2005). *Educating school leaders.* Washington, DC: Education Schools Project. Retrieved from http://www.edschools.org/pdf/Final313.pdf

Mazzeo, C. (2003). *Issue brief: Improving teaching and learning by improving school leadership.* Washington, DC: National Governors Association.

Murphy, J. (2002). Reculturing the profession of educational leadership: New blueprints. *Educational Administration Quarterly, 38*(2), 176–191.

Neumann, R. A. (1994). Reconsidering emergency teaching certificates and alternative certification programs as responses to teacher shortages. *Urban Education, 29*(1), 89–108.

Numbers, R. L. (1988). The fall and rise of the American medical profession. In N. O. Hatch (Ed.), *The professions in American history* (pp. 51–72). Notre Dame, IN: University of Notre Dame Press.

Ravitch, D. (2010). *The death and life of the great American school system: How testing and choice are undermining education.* New York: Basic Books.

Santayana, G. (1980). *Reason in common sense: Vol. 1. The life of reason.* New York: Dover.

Shedd, J. B., & Bacharach, S. B. (1991). *Tangled hierarchies: Teachers as professionals and the management of schools.* San Francisco: Jossey-Bass.

Wirt, F., & Kirst, M. (2009). *The political dynamics of American education* (4th ed.). Berkeley, CA: McCutchan.

8

Should value-added modeling be used to identify highly effective teachers?

POINT: James W. Mahoney, *Battelle for Kids*

COUNTERPOINT: Kathryn Kinnucan-Welsch, *University of Dayton*
Martha S. Hendricks, *Wilmington College*
Suzanne Franco, *Wright State University*

OVERVIEW

For years, the identification of *effective* teachers has been more art than science. For some administrators, effective teachers were those who never sent students to the office. For some parents, it was the teachers who paid attention to their children and who were able to communicate positive expectations about the potential of their young. Further, for others in communities, it was the teachers who remained, over time, in classrooms, serving as a source of stability in an otherwise highly mobile postmodern world.

These intuitive representations of effectiveness served the public's interests for decades, largely because there were no real psychometric tools for assessing whether Teacher A was actually more effective at fostering student academic growth than Teacher B. Things began to change in the 1990s with the work of statistician William Sanders. Sanders was responsible for developing the Tennessee Value-Added Assessment System (TVAAS), which enabled researchers to determine the impact of a teacher on student performance. Up to that point, student progress had been measured against normed groups. Students would take standardized tests, and teachers (as well as parents) could see how a student compared to the broader student population. The problem with this approach is that it places too much focus on the intellectual capital a child brings to school and too little understanding of what specific growth a teacher fosters. Given that socioeconomic family status is closely connected to student academic achievement, teachers in affluent communities could appear to be quite effective because their students could have high achievement while colleagues in very poor communities could appear, on paper, to be quite weak since student achievement scores were below the normed population.

In essence, achievement tends to be tied to family socioeconomic status, but actual academic growth is linked directly to a teacher. As a consequence, suburban teachers could evidence high achievement but low growth since students bring a great deal of academic knowledge to school but learn little from their teacher, or urban teachers could evidence low achievement but high growth if their students bring very limited academic skills and understandings to classrooms but learn a great deal during school years from their assigned teachers. In fact, this is precisely what Sanders found: Some teachers foster real growth while others fail to do so.

The question of import is how such teacher value-added knowledge can and should be used. In other portions of this book authors reference the current controversy in Los Angeles concerning "making public" the effectiveness, based on value-added data, of classroom teachers. The two essays in this chapter represent some of the contentious points that advocates for and critics of value-added modeling (VAM) are making in the professional literature.

James W. Mahoney, President of Battelle for Kids, is an advocate of value-added. His point essay outlines the rationale undergirding VAM and documents, using data from the Houston Independent School District, how the VAM approach can be used to improve teacher performance. In addition, through the use of VAM, Mahoney maintains that it is now possible to begin to isolate some of the characteristics that make some teachers either effective (produce 1 year of academic growth) or highly effective (engender 1½ years' growth). Mahoney describes some of those attributes such as the teacher's ability to differentiate instruction, and makes a clear argument for why the VAM approach now represents an essential part (just not the sole piece) of any established protocol for evaluating teacher performance.

Kathryn Kinnucan-Welsch, Martha S. Hendricks, and Suzanne Franco, all of whom hold university appointments, are not value-added detractors. Even so, these researchers are cautious about how value-added data can and should be used to evaluate teachers. In some respects, these authors share common ground with VAM advocates: They clearly see that VAM data do have a place in the teacher evaluation landscape. However, these authors do not want VAM data used as an exclusive data point for compensation and accountability purposes, and they argue for thinking about the whole range of behaviors that constitute effective teaching and how effective teachers are evaluated.

In reading these two essays, consider these types of questions. First, to what degree, if any, should student growth scores be used to evaluate a teacher's effectiveness? Second, should value-added data represent de facto descriptions of good teaching? If not, what other attributes should be considered?

Thomas J. Lasley, II
University of Dayton

POINT: James W. Mahoney
Battelle for Kids

It is clear that students, parents, educators, policymakers, and others have strong and varied opinions about what makes a "great" teacher. Ask any student about what makes a great teacher, and you might receive the following response: "A great teacher encourages me and makes learning fun." Ask the student's parent, and you might hear this: "A great teacher ensures that my child is challenged and is being successfully prepared for college and the workplace." Policymakers and business leaders may respond by saying the following: "Great teachers know what they are doing is important and hold themselves accountable for student learning." The truth is that great teachers add value to students' educational experiences in many ways—some that can be easily measured and some that cannot.

For decades, experts and practitioners debated how to measure teacher effectiveness accurately. Moreover, in a 2008 synthesis of what is known about the evaluation of teacher effectiveness, Laura Goe, Courtney Bell, and Olivia Little (2008) quoted Cruickshank and Haefele, who concluded that "an enormous underlying problem with teacher evaluation relates to lack of agreement about what constitutes great or highly-effective teaching" (see Cruickshank & Haefele, 1990, http://www.tqsource.org/publications/EvaluatingTeachEffectiveness.pdf). Without universal agreement on the things that characterize good teaching, there will be no universally accepted tools created to measure those characteristics. And, without quantitative data from such instruments, prescriptive advice for making average teachers good and good teachers great becomes difficult.

Should value-added analysis be used to measure teacher effectiveness? Absolutely. It can help to identify extraordinary teachers who, year after year, receive very high academic gains with students. While statisticians may argue over the nuances of value-added modeling, it is clear that this empirical measure can be used to identify outstanding teachers on the tail, regardless of the model used.

Errors of measurement are suppressed by data that consistently show the positive impact on student learning by these teachers year after year. All teachers have had groups of students that they connected with very well and others with which they were less successful. These teachers consistently show growth with all students and different groups of students over a period of years. There is much to be learned from these teachers.

Let's take a closer look at value-added analysis as a productivity measure, how it can be used to empirically identify highly effective teachers, the importance of understanding the characteristics, behaviors and attitudes of highly effective teachers, and what support systems are necessary for educators to improve and become successful.

VALUE-ADDED ANALYSIS: A FAIRER MEASURE OF STUDENTS' ACADEMIC PERFORMANCE

There is no question that what gets measured gets monitored, and what gets monitored gets improved. Value-added analysis brings a critical new dimension to viewing teachers' impact on student learning. Further, value-added analysis brings a different approach to a long-standing challenge in education: how to accurately measure student progress.

For years, achievement was measured by students' performance on state tests. The number of students who passed state tests largely determined school and district performance levels. While providing some useful information on student achievement, state test scores do not provide an accurate view of individual student growth or the progress that schools and/or districts make with the same groups of students. Simply measuring students' achievement without evaluating where students start is akin to knowing how far north or south one is traveling without knowing how far east or west. Not measuring progress invites us to court our own tragic miscalculations of student achievement.

In many respects, value-added analysis provides a lens by which to ask familiar questions and view the answers in a new way. With new answers to age-old questions, schools can begin to interpret the strengths and weaknesses of curriculum, instruction, programs, and practices that influence student learning and whether students are gaining a year's worth of academic progress in a year's time and not merely assess students' achievement as it stands at a particular moment.

From a statistical sense, value-added analysis can set aside the consideration of nonschool-related influences on student achievement (race, socioeconomic factors, culture, language, and others) and, instead, assess the effect that teaching and school-related factors have on student learning. On the other hand, achievement is correlated with socioeconomic status, so value-added analysis has only a slight relationship to measures of socioeconomic status. As a result, value-added analysis has become a compelling means by which to depict and examine student progress.

At the same time, it is important to be clear: Value-added analysis does not replace traditional measures of achievement reporting; rather, it complements them. When taken together, achievement results and value-added information tell us where students are with respect to academic content standards and how effectively the current program is working to move all students toward higher levels of proficiency.

Value-added analysis represents a new approach for measuring the ways in which teaching affects learning and is a fairer and more reliable means of looking at student growth. It has become a powerful motivator for educators because it levels the field and measures the progress of individual students, classes, schools, and districts year-to-year from where they started.

THE IMPORTANCE OF MULTIPLE MEASURES

The onset of value-added analysis has significantly changed the education landscape—shifting the conversation from defining *what* constitutes great or highly effective teaching to *how* to objectively and reliably measure the impact great teachers have on student learning. For the first time in the history of American education, the definition of *great teachers* is grounded in students' academic growth, not just student achievement. The difference is subtle but extremely important.

If "effective" teachers are defined by the number or percentage of students who reach specific achievement levels, then those teachers who create significant, incremental learning in low-achieving students will be overlooked. Likewise, teachers who have classrooms of high-achieving students but do not cause these students to make any significant academic growth will receive unwarranted credit for being effective.

While value-added analysis should be used to improve teacher effectiveness, it should not be used as the sole measure to judge teacher effectiveness. The reason multiple measures are so important is because teaching and learning are complex. It would be a disservice to the teaching profession if we thought the only contribution of a teacher could be measured by one annual student test converted to a simple score. And, on that basis alone, make important judgments about that teacher's future. Equally dishonorable, though, are those who believe test results should never be used as a measure. Of course, they should; students' results are part of a teacher's performance. It's an important piece of datum, just not the whole story.

The only way to suppress errors of measure is to have many data points. An individual student can fail a test because she had a fight at the bus stop, broke up with her boyfriend, or simply doesn't perform well on tests. That single student doesn't negate the impact of the teacher. There are many students whose aggregated scores determine that impact. Furthermore, when you look at a teacher's influence on student learning over multiple years, the impact they make becomes clearer.

Einstein probably had it right when he suggested, "not everything that counts can be counted, and not everything that can be counted counts." Discerning effective teaching must be approached thoughtfully. We can no longer throw our hands up and declare that teaching is too noble of a profession to measure its impact. We cannot treat teachers as commodities. In this challenge lies enormous opportunities to develop multiple measures that help schools discern teaching effectiveness.

THE "RIGHT" PRACTICES MATTER

Developing people and using the right measures also require a corresponding set of high-leverage, effective practices and methods that will allow schools to accelerate student academic progress. As the research confirms that teachers have the greatest influence on students' academic success, it is imperative that we understand what highly effective teachers do in the classroom. We need to tap into the expertise of our highly effective teachers who have helped students maximize their academic growth. To continuously improve, we must create ways to research, mine, and share proven practices that are repeatable and scalable.

During the 2008–2009 school year, the Houston Independent School District initiated a study, supported by the Bill & Melinda Gates Foundation and conducted by researchers from Battelle for Kids, to uncover the practices of highly effective teachers. A group of more than 60 core teachers in grades 3 through 8 in math, science, language, reading, and social studies who facilitated the highest levels of student academic growth participated in the study. These individuals had the highest average value-added Cumulative Gain Index for 2 consecutive school years based on 2006–2007 and 2007–2008 teacher level value-added results provided to the district by its value-added vendor.

This study, similar to one conducted in Ohio, uncovered the following recurring themes across each of the subject area groups. Common across these teachers are

- instruction that supports and engages all students;

- a child-centered focus that fosters relationships and is responsive— teaching to each student's needs;

- a consistent and predictable classroom environment that is positive, safe, organized, and conducive to high quality learning for all students; and

- professional self-efficacy and continuous improvement through collaboration, personalized professional development, and supportive leadership.

Using different types of media and experiences, highly effective teachers' proven practices can be discussed and shared from educator to educator. Principals need to foster a culture of collaboration that supports idea sharing so that proven practices can be taken to scale. Through collaborative learning experiences, educators' collective energy, excitement, and promise will give way to hope, encouragement, and improved results.

DEVELOPING TEACHER TALENT WITH THE RIGHT SUPPORT SYSTEMS

Think of anything you do well. Did you start at that level of proficiency? Probably not. Psychologist K. Anders Ericsson suggests that the real difference between average and superior performance is 10,000 hours of deliberate practice. You build skills and expertise through practice, receiving feedback and improving your performance.

For too long, teachers were given their grade books, lesson planners, boxes of chalk, and red grading pencils before being told to have a good career. There was an expectation that teachers were adequately prepared to teach by their university or college programs. All of the preservice programs in the world rarely prepare teachers for their own class full of students with different abilities, motivations, challenges, and parents.

Teaching is hard work, but we know that with focused and personalized support, teachers can improve their skills and become vastly more effective. Unfortunately, activity is often confused for accomplishment with one-shot professional development marginally related to teachers' real needs. Or it's the "race to the right" where teachers load up on courses that warrant a pay raise and have nothing to do with their role in education.

If we expect teachers to differentiate instruction to meet students' individual needs, then why would we not do the same for teachers' professional development? For example, some teachers may struggle with helping low achievers to succeed while others may want improved ways to work with gifted students. In his recent book, *Drive,* Daniel Pink (2011) argues that mastery—the urge to get better and better at something that matters—is very motivating. What better way to motivate teachers than to provide real support for their practice?

Professional development is absolutely essential to support educators' use of value-added information. Educators can have all the data points in the world, but if they don't understand how to use this information, then it will make no difference for students.

There's an old story, apocryphal in nature but certainly illustrative of the notion. Two woodcutters were engaged in a 12-hour woodcutting contest.

They cut wood in front of each other and an audience of eager onlookers. One woodcutter took a 10-minute break each hour, while the other did not stop. At the end of the session, the woodcutter who took the breaks had cut much more wood. The other woodcutter was shocked. "How could this be?" he asked. The other woodcutter replied, "Maybe it's because I resharpened my axe each hour."

Professional development is resharpening the axe and a critical component when using value-added assessment. Nearly all educator-standards panels endorse the importance of teachers' understanding and applying data-based decision making, yet two problems persist for most educators. First, teachers have had little, if any, training in data-based decision making. Second, teachers have received little data that didn't look like an autopsy—information that rarely, if ever, could actually be used to improve programs or increase student achievement.

Value-added data give teachers starting places to understand where they are and where they are headed. Success stories occur in places that accelerate professional development around value-added measures. Not only do these occurrences help educators understand their results, but they allow them also to review results along with other student data. This combination helps educators plan a new ending for students.

CONCLUSION

While the debate around using value-added analysis to measure highly effective teachers will continue, using it to measure progress is not going away. Statistical discussions certainly will continue throughout the academic community. Ironically, as educators insist on academic rigor for students, some suggest that value-added analysis cannot be used because of its complexity and underlying statistical analyses. With access to the necessary time and professional development opportunities, educators can easily learn to use and benefit from value-added analysis. More important, there are many stories from around the country that showcase how educators are using value-added analysis to improve instruction.

Value-added analysis offers many benefits to assist educators in improving student achievement. It is clearly a tool that can measure progress, promote collaborative dialogue, and make achievement tests more meaningful. However, it may not measure the impact of teachers who can motivate students or inspire a love of learning in students, which also contribute to students' academic success. While traits like motivation and inspiration may not be measured directly, they may be reflected indirectly. The journey to understand and navigate effective measures of both progress and achievement will continue and is of critical importance to understanding and accelerating higher achievement for all students.

It is hard to imagine that any teacher does not want to get better. Simply labeling a teacher according to student performance results is judgment—not improvement. Will every teacher succeed? No. But neither does every salesman, architect, mechanic, or other professional. Teacher ineffectiveness can no longer be tolerated. And we cannot wait for some teachers to gain the experience necessary to become effective because some of them never will.

Teachers are the linchpins to improving student performance. And learning what our most effective teachers are doing in the classroom and the behaviors and attitudes they embody are the first steps toward helping all teachers become more successful. Value-added information gives us a clearer way to help identify the very best teachers.

COUNTERPOINT: Kathryn Kinnucan-Welsch
University of Dayton

Martha S. Hendricks
Wilmington College

Suzanne Franco
Wright State University

Over the past 2 decades, the importance of the contribution of teachers to student learning has been widely acknowledged. Some researchers argued that teachers are the most important factor in explaining differences in student achievement. In previous decades, much of the educational research literature explored differences in student achievement based largely on student characteristics, such as educational attainment of the parents, socioeconomic status, race, and gender. It is only recently that teachers have been placed at the center of research and accountability related to student learning. To put it simply, it is widely said that "teachers matter." Further, recent directions in educational accountability have placed student achievement at the forefront of defining teacher effectiveness. One of the emerging measures of defining teacher effectiveness has been the metric of value-added as based on student performance on standardized tests.

The first section of this counterpoint essay addresses some issues of concern about value-added as an indicator of teacher quality. The second section offers a reframing of the question from indicators of *teacher* quality to indicators of *teaching* quality, and it posits questions that can provide a more robust approach to examining teaching quality. The final section includes thoughts on how to identify and support high quality teaching

OVERVIEW OF VALUE-ADDED AS AN INDICATOR OF TEACHER EFFECTIVENESS

Accountability for student achievement is now embedded in the fabric of our education system and includes monitoring of student achievement on tests or collections of tests in multiple ways. These include, among others, reporting the percentage of students meeting a criterion level (National Assessment of Educational Progress) and comparing average change in performance of a group of students from one year to the next (Adequate Yearly Progress). In the 1990s, the educational research and policy communities began to show increasing interest in a methodology that statistically calculated the attributed contribution of teachers, buildings, and schools to student gains in achievement, taking into account variables such as prior achievement and other characteristics. This analysis is known as *value-added methodology*. The shortcomings of value-added scores as a measure of teaching effectiveness, coupled with a possible alternative approach to measuring teaching effectiveness, is the focus of this essay.

A recent wave of federal and state policies related to education, a variety of reform initiatives, and current research have incorporated value-added measures. For example, the U.S. Department of Education's Race to the Top funding priorities encouraged states to include teacher level value-added scores. In another example, some states, such as Ohio, include a school level value-added indicator among other indicators of performance in annual reporting. Finally, some states and local school boards include value-added metrics in their teacher performance evaluation and compensation policies.

Members of the educational research and policy communities, including the National Research Council and National Academy of Education, have raised serious concerns that high-stakes decisions are being made based on value-added measures, despite the fundamental concerns about the methodology that have not been fully addressed, let alone resolved. These concerns include, among others, lack of evidence supporting reliability and validity of estimates, a reliance on tests that do not fully represent desired educational goals, and the implications of causal inferences linking attribution of teacher, school, and district effects to student achievement in violation of principles of random selection and assignment of students to teachers and schools.

Other concerns highlight the existence of numerous value-added models and that each model is based on different assumptions aligned with different purposes. It is not clear that those who are using value-added metrics have aligned methods and purpose. For instance, some models involve multivariate statistical methods that take into account socioeconomic status, prior testing results, and student factors such as race, gender, native language, and mobility. Some models include the effect of previous teachers as well. To further confuse consumers and other stakeholders, it is not customary for those using the models to specify the model being used in computing value-added scores. A value-added score for a teacher can have a very different meaning for teachers from different states since states use different methods to determine scores.

In addition, realities in schools and states call into serious question the quality of the data linking students and teachers, thus eroding confidence in resulting estimates. These concerns include the questionable technical quality of existing state data systems; the high mobility of students in certain areas, particularly urban; and the fact that students often have more than one teacher in a year to which effects could be attributed.

Value-added measures at this point in time are not sufficiently developed to support the high-stakes decisions for which they are currently being used. So, to return to the question framing this counterpoint essay, Should value-added methodology be used to identify highly effective teachers? The answer is that it depends.

The question about value-added itself falls short of the more fundamental, but complex, questions that ultimately make a difference for all students in classrooms. It is clear that students in the classrooms of effective teachers have higher quality learning experiences than their peers who are in classrooms of less effective teachers. The more important question is, How do we reach the goal of having high quality learning experiences for all students? The goal cannot be reached by simply identifying effective teachers through value-added methodology.

Identifying teacher quality through measures of student achievement, such as value-added, is a circular argument in which teacher quality and student achievement are equated through the one concept of value-added. In other words, teacher effectiveness is defined by the outcome, and the outcome is the same as the measure of quality. The instructional practices, teacher characteristics, and school contexts that contribute to student learning are forgotten in this definition of teacher quality. The question of teacher quality would be better addressed through a more complex picture of the characteristics and contexts of effective teachers and teaching. The next section reframes the question and shifts the focus from high quality *teacher* to high quality *teaching*.

REFRAMING THE QUESTION

Teachers matter, and variables associated with teacher quality include, but are not limited to, teacher characteristics, such as verbal ability and content knowledge; teacher experiences, such as quality and type of preparation, credentials, and years of experience; and attributes such as dispositions toward students, sense of efficacy and persistence, and an interest in continuing professional development. Much has been written about how teacher characteristics relate to student achievement. Still, most agree these characteristics present a partial picture, at best, of teacher quality.

An alternative approach is to identify characteristics of high quality teaching as well as characteristics associated with high quality teachers. Teacher characteristics are important, but are removed from the direct connection with students and student learning. By identifying the characteristics of high quality teaching, the questions shift to where the learning occurs, in the classroom. Previous research on teaching has associated specific, discrete teaching behaviors, or acts, and the conditions in which students were being taught (processes) to student outcomes (products). More recent literature on teacher quality and preparation incorporated a more holistic view of instruction based on cognitive perspective of teaching and learning. Efforts to characterize effective teaching have yielded several tools designed to assess the quality of teaching based on observation of classroom performance or on artifacts of practice, such as instructional logs.

Therefore, the following questions offer a more robust approach to support high quality learning environments for every student: What characteristics are associated with, or identify, high quality teaching? What conditions best support effective, or high quality, teaching? How can the information about high quality teaching maximize learning for all students?

High quality teaching includes understanding both the characteristics of the teacher and what the teacher does. When the questions are addressed together to create a constellation of variables focused on practice and the context in which practice occurs, it is possible to construct a richer understanding of what contributes to high quality learning experiences for all students.

The following illustrations of this approach are drawn from research on novice teachers in the state of Ohio. The Novice Teacher Study was a longitudinal, statewide research project that examined the characteristics, instructional practices, and school contexts associated with novice teachers. Data for this research included observation of teaching using the Classroom Assessment Scoring System (CLASS), an instrument developed by Robert Pianta and his colleagues at the University of Virginia and designed to assess teacher-student interaction in classrooms. Data also included interviews following the observation of teaching and surveys completed by the novice teachers that included multiple scales pertaining to preparation, efficacy, and school context. Case studies of higher performing and lower performing teachers were constructed based on CLASS scores, and from those case studies, descriptions of the characteristics associated with high quality teaching and the conditions that support high quality teaching were developed.

Characteristics Associated With High Quality Teaching

This section of the essay describes the characteristics associated with high quality teaching. It is important to note here that the framework for analysis in the Novice Teacher Study research did include characteristics of teachers, but the foundation for the case studies was based on observation of teaching using the CLASS observation protocol. Observations of teaching, and more precisely student-teaching interactions, using the CLASS observation protocol yielded a score from 1 to 7 in four domains: emotional support, instructional support, classroom organization, and student engagement. The current version of CLASS has dropped the student engagement domain. Higher performing teachers were identified as those whose mean scores were in the 6 to 7 range, and the lower performing teachers were those whose mean scores were in the 1 to 2 range. Teachers in the 3 to 5 range were considered in the midrange. Interview, survey, and school context data were analyzed to construct case studies that contrasted higher performing from lower performing teachers.

Higher performing teachers were able to articulate instructional goals representing what they intended for their students to accomplish. The goals were indicative of rich content knowledge and were connected to the state academic content standards. Students had a clear understanding of the learning goal and instruction aligned with those goals. During the course of instruction, the higher performing teachers adjusted instruction based on whether students were meeting the instructional goal, and teachers incorporated specific, systematic assessment strategies designed to indicate who needed additional instructional support. Adjusting instruction required teachers to have understandings of where students were experiencing challenges, in addition to being able to call on the content knowledge and pedagogy to address the challenges.

Teachers who displayed a rich content knowledge wove that knowledge into their teaching. This is a clear example of how characteristics of teachers related to characteristics of teaching, and it is difficult to separate teacher characteristics and teaching.

Novice teachers who performed higher on CLASS talked about how their instruction could make a difference for students, and they provided specific examples of how they accomplished that. These teachers also reported a high sense of efficacy on related survey items. This characteristic serves as another example of how the variables associated with high quality teaching interrelate as a constellation of variables related to both the attributes of effective teachers and characteristics of high quality teaching.

The research reveals that novice teachers representing high quality teaching used materials that were intentionally chosen to meet specific instructional goals. These resources were often provided by colleagues or found on the Internet, but the teachers had a specific purpose in mind. Technology was often mentioned, but in many cases unavailable, and teachers were often left to improvise and adapt based on limited resources.

At the same time, the research indicates the existence of a common thread across all of the descriptions that novice teachers provided in the post-observation interviews. The teachers who demonstrated higher quality teaching were able to provide a clearly articulated rationale for choices they made, both in planning instruction and in adjusting based on student need. Intentionality was clear throughout the interviews, and when choices did not result in the optimum outcomes for student learning, the teachers had a plan for what they would do next.

Conditions That Support High Quality Teaching

Teachers matter, but so do the contexts in which they are teaching. This is not to say that challenging contexts excuse poor teaching, but it was clear from the Novice Teacher Study research that teaching occurs in context, and to ignore context ignores the complexity of teaching. The novice teachers taught in districts spanning the demographic and academic achievement categories; however, access to resources and indications of integrated use of resources varied across contexts. For the most part, teachers who demonstrated higher quality teaching either had access to needed resources or adapted instruction accordingly.

The other contextual factor that supported high quality teaching was the opportunity to continue to develop as a teacher, and many of the teachers talked about the support they received from other teachers in the building during their 1st year. Opportunities for professional development focused on specific instructional practices such as integration of technology, and summer workshops related to mathematics instruction were also noted by some of the teachers in our research. The current research on effective teaching underscores the importance of ongoing professional development, particularly when it is closely connected to specific content and instructional practice.

USING INFORMATION ABOUT HIGH QUALITY TEACHING TO SUPPORT STUDENT LEARNING

Should value-added modeling be used to identify highly effective teachers? It depends. Value-added metrics alone should not be used to identify highly effective teachers, particularly for compensation and accountability purposes. Identifying high quality teachers through student test scores defines the quality by the outcome, not by the identifiable characteristics and attributes. Furthermore, the research base on use of value-added metrics is still emerging and, in many aspects, conflicting, and does not support high-stakes purposes such as teacher evaluation and compensation. However, should value-added modeling be used in conjunction with other measures of teaching quality, such as direct observation of teaching performance? The answer to that question is a qualified *yes*.

Value-added metrics can play an important role in our developing understanding of what contributes to student learning. It is one piece of information that can be incorporated into a constellation of variables that provide a robust picture of high performing teachers and high quality teaching. Current research, funded by both public and private sources, is exploring teacher quality by relating outcome measures of effectiveness, such as value-added and performance metrics.

Information about characteristics of teachers and teaching can serve multiple purposes. These include improving teacher and administrator preparation programs, supporting novice teachers in their first years of teaching, and teacher evaluation and development throughout a teacher's career. The current climate has emphasized the use of measures of teacher and teaching quality in evaluation, compensation, and school and district accountability. It would be naive to discount these uses, but it would also be a disservice to students, parents, and communities if we ignored the opportunity to improve teachers and the programs that prepare them.

A singular emphasis on teachers or on teaching cannot begin to account for how teachers make a difference in student learning. It is only through an exploration of a constellation of variables, including what teachers know and do in addition to the context of where they are teaching, that policymakers, school boards, teacher educators, and other stakeholders can reasonably account for variation in student learning. Once we more fully understand what accounts for the variation in student learning, then we can begin to make those changes in the education system that will maximize the learning opportunities for all students, regardless of the schooling contexts they find themselves experiencing.

FURTHER READINGS AND RESOURCES

Battelle for Kids. (2010). *Why are some teachers more effective than others? The challenges and opportunities of defining "great" teaching.* Columbus, OH: Author.

Braun, H., Chudowsky, N., & Keohig, J. (Eds.). (2010). *Getting value out of value-added: Report of a workshop.* Washington, DC: National Academies Press. Retrieved from http://www.nap.edu/catalog/12820.html

Darling-Hammond, L., & Bransford, J. (2005). *Preparing teachers for a changing world: What teachers should learn and be able to do.* San Francisco: Jossey-Bass.

Goe, L., Bell, C., & Little, O. (2008). *Approaches to evaluating teacher effectiveness: A research synthesis.* Washington, DC: National Comprehensive Center for Teacher Quality.

Harris, D. N. (2010). Clear away the smoke and mirrors of value-added. *Phi Delta Kappan, 91*(8), 66–69.

Mahoney, J. (2006, March/April). How value-added assessment helps improve schools (D. R. Walling, Ed.) [Entire issue]. *Phi Delta Kappa EDge, 1*(4).

Pianta, R. C., & Hamre, B. K. (2009). Conceptualization, measurement, and improvement of classroom processes: Standardized observation can leverage capacity. *Educational Researcher, 38*(2), 109–119.

Seidel, T., & Shavelson, R. J. (2007). Teaching effectiveness research in the past decade: The role of theory and research design in disentangling meta-analysis results. *Review of Educational Research, 77*(4), 454–499.

Whitaker, T. (2003). *What great teachers do differently: 14 things that matter most.* Larchmont, NY: Eye on Education.

Do strong unions help or hinder school accountability?

POINT: Dennis M. Reardon, *Ohio State Board of Education*

COUNTERPOINT: Elizabeth Lasley Cameron, *Dayton Early College Academy*

OVERVIEW

As this book was being written, there was spirited debate in Los Angeles and nationally about the use of value-added data to assess overall teacher effectiveness. Of course, another argument is raging on about the very future of unions and collective bargaining. On one side of the argument are the unions and union sympathizers. To union supporters, the use of value-added data as a primary indicator of teacher effectiveness represents not just a threat but an inability on the part of the public to really understand the complex nature of teaching as a craft. On the other side of the issue is a spate of policymakers who view the unions as a barrier to sincere and long overdue efforts to assess teacher effectiveness. The critics of unions assert that value-added data and other efforts to reform schools are consistently blocked by teachers and teacher unions; the unions, so the critics assert, favor the status quo and, as a consequence, protect the jobs of all but a few of the most incompetent teachers. Union officials respond that they willingly embrace change but are frequently not included as part of the change process especially when their members, teachers, are evaluated based on metrics or rubrics that are unfair or totally inappropriate.

In this chapter, readers will see something of the active debate evident about the role of unions in American education. The views are expressed by a former executive director of a state affiliate of the National Education Association and a high school English teacher from a Midwestern urban school—a school that started as a public school and then became a charter school, in part, because of conflicts with the local teachers' union. The essays capture powerfully the complexity of the issues around the role of unions in the United States; they also highlight how much common ground often exists even among those with very different views concerning what is needed to foster quality education for students.

Dennis Michael Reardon (Ohio State Board of Education and former executive director of the Ohio Education Association) describes the false argument associated with attributing to teachers' unions the problems endemic to American education. He notes that if unions are indeed the problem, then the 15 states without statutorily authorized collective bargaining should be evidencing performance gains quite at variance with states that authorize it. In fact, data simply do not support the fact that states without collective bargaining (a strong union presence) outperform those with unionized mandates. While Reardon acknowledges that too often teacher unions have failed to exert the leadership needed to effectively link the improvement of teachers' working conditions to high quality learning conditions for students, he argues that teachers and teacher leaders can and must be part of the solution for creating effective schools; they can neither be marginalized nor excluded. Instead, if teachers are purposefully recruited and prepared for classrooms and involved in reform efforts, then, Reardon suggests, they can and will be a voice for teacher members on everything from fostering critical community interest in education to serving as promoters for high quality public education in the United States.

In the counterpoint essay, Elizabeth Lasley Cameron (high school English teacher, Dayton Early College Academy, Dayton, Ohio) describes the fact that unions are essentially too tied to addressing union member needs, too unconcerned with the public good, and too focused on union member perks. Cameron does not assert that unions are inherently "bad." Rather, she describes the different ways in which the self-interests of unions often prevent them from achieving the vision their members espouse and the goals teachers set for the students that they teach. Cameron also claims that unions frequently cling to practices that foster ineffectiveness such as seniority-based hiring while failing to embrace reforms that can truly change schools for the better; the union perks and focus do more to prevent reform than to foster change.

In reading these two essays, consider the following: Would schools in the United States actually be better and stronger if no unions existed? Why or why not? Also, if unions are going to be a positive force for change, what types of transformation of existing practices need to occur to ensure that in the future they are part of the accountability solution and not a barrier to real educational reform? Finally, there are some who might argue that because of the rapid changes occurring around collective bargaining (e.g., Wisconsin and Ohio) that unions are necessarily reforming themselves to meet the emerging working conditions. Do you see this occurring in your state? If it is not evidenced, why might that be the case? If it is occurring, who is forcing the change, and how are the unions responding?

Thomas J. Lasley, II
University of Dayton

POINT: Dennis M. Reardon
Ohio State Board of Education

As the American economy struggles with the harsh effects of wide-ranging technological, economic, and social change, the capacity of America's public schools to prepare our students adequately to succeed in the 21st century has become the focus of a spirited, national debate. Central to this debate are questions regarding the role that unions representing teachers, support professionals, and, in some school jurisdictions, administrators are playing in reforming America's schools. Thus, against a national backdrop on what may be the future of unions and collective bargaining, the question presented for discussion in this debate examines whether strong unions help or hinder strong accountability in America's schools.

The role and influence of labor unions have historically generated vigorous debate in the United States. Yet during the past 30 to 40 years, unions often have been cited as a principal cause of the failure of various sectors of the U.S. economy, including auto and aircraft manufacturing, mining, and steel production.

As opposed to attempting to understand the complex dynamics affecting the state of America's schools, some opponents of teacher unions have identified them as a major obstacle to improving our nation's schools and charged them with placing the interests of their members above the welfare of students. These critics have accused teacher unions of unreasonably opposing school reform efforts and imposing burdensome administrative rules and procedures on school administrators, thereby, making it nearly impossible to discharge incompetent teachers.

If unions were a principal determinant of a quality education in America's schools, it seems reasonable that the schools located in the 15 states in which collective bargaining is not statutorily authorized would demonstrate higher student achievement and superior high school graduation rates than schools in those states that allow collective bargaining. However, as confirmed by data from the U.S. Department of Education's National Center for Education Statistics (National Center for Education Statistics, 2009), this is not the case.

STRUGGLE FOR POWER AND INFLUENCE

One of the primary points of tension in the debate about the impact of unions, a point that generally is not addressed in such direct terms, involves power, which is the capacity of one or more groups such as administrator organizations, school board associations, teacher unions, and/or business groups, to name a few, to influence and control the direction of education in the United States to achieve their interests. The fact is, if unions were to be outlawed within the education enterprise, the battles over power and influence would continue among the remaining groups.

I do not approach this debate as an unflinching supporter of education unions: Some unions are positive forces in school systems; others are not. During my service from 2001 to 2008 as the executive director of the 130,000 member Ohio Education Association, I had frequent opportunities to learn, again, and again, one of life's ever-present lessons: Members of teacher unions, with their wide range of beliefs, biases, fears, and strengths, react to change that they believe threatens their security in much the same way as do members of school boards and administrator groups, auto workers, and airline mechanics, among others: They resist change that they perceive as hostile.

This essay argues that the only way to achieve meaningful reform in America's PreK–12 education system is to take effective steps to engage in the design and implementation phases of school reform the frontline educators on whom we must rely to create excellent schools. Educational leaders must develop the capacity to create and nurture productive relationships with a wide range of stakeholders, including teachers and their unions, to create systems that prepare every child to succeed as an informed and engaged citizen. Educational leaders must take seriously the importance of engaging, involving, and collaborating with teachers—and their unions. Although relying on positional power or formal authority to impose the desired change undoubtedly would generate more debate and drama that could be exploited for political purposes, it will not markedly improve America's education systems.

In an effort to address objectively whether strong unions help or hinder accountability in America's schools, it is important to define the terms *accountability* and *strong unions* while identifying which aspects of the American education system teacher unions affect in significant ways. The term *accountability* is defined in many different ways. For purposes of this essay, accountability refers to the relationship between responsibility and authority; that is, it refers to the responsibility that accompanies the authority to accomplish certain outcomes that satisfy a set of stated or agreed outcomes and standards including such elements as well-prepared students, high quality, and fairness.

By definition, a strong union must demonstrate attributes of strength. For example, a strong union should be able to recruit and retain a high percentage of voluntary members among the employees it represents; enlist members' support for the union's vision, agenda, and methods of operations; when appropriate, persuade its members to revise their professional practice, in order to meet the shifting needs of students; elect or appoint representatives who not only understand and appreciate the conditions under which their members work but also strive to create conditions that will allow their members to succeed in their professional practice; and build and foster strong working relationships with school administrators for the purpose of making the school system and, in turn, the union's members successful.

Although a number of teacher unions have demonstrated their strength according to such standards, in too many instances, union leaders have failed to anticipate the social, political, and economic dynamics that are driving the need for reforming America's education systems. They have failed to recognize the essential link between teachers' working conditions and the conditions that promote student learning. As a result, these union leaders have sacrificed opportunities to engage administrators in improving the conditions in which their members work—and that could positively affect student learning. Drawing on a heritage of outdated, industrial-period unionism, some teacher unions have tended to focus almost exclusively on pay, benefits, and working conditions that address the employees' workplace needs, such as the length of school days and school years, planning time, sick and vacation leave, and the like.

Unions must now expand their efforts to ensure that their members' working conditions also promote student learning. Unions' failure to respond to these concerns with a more collaborative, problem-focused attitude will result in further loss of moral standing with the public—and in the eyes of many of their members and potential members.

ROLE OF TEACHER UNIONS

Invariably, as this debate ensues, it tends to focus on the two dominant, national teacher unions, the National Education Association (NEA) and the American Federation of Teachers (AFT). The NEA and the AFT are, in simple terms, federations of state level affiliates that, in parallel structures, consist of hundreds of local affiliates that represent the wide array—and frequently conflicting interests—of large urban, small rural, and suburban school districts, communities, and educators. This high level view of teacher unions overlooks a key component of this system: The two national unions are made up of thousands of local affiliates that belong to, but are not controlled by, the national unions.

In stark contrast to the claims of opponents of teacher unions, they are not top-down, centralized organizations commanding ranks of disciplined troops who are committed to achieving a focused, tightly scripted agenda. Teacher unions are made up of members who expect their leaders to practice a form of organizational democracy that, all too frequently, challenges the unions' ability to pursue rapid and dramatic change, setting the stage for a wide variance in the affiliates' subscription to and alignment with the policy direction adopted by the parent union.

It does not appear that opponents of teacher unions have meaningfully examined the structural and cultural forces that govern the operation of the NEA and AFT or the thousands of their state and local affiliates. Neither do the opponents appear to have researched the effects these dynamics have on the ability of the two national unions and their state level affiliates to persuade their local affiliates and members to blindly support, or at least not skeptically resist, school reform efforts such as the federal Race to the Top competitive grants.

So what roles do teacher unions play? Among a range of services, unions provide a voice for their members regarding professional issues; they lobby the executive and legislative bodies of government on behalf of their members' interests; they negotiate labor agreements; they provide administrative and legal representation for members who are dealing with employment-related matters; they offer their members a wide range of professional services, including professional development opportunities; and they serve as one of public education's major defenders and promoters.

In citing teacher unions as a major contributor to the alleged failure of America's education systems, opponents ignore not only the effects that wrenching changes in America's social, economic, and technological structures including poverty, divided families, high rates of mobility, and inadequate social support systems have had on the ability of children to learn, but also they ignore the profound, systemic deficiencies that exist within America's school systems. Widespread examples of these institutional problems include unstable funding systems and the inequitable distribution of resources in our schools; outdated and inadequate policy frameworks; a wide disparity in the ability of school boards to carry out their strategic leadership function; leadership and management capacity that has not kept pace with the increasingly complex demands of reforming and leading challenged school systems; expecting educators to fulfill many of the basic obligations that traditionally have fallen to parents and guardians, thereby setting the stage for educators to be blamed for failing to fulfill an ever-expanding scope of responsibilities; the ill conceived subscription by school leaders to "flavor-of-the-month" instructional programs; and the use of performance assessment systems that fail to provide meaningful and timely feedback to administrators, teachers, and students.

RECONFIGURING INSTITUTIONAL RELATIONSHIPS

As Thomas Friedman noted (2006), the fundamental rules governing relationships between and among individuals, groups, nations, and societies are being reconfigured in ways that are disrupting and challenging long-held assumptions, traditions, and practices around the world. In America's schools, this wrenching change is reflected in a wide array of relatively recent initiatives, including the unparalleled expansion of federal involvement in public education at the state and local levels and the associated tensions such interventions trigger in the context of "local control"; the extensive adoption of academic standards across states; a strong focus on personalizing each student's academic program; the expectation that teachers assume new and more challenging roles as "learning agents"; the unraveling of hierarchical structures, authority, and power within the education sector, including the privatization of education services and the expansion of school options; and a growing demand for STEM (science, technology, engineering, mathematics) programs.

A good part of the resistance that teachers and their unions have expressed about these changes is grounded in the twin beliefs that many of these reform efforts are based on untested concepts and practices and that if the unproven practices and programs are not successful, educators will be blamed. Given the long list of school reform efforts that have been debunked after experience highlighted their deficiencies or that were unilaterally jettisoned by a change in state or school district leadership, it is not surprising that educators will not blindly follow the preferences of individuals who they believe do not understand the scope and depth of their daily challenges. Recent, highly publicized debates regarding the Obama Administration's and various state governments' efforts to reform education reflect such concerns.

In terms of addressing the claim that teacher unions unreasonably burden the PreK–12 education system with unnecessary regulations and obstructionism, let's examine the actual power structure within school systems.

With extremely rare exception, teacher unions do not play a role in hiring, evaluating, and/or firing staff; determining schools' graduation requirements; or designing, negotiating, or adopting state or district education policies, funding formulas, or school budgets. In those school jurisdictions in which teacher unions are authorized to negotiate rules and procedures governing the working conditions of their members, it is important to recognize that there is no setting in which a teacher union can unilaterally impose rules or procedures obstructing school reform efforts or establish unreasonable working conditions, including prohibitions against firing incompetent teachers or those who violate certain standards of conduct. Invariably, teacher union representatives must negotiate those rules and procedures with higher ranking administrators, who have the authority—and, I would argue, the responsibility—to challenge and reject those proposals that threaten the effective operation of a school system.

THE KEY TO EFFECTIVE EDUCATION REFORM

Research conducted by the Center for Teaching Quality confirms that teachers' perceptions of certain working conditions strongly correlate with the ability of schools to meet required gains in student achievement. The effect of these critical working conditions is strongly influenced by the ability of school administrators to engage teachers in creating a school climate engendering trust and mutual respect, understand the dynamics of empowerment while responding positively to teachers' concerns related to their authority to make important education decisions, support teachers who take on teacher-leadership responsibilities, and provide teachers adequate time and opportunity to work with colleagues regarding education issues (Berry, Smylie, & Fuller, 2008). Creating such supportive conditions requires school administrators and teachers to possess the knowledge and skills needed to effectively lead and transform modern organizations. Thus, it seems reasonable to expect governors, legislators, and educational leaders to invest the resources needed to develop that capacity within school systems. In too many cases, that critical link appears to have been overlooked—or intentionally ignored.

Some opponents of teacher unions may never accept the proposition that they could meaningfully and positively contribute to an effective education system. However, unions can and, in many cases, have done so. For example, in 2009, the New Haven Board of Education and the New Haven Federation of Teachers Union (2010) reached agreement on a new approach to teacher professionalism and growth, placing a special emphasis on a joint commitment to turn around low-performing schools. The notable provisions included authorizing principals to select their schools' staffs, redesigning work rules, adjusting the length of the school day and school year, and modifying scheduling and instructional programs. For some years, the Columbus Education Association and the Columbus Board of Education have administered a peer review program that commits the union to maintaining high quality instruction in the classroom (Columbus Education Association and the Columbus Board of Education Master Agreement 2009–2011). In the Intelligence Squared U.S. debate on March 16, 2010, Gary Smuts, superintendent of the ABC Unified School District in Cerritos, California, stated,

> Don't blame my district's union for failing schools. They're one of the reasons my district is successful. Student achievement is the main work

of our teachers' union. In fact, last year the union reps changed their title from "union rep" to "learning rep." And they were told by the union president, your number 1 job is student achievement. (Intelligence Squared U.S., 2010, p. 12)

KnowledgeWorks Foundation, a Cincinnati-based pioneer in facilitating high school redesign efforts in Ohio, recognized the critical role that unions could play in successfully reforming high schools. One of the Foundation's "non-negotiable" provisions in its agreement with participating school districts was a requirement that they enlist the involvement of their teacher unions in those redesign efforts. KnowledgeWorks found that although the unions initially tended to react skeptically to the redesign initiative, their resistance could be addressed by involving them from the outset in the redesign efforts and ensuring that they remained engaged in the discussions throughout the process (KnowledgeWorks Foundation, 2009, p. 13). As Michael Fullan (2010) noted, "there is no way to make whole-system reform work without the entire teaching profession and its leaders" (p. 96).

The demands and expectations placed on America's education systems have significantly changed in the last 20 years. At the national level, and in some cases at the state level, the major organizations representing teachers, administrators, and school boards have reached a shared understanding of some of education's major challenges and have joined together to address them at the policy level. However, these national stakeholders have been less successful in assisting their affiliated groups at the state and local levels, where theoretical solutions confront the complexity of real-world application, to adopt more collaborative attitudes and acquire the skills needed to work together to solve common problems. That is not to say that some state and local unions are not successfully working with administrators and school boards to improve education; there are, as noted above, multiple examples of effective union collaboration and innovation within school districts. But for too long and, regrettably, in too many cases, the education establishment including teacher unions, administrator organizations, and school board associations has allowed teachers, administrators, and school boards at the local level to conduct their relationships according to practices that no longer serve the best interests of public education. While such a circumstance does not apply to every school or school district, it is common enough to represent a pattern undercutting the public's perception of the quality of America's education system.

Successfully reforming an institution requires time, other resources, and a constructive approach. The governance model used in many school systems is no longer adequate. The combative style of collective bargaining that often was practiced between the industrial giants and their employees' unions does not fit the service-oriented environment of emerging 21st-century schools. Success in today's environment requires a higher level of engagement, involvement, and collaboration. The tendency to rely on power and control to produce change must give way to creating collaborative partnerships. As opposed to relying on a "win-lose" perspective, the union leaders, administrators, and school board members must learn to create "win-win" relationships.

Learning to "work with," or collaboratively, with the representatives of the other party, as opposed to imposing the desired change, may require leaders in all segments of the education enterprise to acquire new sets of knowledge, skills, and attitudes. In some cases, union leaders, administrators, and school board members will have to modify their attitudes toward the role and legitimacy of the other parties. Unions must learn to recognize and appreciate the importance of the administrative and management functions that school administrators perform and the governance function that school boards fulfill. Alternatively, administrators and school boards must recognize the essential representative role that unions fulfill. And all of them must adopt a shared vision that places the student at the center of the education enterprise and recognizes that they share responsibility for ensuring that each student becomes a successful and productive citizen. The success of America's education systems requires nothing less.

COUNTERPOINT: Elizabeth Lasley Cameron
Dayton Early College Academy

Unions have made positive and negative contributions to education. Prior to the creation of unions, administrators had all of the power. Even the National Education Association was initially controlled by administrators. In the 1960s, states slowly began adopting laws encouraging teacher collective bargaining. By the 1980s, collective bargaining, at least in some forms, was a staple in districts and states across the country. Unions gave teachers a voice and provided a job security unmatched by most other professions (Moe, 2006). Unions were created to balance the power between administrators and teachers, but in the process of balancing power, unions put a tight grip on the public schools in this country, threatening data-driven, student-centered, and thoughtful decision making at a time when the American education system is struggling to compete globally. The union grip on public schools must be loosened if public schools intend to undergo significant change.

THE CURRENT ROLE OF UNIONS

According to Terry Moe (2006), "the unions now shape the public schools from the bottom up through collective bargaining agreements that affect virtually every aspect of school organization and operation" (p. 229). That union "shaping" has created an imbalance within the school culture. The American education system must strive for balance while continuously prioritizing student needs. A balance of power in this country's schools has yet to be achieved; loosening the union grip in America's schools will provide an opportunity for policymakers and progressive educators to once again drive educational practice toward excellence. Educators at all levels must fight for a balanced power structure in schools as schools undergo reform in a desperate attempt to keep up with our global competition and transition more students to college. Yes, teachers' voices are necessary, their working conditions do affect student learning, and, in this regard, unions are helpful. However, for real change to occur in America's schools, unions' financially draining collective bargaining practices, unconditional support of teachers (unfortunately, of far too many ineffective teachers), and seniority-based hiring and firing practices must come to an end.

As reflected in the current firestorm over collective bargaining, an argument can be made that unions far too often function in their own interest: "The problems of power are inherent to the unions as organizations" (Moe, 2006, p. 230). Unions spend far too much time recruiting members and fighting for resources. This fundamental "self-interested" objective drives decision making in many schools; the students' needs become an inconvenient afterthought. As with any organization, the union fights for anything that improves the status of its objective.

Unions have been known to fight for numerous school policy issues, including higher salaries for teachers, protecting teacher jobs, and even minimizing class sizes. Many critics agree with union efforts to support these issues, but the rub lies in the reality that far too often, the unions are not supporting issues because they agree those issues reflect the best interests of the students; rather, a union supports a given cause because it helps the union meet self-interested objectives. Unions, self-centered by design, also make decisions that hurt schools, such as protecting bad teachers. "The real problem . . . is not union power per se, but employee power operated on behalf of employee interests" (Moe, 2006, p. 233). The fact that the unions are protecting teachers elucidates the misguided nature of the union machine. The teachers' rights should not be taking precedence over the students' needs.

MISGUIDED UNION SUPPORT AND ITS EFFECTS

Such misguided union support is evidenced in the displacement of several effective teachers at Dayton Early College Academy (DECA) in 2007. DECA is among a small number of early college schools in the country employing reformative, innovative, and strictly college preparatory curricula to first generation college students. When DECA was created, it was simply another option within the Dayton Public School District. Interdistrict choice *is* something unions helped to push forward. However, the misguided role seniority plays in the hiring and firing process, and the power that unions have in this process became clear when a 2007 operating levy failed to pass in the Dayton Public Schools. The failure of the levy meant that at least 200 teachers and myriad extracurricular activities would be eliminated. To ensure the seniority of all Dayton Public Schools faculty, senior teachers from all over the public school system were assigned to DECA, displacing 10 DECA teachers. Seniority took precedence over teacher effectiveness.

Part of DECA's spark lies in its teachers' drive to truly reach all students, personally and academically, as well as their interest in the pedagogy necessary to prepare learners for college. DECA uses a unique grading system based on skills acquired rather than letter grades, a series of independent projects and presentations aids in the college transition. The teachers visit their students' homes and build mentoring relationships with assigned advisees. Last, the teachers are provided cell phones so they can be on call for their students, specifically their advisees, after hours. Not just anyone should be thrown at random into DECA's environment—or at random into any school culture.

Teachers are not cogs in a mechanical system. The culture and mission of a school must reflect the teachers' mission and goals to ensure teacher effectiveness in the classroom. As a result, the hiring process at DECA involves deep discussions with teacher candidates regarding their willingness to adapt to the school's curriculum delivery model. Assigning teachers to a school like DECA at random was a decision that many administrators, students, and teachers feared would destroy a school that was obviously successful but in a culture where success is far from normative. Many effective teachers were facing the prospect of handing their classrooms to teachers who had expressed no real understanding of the mission of the school or even the intention to engage in reformative education practices.

DECA solved the problem by becoming a charter school sponsored by the Dayton Public Schools. DECA's decision to become a charter school did not occur without resistance from the union. The union's focus appeared to be on protecting the senior teachers. DECA's mission was clear: to protect the interests of the students. As it became increasingly clear to DECA's small staff and student body that half the staff would soon be replaced by teachers who had no specific interest in the school and its mission, becoming a charter appeared to be the only option. The point is not that the unionized teachers were not effective in the classroom but rather that the union seemed willing to compromise the educational performance of a school by saving jobs for senior level teachers.

Decisions about who should teach must be data driven and based on teacher evaluation and student performance. Basing decisions on teacher effectiveness has been a struggle because teacher evaluations are too limited in scope and infrequent. Usually, the teacher knows in advance that he or she will be observed by an administrator, and anyone can put on a show for a day. Teacher evaluation methods must be analyzed and improved as this country strives for reform and increased effectiveness. Furthermore, effective teacher evaluations would help educators make data-driven decisions about who stays and who must go.

The costs of collective bargaining are hurting the students as well. The former dean of the University of Dayton School of Education and Allied Professions fought for the needs of the students at DECA and witnessed the costly nature of process: "Because of the inability of the teachers' union to embrace the spirit of the Collective Bargaining Agreement and find appropriate alternatives to the seniority provision of the union contract, I would estimate that it has cost DECA at least $1,000 per student per year in operating dollars" (Thomas J. Lasley, Interview, August 1, 2010). Too often, the fight for teachers is taking money from the students.

Paul T. Hill (2006) argued against the costliness of collective bargaining agreements. He defined the role unions play in the problem: "When a union gets money, privileges, and job protection for teachers, it is only doing its job" (p. 90). It is the school boards, Hill continued, that enter agreements that unwisely spend money or "ensure that the neediest students will get inequitably small shares of funds and teaching talent" (p. 90).

Unions are clearly not the problem entirely, but they do create a safe harbor for problems to grow because their decisions are not made with the students' needs first; teachers are naturally playing into a system that is alluring with promises of pay increases and job security.

One of the major contributing factors to driving up costs is the requirement that all tenured teachers be placed prior to the hiring of new teachers (Hill, 2006). This particular requirement does not consider the quality of teachers. When school budgets are in the red, the most expensive teachers usually keep their jobs while the least expensive teachers lose their positions. Tenured teachers' indisputable rights can be costly to preserve. No matter what, districts cannot hire new teachers into the district until all senior teachers have been placed. Much like the incident at DECA, the teachers with seniority oust everyone "below" them and essentially drive costs up without regard for quality. Sometimes, administrators will work around this obstacle by postponing a posting until all the senior teachers in the district are placed; this way, an administrator has the freedom to hire whomever they choose. Urban districts are more vulnerable to hiring limitations than suburban districts, according to Hill, because urban districts' placement processes tend to take longer. By the summer, the teacher candidate "pickings" naturally get a bit slimmer in terms of teacher quality; this reality puts urban districts at yet another disadvantage.

The safety of tenure guaranteed by unions is another compromising force. Some teachers acquire tenure after only 5 or 6 months of teaching, while most teachers are granted tenure after only 3 to 5 years of teaching experience (Hill, 2006). When this reality, ensured by unions, is juxtaposed with the fact that the United States, when compared internationally with European school children, did not even make the top 10 (Thomas, Wingert, Conant, & Register, 2010), it becomes apparent that the current tenure system may not support quality. Despite the problems in the American education system, firings are rare, and many ineffective teachers continue to be responsible for educating young people. Thomas et al. (2010) cogently wrote,

> In New York City in 2008, three out of 30,000 tenured teachers were dismissed for cause. . . . The percentage of teachers dismissed for poor performance in Chicago between 2005 and 2008 was 0.1 percent. In Akron, Ohio, zero percent. In Toledo, 0.01 percent. In Denver, zero percent. In no other socially significant profession are the workers so insulated from accountability. . . . Teachers are treated as if they are unconditionally entitled to their jobs. (p. 24)

The unions perpetuate a misguided system where the teachers are coming first, and seniority carries greater weight than job performance. Illustrative of the fact that too little attention is given to assessing teacher quality is the fact that 99% of all teachers in the United States are rated "satisfactory" by their school systems (Thomas et al., 2010). This positive teacher performance assessment implies that teachers in the United States are effective; yet the United States continues to fall behind globally. Ineffective teacher evaluations combined with union pressure have created an education system where many ineffective teachers are left in the classroom, and this must be considered as a possible contributor to this country's failure to compete globally in education.

Administrators should not be pushed to tolerate teachers who prove ineffective in the classroom. This system places too much power in job protection and less power to informed, data-driven decisions: "Principals must often oversee teaching staffs that they did not hire, cannot fire and that are perfectly free to cooperate or oppose any effort to improve instruction" (Hill, 2006, p. 99). The unions make possible the teacher-centered approach to hiring and firing rather than a student-centered one.

Many educators blame school administrators, not unions, for the consistent retention of "bad" teachers. However, Judy Hennessey (Interview, March 29, 2010), CEO and superintendent of DECA, who has worked in school administration for 30 years, argues that administrators face a challenge when attempting to fire an ineffective teacher. Administrators, she maintains, are usually on their own, and with the unions to face, those seeking to fire ineffective teachers face an arduous and costly process. They must allow teachers time to make progress, and if any progress is shown, the administrator must give the teacher more time. In a sense, this is an understandable and appropriate concept; however, what parent wants his or her child in a classroom with a teacher who was so ineffective that the administrator pursued termination? Why would or should any school patiently wait for a teacher to be effective? Unless the teacher is in his or her 1st year, this practice is not putting students first.

Teacher salary guarantees are another union protection that can prove detrimental to school budgets and teacher quality. Teachers must receive appropriate financial reward for their jobs. Teachers are essential to our society, but their true value is in their effectiveness in the classroom; it is this quintessential aspect of education that our society has failed to nurture and protect. Teachers do not need a guaranteed salary in most schools based on years of teaching experience and postgraduate work (e.g., a master's degree). If anything, it is the guarantee that lowers the quality of education and obliterates the competitive edge from the teaching profession.

Currently, the teaching profession is attracting a disproportionate number of students from the bottom third of high school graduating classes into the teaching profession (Thomas et al., 2010). If, instead, the goal is to attract a greater proportion of students from the top third of high school graduating classes and to improve teacher quality, then mechanisms need to be found to reward teachers more on performance than longevity in their classrooms. Teachers should benefit financially from their respective effectiveness in their classrooms rather than for the number of years in their classroom. In essence, quality-conscious educators are becoming increasingly frustrated with unions because the current system promises money to teachers without regard for effectiveness and/or long-term budget issues.

Teachers' guaranteed pay scales create deficit problems for schools. Hill (2006) illustrated by describing the inflatable salary of a teacher in Chicago over the first 4 years of teaching. Between the annual percentage increases of 2%, which is supported by unions, Hill demonstrated that with the guaranteed steps in the pay scale and the teacher's acquisition of a master's degree, the teacher experienced a pay increase of 38.6%. Although merit-based pay may also create budget challenges, it may have a positive effect on quality, as competition can often bring about greater effort and excellence.

INNOVATION FOR EXCELLENCE

Reforms such as merit-based pay must be explored and encouraged by unions as well as administrators, teachers, and educational policymakers if the United States intends to catch up with its global competitors. With limited exception, unions consistently resist merit-based pay and similar reforms, and although there is no guarantee that changing the way teachers are paid would improve schools, a more competitive playing field for teachers could feasibly improve teacher quality. For many teachers, skills and effectiveness in the classroom stagnate after the first 5 years. A competitive climate for teachers could provide the motivation necessary to improve and reward those who are most effectively maintaining environments conducive to learning.

The American dream is rooted in competition and individualism; yet despite these foundations, we have created an environment for teachers where competition, excellence, and hard work must be intrinsic. Education has the potential to attract the highly educated teacher candidates and encourage appropriate, professional competition. Daniel Weisberg, general counsel of the New Teacher Project and coauthor of *The Widget Effect,* a study of the state of unions and education in this country, emphasizes the importance of competition: "You know, the Marine Corps never has any problem meeting its enlistment goals, because it's an elite corps, and people want to be part of something that is seen as the best" (qtd. in Thomas et al., 2010; see also http://www.newsweek .com/2010/03/05/why-we-must-fire-bad-teachers.print.html).

The competitive edge has been removed from the teaching profession, which stifles motivation and may deter the more ambitious candidates from pursuing a career in teaching.

Dennis Michael Reardon, in his point essay, writes that the members of teacher unions simply react to changes that threaten their security, just like autoworkers and airline mechanics. I want security just as much as the next teacher. Nevertheless, job security should be taken only so far. The profession as a whole must be redefined and highly valued. As a mother, I would rather take my child to a school where teachers take their jobs as seriously as doctors in an emergency room than a school where teachers' main motivations are job security and guaranteed salary increases.

Unfortunately, and as noted, current forms of teacher evaluation are inadequate; to apply merit-based pay models, teacher evaluations would have to be improved considerably. New methods of evaluation are emerging that reward effective teachers and "encourage" ineffective teachers toward other professions. However, innovations like merit-based pay will be impossible without union support.

Merit-based pay is not the only innovative idea hitting the roadblock of union power. Ideas that challenge union power or values generally fail to come to fruition in union schools. It is for that reason that reform schools and non-union charters have become a necessity. Even so, the divide between reform and union can no longer continue. Reform must become a reality if this country intends to compete globally and improve a struggling system, and as schools in this country undergo change, the role and function of unions change to facilitate reform. Union support of seniority-based hiring and firing practices, financially draining collective bargaining processes, and unconditional support of teachers impedes innovation and reform. Reform and innovation must become the union goals if we intend to literally "race to the top," as President Obama's education initiative declares.

Reardon makes a good point when he argues that unions are not the only problem with the current education system in the United States. Unions are not in every school, and unions are not always misguided. However, unions are a part of the problem, so they must be a part of the solution. Both of us agree that specific change must occur in the current system, but we also agree that some unions have yet to approach the very real problems facing education in this country with problem solving that focuses on ways to improve working conditions that promote student learning. If these out-of-date unions pushed progress and a student-centered approach to decision making, the current climate in this country's education system would dramatically shift to prepare for the future. The problem with education is multifaceted. Yet overcoming the hold unions have on the fate of many schools in the United States is a necessary change that will be a catalyst for reform and progress in America's schools.

FURTHER READINGS AND RESOURCES

Berry, B., Smylie, M., & Fuller, E. (2008). *Understanding teacher working conditions: A review and look to the future.* Retrieved from Center for Teaching Quality website: http://www.teachingquality.org/pdfs/TWC2_Nov08.pdf

Columbus Education Association. (2009). *Master agreement between the Columbus Board of Education and the Columbus Education Association 2009–2011.* Retrieved from http://www.ceaohio.org/GD/Templates/Pages/CEA/ceaDefault.aspx?

Friedman, T. (2006). *The world is flat.* New York: Farrar, Straus & Giroux.

Fullan, M. (2010). *All systems go: The change imperative for whole system reform.* Thousand Oaks, CA: Corwin & Ontario Principals' Council.

Hill, P. T. (2006). The costs of collective bargaining among teachers. In J. Hathaway & A. J. Rotheram (Eds.), *Collective bargaining in education* (pp. 89–110). Cambridge, MA: Harvard Education Press.

Intelligence Squared U.S. (2010, March 23). *Debate: Are teacher unions to blame for failing schools?* National Public Radio. Retrieved from http://www.npr.org/templates/story/story.php?storyId=125019386

KnowledgeWorks Foundation. (2009). *Delivering success to Ohio's high schools.* Retrieved August 29, 2011, from https://exemplarpr.com/uploads/KnowledgeWorks_Foundation_Ohio_High_School_Study.pdf

Moe, T. M. (2006). Union power and the education of children. In J. Hathaway & A. J. Rotheram (Eds.), *Collective bargaining in education* (pp. 229–255). Cambridge, MA: Harvard Education Press.

National Center for Education Statistics. (2009). *Dropout and completion rates in the United States: 2007.* Retrieved from http://nces.ed.gov/pubs2009/dropout07

New Haven Federation of Teachers. (2010). *Master agreement between the New Haven Board of Education and the New Haven Federation of Teachers, Local 933, AFT, AFL-CIO.* Retrieved from http://ct.aft.org/nhft/index.cfm?

Thomas, E., Wingert, P., Conant, E., & Register, S. (2010, March 15). Why we can't get rid of failing teachers. *Newsweek, 155*(11), 24–27.

10

Should the Carnegie Unit be eliminated?

POINT: James L. Olive, *Ashland University*
COUNTERPOINT: Tracey R. Smith, *University of Dayton*

OVERVIEW

During the past century, school reform has been a focus of policy efforts by a wide variety of governmental agencies as well as nonprofit organizations. Since the late 1800s, those concerned with the quality of life in the United States have recognized the relationship between education and economic vitality. It is well documented that those without a high school education are more likely to live in poverty (nearly 25% do so). At the same time, those with a college education earn much more and have the intellectual capital to explore career options in ways that are virtually impossible for those with less education.

In the early 20th century, the United States was emerging as a global economic power. Critical to the development of the United States was the creation of an education system that would more fully maximize the intellectual potential of all its young people. Those in positions of power realized that without a better way of monitoring and documenting the progress of a student's academic work, it would be impossible to create a truly educated populace.

The National Education Association's Committee of Ten proffered a solution to the "academic tracking" conundrum. Among the committee's recommendations were such suggestions as providing fewer course electives, most notably offering courses that would last a year and meet every day (or at least 4–5 times weekly); then, as a result, matriculating students would be awarded Carnegie Unit credits. Since that time, groups concerned with the structure and content of the high school curriculum have proffered many other reforms at the secondary school level. For example, the *Cardinal Principles of Secondary Education* report identified a specific set of goals for high schools, such as command of academic skills and the appropriate use of leisure time. The one constant over the past century, through all the curricular changes and structural modifications, has been the Carnegie Unit.

In this chapter, James L. Olive, of Ashland University, and Tracey R. Smith, of the University of Dayton and a Greene County administrator and former state school board member in Ohio, critically examine the Carnegie Unit issue. Both essays track the historical roots of the Carnegie Unit even as they also come to different conclusions about the efficacy of the "unit."

Smith makes the case for the Carnegie Unit. For Smith, the unit is not a perfect measure, but it is a necessary one, especially at a time when the United States is rapidly moving toward adoption of common academic standards. Smith points out that the Carnegie Unit was created to standardize the exposure time of students to content; such standardization was essential given the mobility of the student population and the need of colleges and universities to know what students applying for admission to college had actually experienced in high school. True, for Smith, the Carnegie Unit can be and often is imperfect; equally true, it represents a "standard" that is essential for a student population that is increasingly mobile.

Olive takes a different view. Olive contends that the unit's utility is no longer warranted and that more functional and appropriate alternatives now exist. According to Olive, the 21st century enables educational content to be delivered in ways that were unheard of 100 years ago when the Carnegie Unit was conceived. With all the innovative delivery systems, Olive maintains that it no longer makes sense to use *seat time* as the essential marker of and for student academic progress. In this regard, he recognizes that students often come to school with rich academic experiences; it is now possible to assess what students know so that they are not needlessly learning (or relearning) information that they already possess. Olive thus proposes the "retirement" of the Carnegie Unit and proffers an example of a viable and perhaps necessary alternative: *flexible credit.*

In reading the essays in this chapter, consider the following questions: First, does the Carnegie Unit assume that each student has experienced a rigorous academic curriculum? Second, should flexible credit be permitted to be acquired through independent study or travel and be used in place of the Carnegie Unit? And, third, if used, what problems do you perceive emerging with such alternatives?

Thomas J. Lasley, II
University of Dayton

POINT: James L. Olive
Ashland University

What is the best way of measuring knowledge? How can educators know when students have obtained enough knowledge so that they may move to the next level or grade? Are the scores that students attain on specified tests accurate assessments of what they know? This approach proves problematic when one considers the diversity of our population, the differences in curricula taught across the nation, the subjective value that is placed on certain types of knowledge, as well as the decision to test in some areas but not others. For instance, are mathematics and science truly more important than music and art? One would presume this is the case given that mathematics and language arts are tested areas in most states whereas music, art, and physical education are untested.

The challenge of equally assessing all students' knowledge and readiness for higher education was a dilemma that many colleges and universities faced during the late 1800s as an increasing number of students, originating from a wide variety of schools, applied for admission to college. Higher education institutions clamored for a standardized method of ensuring the quality of a high school education. In response to this demand, the Carnegie Unit was born and adopted in the early 1900s.

Unfortunately, after nearly a century of use, many within education argue that the Carnegie Unit has proven itself to be more of an obstacle to educational creativity and flexibility than as an effective tool with which to "mark" students' academic progress. In fact, in 1993, Ernest Boyer, the then-president of the Carnegie Foundation, the organization from which the unit bears its name, "officially declared the Carnegie unit obsolete" (DiMartino & Clarke, 2008, p. 147). In agreeing with Boyer and other critics who question the relevancy of the Carnegie Unit, I propose that it is time for the Carnegie Unit to be eliminated and replaced by a better alternative that more effectively meets the needs of today's young people.

OVERVIEW OF THE CARNEGIE UNIT

To form a justifiable opinion on the Carnegie Unit, one should be familiar with its history and its definition. As mentioned above, the unit's name originates from the Carnegie Foundation for the Advancement of Teaching, which was founded by Andrew Carnegie in 1905. Since its inception, the Carnegie

Foundation has served as an independent policy and research center on American education.

The Carnegie Unit was developed in 1906 as a means of measuring the amount of time students studied subjects in high school. The unit's creation stemmed from two events, or circumstances, that occurred during the late 1800s. First, many of the comprehensive examinations that were used by colleges and universities to make admissions decisions were found to be highly subjective in their scope and interpretation as well as unreliable in their use. Consequently, in many cases, the standards of one institution were not comparable to those of another institution. The second impetus for the unit occurred when a standardized unit of education was envisioned by a Harvard University academic named Charles W. Eliot, who perceived a need for standards in secondary education. Eliot's proposed unit of education was subsequently endorsed by the National Education Association in 1894.

Introduced in 1906, use of the Carnegie Unit did not gain momentum until the Carnegie Foundation stated in its 1907 annual report that institutions must use it (the Carnegie Unit) as an admissions requirement if they wanted to participate in a new faculty pension fund that was being established. Thus, by 1931, more than three quarters of the nation's schools and colleges had begun using the unit. The Carnegie Unit has since become a key component in class scheduling, staffing decisions, grading, course sequence, and higher education admission procedures.

The Carnegie Foundation's website provides the following definition for the calculation of the unit:

> The unit was developed in 1906 as a measure of the amount of time a student has studied a subject. For example, a total of 120 hours in one subject—meeting 4 or 5 times a week for 40 to 60 minutes, for 36 to 40 weeks each year—earns the student one "unit" of high school credit. Fourteen units were deemed to constitute the minimum amount of preparation that could be interpreted as "four years of academic or high school preparation." (n.d., "FAQS: Questions about publications")

WHY THE CARNEGIE UNIT SHOULD BE ELIMINATED

Many within the educational community criticize the Carnegie Unit. The crux of these arguments is that the unit is based on an arbitrary length of time that is supposed to measure how much students have learned. In other words, this measures the seat time of students in classrooms. This seems highly unfair when one considers that all students learn differently and at their own pace. In addition, this is not to mention that each subject, teacher, department, school, and institution are also unique and can also play a critical role in the educational process of students.

The Carnegie Unit has become a cornerstone in the organization of the educational curricula in high schools. Unfortunately, its inflexible nature acts as a deterrent toward interdisciplinary teaching since educators are left with the daunting task of assigning specified numbers of units to each separate discipline. A consequence of this approach is that a level of subjectivity is infused into the curricular planning process, which may result in an unequal balance of units based on a perceived value of one subject over another.

Since the early 1900s, our system and process of education in the United States has evolved as we have learned more about the different ways in which people learn, such as by sight (visual), by sound (auditory), and through motion and physical contact (kinesthetic). The changing demographics of the U.S. student population have also had a profound impact on today's classrooms. Many instructors now organize and structure their curricula and the way they teach them based on the composition of classes. Faculty who have used innovative and interdisciplinary approaches have found the Carnegie Unit to be a frustrating obstacle to the learning process since it restricts not only their time with students to a predefined, arbitrary segment of each day, but also it significantly impacts the amount of instructional time each subject is given.

Quite simply, the amount of time students sit in classes is an inadequate measurement of how much they have learned. It is time for schools, administrators, and schedules to become more flexible about how student learning progress is measured so that all pupils are actively engaged in the learning process and effectively assessed.

Other, more recent, developments in education also pose a challenge to the Carnegie Unit while providing further justification for its elimination. The first of these developments has been the increase in out-of-classroom excursions, such as field trips. Among the many benefits that they provide, field trips offer valuable experiences that would otherwise not be possible in classrooms. Field trips can also provide alternate paths that teachers may choose in their approaches toward topics.

At the same time, field trips provide students the chance to learn hands-on in new environments. For kinesthetic learners who learn better through motion and touch, field trips can provide terrific opportunities for actively participating in events and activities while they learn. Moreover, field trips function as *equalizers* among the different ways students learn. Whether students are auditory, visual, or kinesthetic learners, all become part of the overall experience so that they are free to learn topics in their preferred manners.

Field trips sound like a useful instructional tool. However, field trips often-times do not fit easily within the structured Carnegie Unit model of education. In many cases, since the time spent engaging in such activities does not equally relate to typical class periods, assigning "credit" can be a challenge. Additionally, issues can arise when teachers attempt to grade or assess out-of-class projects or activities.

A second educational development over the last few decades that does not mesh well with the Carnegie Unit involves *performance* or *portfolio-based assignments*. Performance-based assignments use student activities instead of tests or quizzes as the basis for assessing skills and knowledge. Measuring through performance facilitates the learning process since students and teachers are able to build collaboratively on daily assignments and projects as well as on examination materials.

While traditional assessment techniques, such as tests or quizzes, are based on the belief in there being one correct answer or way of doing something, performance-based assessments use more realistic methods of grading. When students' aptitudes are measured in a holistic way, they are given opportunities to capitalize on their unique strengths. Further, it should be noted that life itself does not consist of purely objective knowledge or facts that can be judged or learned along the lines of true and false, black and white, or right and wrong; this is a crucial notion about the nature of knowledge that students should learn early in life.

If educators were to ignore the benefits gained through a more realistic form of assessment, one could still point to the large body of research that suggests performance and portfolio-based projects help students in a number of other ways. When students work on performances or portfolios, they are often-times more engaged in the active learning process both in and out of class-rooms. Additionally, students are provided with more opportunities to infuse their own creativity into projects such that the motivation to complete assignments is usually higher since students are typically more interested in the topics. When structured appropriately, performance and portfolio-based assignments also enable teachers to gain a more in-depth understanding of students' knowledge bases and skills.

Sadly, the Carnegie Unit does not support such divergence in standard instructional practices. As with field trips, performance and portfolio-based assignments prove problematic when the time comes for grading since they may not conform to standard slots of time or predesigned "packages" of curricula.

Distance learning and other forms of independent study also run counter to the notion of standardized measurements for student learning because individuals are able to take as much or as little time as they need to learn material;

distance learning is not at all connected to seat time requirements. The benefits of this learning strategy are somewhat obvious: Students are able to learn on their own time schedule, course content can be completed virtually anytime and anywhere, and the student is responsible for meeting deadlines, which encourages responsible planning skills. Where distance learning and independent study run into problems regarding the Carnegie Unit is that in many cases, it is nearly impossible to validly quantify the amount of time a student spends in his or her "seat." Moreover, in such an independently structured situation, proving beyond a shadow of a doubt that the student has completed his or her own work is just not feasible.

ALTERNATIVES TO THE CARNEGIE UNIT

There have been proposed modifications to the Carnegie Unit since its inception. One suggestion has been to create a series of *equivalency tests* to measure students' competences in specific subjects or areas. Regardless of the amount of time students spent in class, passing equivalency tests would award them credit for the subject. This method of granting credit has been in use by higher education for some time. However, this approach does pose a challenge since a nationally standardized curriculum does not exist. Interestingly, with the emergence of common academic standards across most of the states, this option may become more viable in the future.

Another proposed modification to the Carnegie Unit has been to "break" the unit into smaller pieces, which can then be allotted with more flexibility. Choosing this route, though, introduces a level of subjectivity that many Carnegie Unit supporters argue against. For instance, how one school board chooses to divide its Carnegie Units might in no way match the methodology selected by educators in another district.

Fortunately, many states have recognized that the benefits of innovative instructional strategies such as the ones that were described above far outweigh any potential drawbacks associated with the elimination of the Carnegie Unit. In 2005, the New Hampshire State Board of Education became the first governmental organization to abolish the unit officially. In its place, school boards in New Hampshire were directed to create and implement competency-based systems of assessment.

Today, nearly half of the nation's states permit movement toward some type of an alternative to the Carnegie Unit. Many of these alternatives come in some form of what is commonly referred to as *flexible credit*. With flexible credit, students are able to earn credits through a number of nontraditional means such as testing out of subjects, proving the mastery of subjects in some other way, such as performance or portfolio-based assessments, and through alternate forms of education, such as distance learning, independent study, or internships.

Ohio's flexible credit program, for example, implemented during its 2010–2011 school year, is widely perceived to be one of the most broad and comprehensive. Under what Ohio calls its "credit flexibility" plan,

- local boards of education were required to adopt a credit flexibility policy by the start of the 2010–2011 school year and are mandated to communicate their plans to parents and students on an annual basis;

- any and all subjects can be considered for credit under a school board's credit flexibility plan;

- school boards are not permitted to limit the number of courses or credits taken via flexible credit approaches;

- any students within districts are eligible to be considered for flexible credit;

- any students are able to test out of the second semester of courses after they have "sat" for the first semesters of the same courses;

- the "educational options" that students may use to obtain flexible credit include distance learning, internships, educational travel, after school/tutorial program, independent study, community service or engagement project, and extracurricular activities;

- schools *must* accept credits earned via credit flexibility for students transferring from any school in Ohio that meets the state's minimum operating standards. However, schools are not obligated but *can* accept credits from other educational providers, including online providers.

CONCLUSION

History has shown that fundamental change usually takes a long time and perhaps this is even truer for America's system of education. The steps that New Hampshire and Ohio have taken make it clear that the time has come for the official retirement of the Carnegie Unit. Regardless of whether flexible credit proves to be an effective solution to the problem of learning assessment, few would argue against the benefits of a truly personalized education for each student.

COUNTERPOINT: Tracey R. Smith
University of Dayton

The Carnegie Unit continues to be relevant into today's educational setting, as it consistently measures what it was intended to measure. However, it has also been misused by educators, administrators, and college admissions counselors, leading some to believe that it is no longer applicable. This essay posits that the Carnegie Unit should not be eliminated but rather that its purpose and use should be redefined.

ORIGINAL INTENT OF THE CARNEGIE UNIT

The Carnegie Unit was created in response to the 1893 Committee of Ten on Secondary School Studies recommendations to the National Education Association, which emphasized specific school models of preparation for success in college, including a more standardized curriculum. The chair of the Committee of Ten was Harvard University President Charles W. Eliot.

In 1909, Andrew Carnegie's Foundation for the Advancement of Teaching offered colleges money intended for use in enticing professors to retire; in essence, the intention was to provide financial incentives to buy out aging professors. Carnegie's ultimate goal was to create openings for young faculty members to fill thereby bringing new, fresh ideas and approaches to higher education. Insofar as the money was to flow directly from the Carnegie Foundation to the colleges and universities, Carnegie and his board of trustees, which happened to include Charles W. Eliot, had the opportunity to influence the college presidents.

The Carnegie Foundation began with creating a set of standards to be used at colleges in order for the institutions to qualify for pension disbursements; one of those standards spoke in particular to a growing frustration with the college admissions process in the United States. More specifically, there was concern that colleges and universities were not uniform in selecting who to accept or what high school coursework they were expecting the entering 1st-year students to possess. As a result, for any institution to be considered for funds by the Carnegie Foundation, enrollment offices could only accept students exiting high schools with the successful completion of 14 units of coursework. Each of the fourteen units was to represent 120 instructional hours.

The Carnegie Foundation also identified the types of subjects that were acceptable as "units." Colleges and universities that were in competition for

Carnegie money exerted pressure on high schools to adopt this new system of measuring course completion when developing teaching schedules and construction course curriculum. As a result, the unit very quickly was widely referred to by those in education as the Carnegie Unit.

By 1909, and after its approval by the College Entrance Examination Board, the Carnegie Unit was in place in practically every high school in the nation. To many, the system of American education now had a "solidly constructed ladder upon which the aspiring could rise" (Perkinson, 1991, p. 133). Thus, began an era of school leaders, teachers, parents, and students thinking about accountability in education.

Before the Carnegie Unit, state universities were overseeing the academic standards at high schools to ensure that teachers were properly preparing students for university level work. It quickly became impossible for postsecondary institutions to engage in this practice as the number of public high schools dramatically increased after the turn of the 20th century. As a result of the development of the Carnegie Unit and, for the first time, all schools were unified in how they measured educational attainment, especially important as the population of the United States became more transient and mobile during the industrial revolution and as more and more children moved between school districts, attempting to take credits with them to new school assignments.

ADVANTAGES OF THE CARNEGIE UNIT

The adoption and use of the Carnegie Unit eliminated a great deal of confusion in education in the early 1900s. The unit is still a necessary "structure" today, especially in an era of an increasing number of high school students seeking admission to college. The Carnegie Unit standardizes the amount of time, so colleges can be assured a student has been exposed to a certain subject. College and university officials know that students with credit in algebra I have had the same amount of time in the course as those in different districts. The second strength of the unit relates to competition for entrance into colleges or universities. The Carnegie Unit carries the same "time" definition for all secondary schools thereby leveling the field for aspiring first-year college or university students, allowing admissions departments in these institutions to make comparisons with confidence that the transcripts sent have the same credit baseline.

Each state legislature or board of education has prescribed an agreed on quantity of material to be delivered over 4 years for completion of a high school diploma, and the Carnegie Unit provides a way to break the material down into manageable and transferable units. The unit helps clarify students' programs while providing a coherent track for acquiring diplomas. At the same time, the Carnegie Unit does not, nor should not, stand alone. Rather, the Carnegie Unit should be combined with other information such as a school's curriculum, catalog description, prerequisites, grade, and grade point average (Fryshman, 2010).

Assuming that educators can reach a consensus about the content, rigor, and intellectual challenge of curricula, a course of study emerges that is sufficiently descriptive so that all involved with education can understand what has been achieved. Therefore, allocation of Carnegie Units for each course becomes more meaningful and lends itself to useful and easy interactions between instructors, departments, and schools because the structured details have been agreed upon before the course reaches a course composite and enrollment commences.

Schools need to return to making rigor and intellectual challenge a focal point when devising or revisiting courses as a way to determine the number of credit hours to be assigned to those courses; there should thus be a direct correlation between the number of Carnegie Units and curricular rigor. In other words, one important aspect of the Carnegie Unit at its inception was using it as a way of not only addressing seat time in class but also as a means of measuring the intensity and rigor of the work that occurred in a class. If common norms are accepted, then the validity of the Carnegie Unit will be preserved. In fact, primary and secondary schools have accrediting bodies, such as North Central Association of Colleges and Schools and Middle States Association of Colleges and Schools, among others, auditing their course offerings to ensure that curricular units are what they say they are.

RENEWING THE RELEVANCE OF THE CARNEGIE UNIT

The Carnegie Unit once sought to indicate student learning and mastery of subjects to colleges and universities, with some educators hopeful that use of a standardized unit would eliminate the need for entrance examinations. Certainly, in that light, the Carnegie Unit is not relevant. Most would agree that measuring time in class does not equate to mastery. Yet this was not the intention of the Carnegie Foundation. The Carnegie Foundation explicitly argued against placing limits on the curricular freedom of secondary schools or colleges and universities, instead professing only to develop academic "counters" for institutional use (National Association of Secondary School Principals [NASSP], 1964). The Carnegie Unit has long been criticized for not being a strong measure of success. Specifically, critics suggest that measuring seat time does not measure student mastery of a subject. While that might have been true for years, the pendulum of education is swinging and bringing more importance to the use of the unit. If the argument that seat time does not equal academic success was once valid, then the argument will likely lose validity in light of the emergence of the national Common Core standards and assessments. In fact, a national set of "common standards" is emerging that appear to be exactly what the president of the College Entrance Examination Board had in mind before passing the recommendations of the Carnegie Unit. In its *Third Annual Report* (National Association of Secondary School Principals [NASSP], 1907–08), the NASSP's justification for the recommendations was given:

> The time has now come when the efforts which have been made independently in various parts of the country may be crystallized into one standard which shall be national in scope. We have passed through an experimental epoch out of which we should seek principles and conclusions which shall be practical and national. (p. 12)

Common Core standards in mathematics and English language arts that were released for adoption in 2010, with common assessments soon to follow, may be an opportunity for the Carnegie Unit to renew its relevance. For states choosing to adopt the emerging standards, it will be assumed that basic levels of common education will be imparted to students with a benchmark for success and mastery clearly indicated. In this light, the Carnegie Units will once again, or maybe even for the first time ever, very clearly indicate that for each credit earned a common set of curricular concepts were disseminated to learners. State curricular leaders from most states have engaged in serious deliberation, debate, discussion, and vetting of the emerging standards to stakeholders as well as international benchmarking when writing the common standards. Arguably this exercise has increased the seriousness in curricular discussion and faith that educators have to guide the teaching of what is valuable, timely, and relevant to educating youth to be productive members of society.

Framers of the national curriculum are encouraging the dissemination of curricula in a way that is clear, concise, and deep. In this regard, the Carnegie Unit of instruction will be a perfect partner to *clearly* and *concisely* show that students have engaged in this intelligently structured education process. The process of adopting standards, model curricula, and end-of-course assessments will require continued dialogue between educators, stakeholders, and subject experts about rigor. A reliable and valid assessment can be a perfect "partner" to the Carnegie Unit, thereby showing a connection to seat time and skills or knowledge.

Critics of the Carnegie Unit would like to argue that assessments themselves are tied to traditional short answer, multiple choice, true/false, and similar items. These critics may believe that the Carnegie Unit is not applicable to performance-based or formative assessments, such as portfolios, arguing that the curricular rigidity of the Carnegie Unit and flexibility cannot be partners. This assertion is without merit. Classroom organization, assessments, and grading can be extraordinary and innovative within a Carnegie Unit system. Educators create and score the assessments and clearly set standards within all measurements related to what is proficient and accelerated while tying these to whether students have successfully earned Carnegie Units.

Trouble with a Carnegie Unit occurs only when one does not understand its limitations. A Carnegie Unit is a *medium of exchange*, a common language, a *lingua franca*. It is for this reason that during a state's deliberation and adoption of credit flexibility plans, or other similar programs, that Carnegie Units continue to be embraced. No state has argued that the Carnegie Unit is antiquated to the point that it needs to be eliminated. In fact, instead of being an impediment to flexibility, the Carnegie Unit can be a brick and mortar template through which to create credit flexibility options.

Learning can occur outside of the traditional classroom, and if students "in the field" are held to the same standards and rigor as those in class, then as proven by mastery of a common assessment, assignment of Carnegie Units should occur in ways that enhance accountability efforts. The traditional assigning of the Carnegie Unit, because it was done with thoughtful, professional deliberation, and the creation of course objectives can be achieved in the case of nontraditional study as long as the requirements set forth are met.

Therefore, perhaps the consideration in defense of the Carnegie Unit should be to revise or redefine its purpose and use it in such a way that clearly acknowledges its use for today's society. For example, a student earning a D will get credit for a course. The Carnegie Unit credit shows attainment, while the grade shows *level* of that attainment. In this way, while an argument can be made that grade inflation has occurred in schools, there is rarely a proper argument for credit hour inflation. Perhaps the argument should not then be about the Carnegie Unit but about creating a unified grading system or a rubric for performance review.

The United States is moving toward common assessments as a next step to the adoption of Common Core State Standards. Two options of common, national assessments are being debated. Each of these assessment approaches includes quarterly testing, performance-based tasks to be measured by educators, listening and speaking components, and formative projects. Both models are rigorous in that they include varied methods of assessing and scoring with the intention of capturing all types of learning as well as auditing learners for deep understandings of material. Both are able to assign Carnegie Units as a measurement for successful completion of course material. Clear, concise, and commonly agreed on standards will lend themselves to common assessments for students in most states, which in turn will mean a common rubric or scores indicating levels of mastery. In this light, perhaps more trust will be placed in credit attainment and the meaning behind a Carnegie Unit.

CONCLUSION

In essence, the Carnegie Unit itself is not at issue or flawed. It has consistently measured what it was intended to assess: the time allocated to ensure defined course content is taught. The problem relates to "user error." Specifically, the difficulty arises in the way school officials have focused on seat time rather than on defined academic outcomes; this has weakened the original intent and message associated with the Carnegie Unit. Each time educators, administrators, or college admissions counselors accept units and interpret them as mastery of subjects, sight unseen, the units are misused. Instead, course grades, teacher comments, and college entrance examinations should all be used in tandem to attain accurate assessments of student achievement for given subjects. Ultimately, candid discussions must be conducted at the national level about the Carnegie Unit with a clear decision made regarding what rubrics or metrics will be paired with it, nationwide, to ensure ease of credit transfer. This exercise should occur because, in reality, unless educators and legislators can agree on a more meaningful representation of knowledge gained from secondary level courses, the Carnegie Unit will continue to be used and, unfortunately, compromised in terms of its value.

FURTHER READINGS AND RESOURCES

Carnegie Foundation for the Advancement of Teaching. (n.d.). *FAQs: Questions about publications and previous work.* Available from http://www.carnegiefoundation.org

DiMartino, J., & Clarke, J. H. (2008). *Personalizing the high school experience for each student.* Alexandria, VA: Association for Supervision and Curriculum Development.

Fryshman, B. (2010, January 22). The Carnegie Unit: Articulate and expressive. *Inside Higher Ed.* Retrieved from http://www.insidehighered.com/views/2010/01/22/fryshman

Graham, D. A. (2010, August 11). States experiment with out-of-classroom learning. *Newsweek.* Retrieved from http://www.newsweek.com/2010/08/11/states-experiment-with-out-of-classroom-learning.html

National Association of Secondary School Principals (NASSP). (1964). The history of the Carnegie Unit. *NASSP Bulletin, 48,* 5–25.

Ohio Department of Education. (2010). *Credit flexibility guidance documents.* Retrieved from http://www.education.ohio.gov/GD/Templates/Pages/ODE/ODEDetail.aspx? page=3&TopicRelationID=1864&ContentID=82751&Content=90088

Perkinson, H. J. (1991). *The imperfect panacea: American faith in education, 1865–1990.* (3rd ed.). New York: McGraw-Hill.

Is school funding sufficient and adequate for helping schools meet the emerging accountability demands?

POINT: C. Daniel Raisch, *University of Dayton*

COUNTERPOINT: William L. Phillis, *Ohio Coalition for Equity and Adequacy of School Funding*

OVERVIEW

Throughout the 20th century, debates raged about the adequacy of funding for American public schools. No state could be excluded in terms of individuals or groups perceiving either that schools had too few resources or that they were inefficiently and ineffectively using the resources that were available. In addition, no rush to a common solution occurred with regard to school funding despite the fact that there was a significant amount of litigation on this contentious issue. As a result, school funding palliatives emerged that varied from state to state. However, during the early part of the 20th century, *minimum foundation programs* surfaced, which proffered a minimum level of financial support per child using state and local resources. More than 20 states currently rely on some form of state foundation formula for calculating how much support to provide city and local school districts.

One aspect of the debate relates to equity: Are sufficient resources available to provide a proper and effective education for all children in public schools? Not surprisingly, as noted, there has been significant litigation about whether equitable funding per child was available and whether the real inequities that were evidenced constituted a violation of state level constitutional provisions. Perhaps the most prominent dispute was *San Antonio Independent School District v. Rodriguez* (1973), the only school finance case to reach the U.S. Supreme Court. In this case, Demetrio Rodriguez, a poor sheet metal worker, questioned the adequacy of his children's education as compared to that of young people living a short distance away in an affluent community. Rodriguez's children went to a school that lacked necessities such as books while students in a neighboring district were blessed with apparent literacy abundance. The Court, interestingly, asserted that since education was not a constitutionally protected right, Rodriguez's children did not have a federal Constitutional right to protect them against their continuing to be educated in substandard conditions. In other words, the Court held that since education was a responsibility of states, plaintiffs had to seek remedies under their state constitutions.

State courts subsequently ruled that school finance structures that permit wide per-pupil funding discrepancies are not "thorough and efficient" (in some states described as a "uniform system of education") and have set aside the impact of *Rodriguez,* but have still not fully "corrected" the equity issue. Among the more notable state cases at the leading edge of the deluge on school finance, often leading to multiple rounds of litigation, were *Serrano v. Priest* (1971, 1976, 1977) from California and *Robinson v. Cahill* (1973a, 1973b) from New Jersey, both of which addressed school financing under state constitutions. With all the legal machinations, the question persists: Are sufficient funds provided to educate each child in a thorough and efficient manner?

In this chapter, C. Daniel Raisch (University of Dayton) and William L. Phillis (Ohio Coalition for Equity and Adequacy of School Funding) debate the school funding issue. Raisch does not question whether equitable school funding models are needed within the approximately 14,000 school districts across the United States. He does question whether funds are being spent effectively and efficiently. Are some schools overstaffed? Raisch points out that over the past 40 years, public school employment has grown 10 times faster than student enrollment, yet academic performance by students in reading, for example, has remained unchanged. He examines different aspects of school operations such as transportation, concluding that the issue may not be the sufficiency of available dollars but rather how the available dollars are spent.

Phillis takes an opposing view. He argues that the diverse needs of students coming to school necessitate a sufficient and adequate funding model. Part of the problem relates to the heavy reliance on property tax, which engenders inequities in per-pupil funding across school districts. These funding variations clearly suggest the inherent flaws associated with the current financial models used by states to ensure thorough and efficient educational programming. Phillis uses one state, Ohio, as an illustration, but clearly the problem is not unique to that state. The litigation on school funding across the United States suggests the universality of the school funding issue.

In reading this chapter, consider these two questions: First, what other approaches to funding schools do you think would create a thorough and efficient approach? Second, is there "financial waste" in education that you think appears clear based on the educational experiences you have had in schools?

Thomas J. Lasley, II
University of Dayton

POINT: C. Daniel Raisch
University of Dayton

Some would argue that funding cuts brought on by the recent economic recession will mitigate the ability of schools to be held accountable for results. I assert that the cuts, though regrettable, do not and should not hinder schools from performing effectively. For far too long, educators have made excuses for the poor performance of their students. It is time to drop that mind-set. Schools need to perform regardless of what resources are available; they need to (and teachers must!) be held accountable for results.

In 2007, a financial blizzard hit school systems, slashing state and federal support while local tax collections began to plummet; schools must therefore gear up for years of static if not sinking revenue. A recent study conducted by the National Council of State Legislators found that schools should anticipate nearly a $145 billion shortfall from the $600 billion normally collected to support schools in coming years. How can schools weather the storm? Should they prepare for future losses? There is clear indication that the housing and commercial real estate markets have yet to hit bottom. Assuming that this analysis is economically correct, public schools are in for lean years. With taxpayers saying "no more taxes," schools and other public organizations must implement reductions, which probably means reducing employees, seeking alternative means of delivering instruction or other services, and generally running their operations more efficiently.

As examples of the most recent financial concerns for schools, the governors in the states of Ohio and Wisconsin are dramatically changing the landscape regarding funding for schools in their states. Legislation has been passed and will soon be implemented that will alter the control and funding of education in each state. While many may not agree that cutting funds for education is the way to solve a funding crisis in most states, it clearly is one of the avenues that must be explored. Generally, in a crisis, creative and good ideas emerge, and what we are seeing now is but one example of problem solving for supporting public education.

Legal action to increase state funding has been filed in at least 45 states. Courts have found for the plaintiffs in more than half of those cases on the basis that schools are not "adequately" funded. This has changed the way public education is funded, moving decision making from local boards and state legislatures to the state courts. Where educators once were involved in the political process of securing funding, they now hire teams of attorneys to evaluate the adequacy of school funding. Can the public continue to win the majority of court battles? Recent judicial trends seem to indicate no. If not, are there other options beyond property and income taxes to appropriately fund PreK–12 education?

There are few signs of educational leaders running their organization more efficiently through belt tightening, reducing services, or reorganization. While it is not unheard of to have a school treasurer work for more than one board, it was unusual to learn only recently of a superintendent in Ohio who was employed by two boards. Given the size of some districts in most states, probably many schools are overstaffed. Why would a PreK–12 district of 500 students need a treasurer and a superintendent when one district with 5,000 pupils operates with one treasurer and two assistants and one superintendent and two assistants? The numbers do not correlate. One could combine the administration of 10 districts of 500 and reduce staff by 14. At an average cost of $100,000 per central office employee ($80,000 salary plus 25%–30% fringe benefits), that adds up to a saving of nearly $1.5 million.

This essay does not urge communities to close schools, although some should. Rather, this essay argues for leaders to look at ways to appropriately fund and manage schools. It will take years of thoughtful planning to figure out how to coordinate public educational services without decimating a local community. One working model in progress is Ohio's reduction in its number of county offices, now called educational service centers, or ESCs. Ohio, a few short years ago, had 88 ESCs; today, the number has been reduced to 52 and should be further reduced. It has taken time, some legislative push, and the collaboration of a number of ESCs to figure out how to offer the same, often better, services more efficiently and effectively. PreK–12 public school districts should do the same. It is difficult to justify how the United States can efficiently operate nearly 14,000 school districts with an average of 3,400 students in each district.

Based on data in the most recent *Digest of Education Statistics* (National Center for Education Statistics, 2009), 48,183,858 students attend 13,924 regular public school districts; this does not include joint vocational schools and the like. There are 98,916 school buildings within those districts. Nearly 70 of those districts have less than 2,500 students in attendance, or about 17%, of the total student population. Nearly 50% of the districts have less than 1,000 students in attendance accounting for about 5% of the total student population. Those 1,000 or less student districts, in aggregate, account for 6,389 of the 13,924 districts, or approximately 2.6 million, of the 48 million students. Thus, the median size district in the United States is just over 1,000 students. Finally, 19.6%, or 2,724 of the districts, have 299 or fewer students. There are 288 one-teacher schools, mostly due to the fact that they are located in sparsely populated areas. Given these numbers, the cost of school administration should be much more transparent with boards entering into shared services agreements in an effort to operate more efficiently and effectively.

Granted, size alone is not a silver bullet, but can efficiencies of scale improve learning and dollars saved? Based on the previous numbers, the answer is yes. Visionary leadership can save community schools where appropriate while saving taxpayers significant sums of money as they maintain the same or improved levels of student learning.

VISION

Most teacher education programs begin with courses in philosophy or foundations of American education. These courses contain sections on the history of education and philosophical underpinnings of the American educational process, generally focusing on the "past," but they provide little information and excitement for the future of education. In other words, very little time is spent on the *vision* for education. As universities prepare future teachers, these new educators must be prepared for what the future may hold; they must explore pioneering, inventive ways to educate students. What will the jobs of the future and students of the future look like? Does teacher education always need to be completed in face-to-face settings? Could a dynamically developed online educator preparation program be an option? With innovative technology that is available and on the horizon, some universities are offering or planning to offer various options to those who wish to enter the teaching field.

Having apprentice teachers is a model that allows highly qualified master teachers to work with new teachers. This model is one way to reduce cost yet reward the true master teacher. Put another way, teachers who teach in a way that adds value to what they do deserve additional compensation and should be the ones training and mentoring apprentices. In addition, apprentice teachers need a comprehensive, high quality induction program that addresses the high attrition rate among new educators and accelerates their performance growth.

21ST-CENTURY EDUCATION

What does it mean to American education that in the past 30 years we have moved from the information age to the *shift age* (Houle, 2007)? We are shifting from the age of computers, laptops, DVDs, fax machines, smart phones, the

Internet, distance learning, and connected classrooms to an incomprehensible future. Just a few years ago, we did not know or understand any of the terms just listed; the transformation in the next few years will be at a pace most of us cannot comprehend. Will education, and more important, educational leaders, be on the front or back edge of this shift? Public education is still based in the industrial age; it has not yet fully entered the information age, and the rest of the world is moving into the shift.

Some of the trends to look forward to in the shift age include accelerated electronic connectivity of the planet—not schools or districts or regions but the planet. There are over 6 billion humans, and 4 of 6 have cell phones. Neither time nor distance limits human communication.

"Location" is increasingly less important. We can work, teach, learn, study, and perform "team" functions anywhere and at anytime. We no longer worry about distance, time, place, or delivery method. Are schools implementing connectivity and the collaborative opportunities that this affords? Classrooms are rapidly becoming less of "confined" spaces. Most students are *digital natives* while most teachers are not. Is it possible that those institutions that do not catch up to and keep pace with the digital native will not be in business in the next 20 to 30 years? Many educators bring the world into the classroom, but only a few take the classroom to the world. Schools and colleges must address the issue of online learning. As one example, the Monterey Institute's National Repository for online courses provides access to an entire online high school curriculum free of charge. This and hundreds of other examples make it obvious that students now have entrée to a growing number of free learning alternatives that were inconceivable a few years ago.

Digital natives are the current residents in and entering our schools. The digital landscape is their native territory. They cannot remember their parents not having cell phones, computers, or the Internet. We digital colonizers are having a difficult time understanding the "language" of the natives. Our students are different; they seem to be able to concentrate on multiple things at the same time. We cannot possibly envision their capability to work on multiple tasks at the same time. In reality, the natives will grow up with an increased capacity for combining information, data, and concepts.

EQUITY AND ADEQUACY

Equity is generally understood as a distributional concept involving a comparison across schools and school systems. Equity can be defined in terms of inputs or outcomes. When defined as *inputs*, an equitable school finance system is one in which all schools have equivalent resources for inputs, often referred to as *horizontal equity*. Equity of inputs is not always the same in every situation. For example, one school may offer the community specific class sizes while another may offer other special services to meet the student's needs.

When equity is referred to as *outcomes*, it is generally discussed in terms of ensuring that schools and districts obtain sufficient resources to achieve similar results. In other words, one school may receive more resources than another based on the particular needs of the students being educated. Equal outcomes often require unequal resources depending on the needs of the students.

Adequacy is generally defined as assuming an absolute target and is interpreted either in terms of inputs or outcomes. Using the outcome viewpoint, districts or schools meet the adequacy standard if all schools have adequate resources to attain specific outcomes given the particular group of students served. For example, the target might be 75% of a given group passing a state proficiency examination.

Conceptually, equity and adequacy are relative terms. Schools may never have either, or they may have either or both depending on how they are managed. The point of this section is to encourage leaders to review and reflect on internal district operations. Most organizations do not operate with total efficiency. Perhaps it is not possible, but it should be one of the fiduciary responsibilities of the leadership.

WEIGHTED STUDENT FUNDING

Despite nearly 3 decades of blue ribbon studies, expert witnesses, court rulings, legislative changes, and expenditures of millions of dollars, public schools in the United States do not have school funding systems that deliver the results school-age children need. In fact, about half of the State Supreme Court cases ruled against school funding systems. Are these models flawed or are there simply not enough dollars available to meet the educational needs of all school-age children?

One solution that can help to reduce funding inequities at the school and district levels while simultaneously addressing the antiquated nature of the current funding system is the concept of *weighted student funding* (WSF). The Fordham Foundation cites the following as keys to WSF: Full state funding follows the child to the public school the child attends. Per-pupil funding amounts are weighted according to the child's individual needs and circumstances. It is worth noting that most states have some form of WSF in place especially with regard to special needs children. Under WSF, resources arrive at the school as real dollars that can be spent flexibly with an emphasis on results rather than on predetermined and inflexible programs or activities.

WSF offers an option to states' school finance challenges by directing more funds to schools serving high proportions of disadvantaged children, regardless of where they live; ensuring that schools receive all of the resources generated by each student; and allowing school-level leaders to allocate resources in ways that meet the needs of their specific children. WSF cannot be implemented overnight but immediately starts funding children by addressing their specific needs via decision making at the level of the child, not some central distribution point. Under WSF, public funds are allocated fairly, efficiently, and with accountability in place when dollars follow the student based on the student's individual need. School boards and officials must be accountable both for continuous academic growth for their students and for making progress toward and meeting minimum state and federal academic standards.

EXTRACURRICULAR ACTIVITIES, OPTIONAL?

In many foreign nations, offering extracurricular activities, especially athletics, directly through public schools, is virtually unheard of. How many thousands of dollars does the average district pay for the support of extracurricular activities? If one includes the facilities, personnel, utilities, maintenance, transportation, and administration of each program, could costs of operating a school be reduced? More and more school boards are implementing *pay for play* fees to families of athletes. Schools across this country spend millions of dollars on extracurricular activities. Is this fair to the taxpayer? Is it in the best interest of our students not to support these types of activities?

ADVANCED LEVEL COURSES

If school boards charged for the actual cost of some nonrequired curricular options, would parents still support them? When discussing athletics, the answer is probably yes. But how about advanced levels of honors, advanced placement, or classes that have very low enrollments—such as Level 4 or 5 of foreign languages? In larger districts, it is reasonable to assume that it would be possible to fill AP European History classes, but the vast majority of systems would never be able to do so. What is the cost of unfilled classes? Are there options for those students in the smaller districts to have similar courses?

STAFFING, RATIOS, AND CLASS SIZE

Some scholars claim that there is a connection between student achievement and class size or between achievement and money spent coaching educators who struggle to achieve even minimum growth in their students. Clearly, some evidence supports small class sizes in early grades, but the results are not widespread. Parents like small classes because they believe this approach provides more "private" instruction for their children. Educators love it because their workload and discipline concerns decrease. Politicians like it because it offers a model of education reform. Unions like it because it gets more teachers in their membership. Students should benefit but the long-term results are not plentiful.

The centerpiece of the class size study was the Standardized Testing and Reporting (STAR) research project in the 1980s conducted in Tennessee. Students were randomly assigned in three types of classes as they progressed from kindergarten through the third grade. Group A was a regular size class of approximately 24 students with one teacher; Group B was a similar size class with the support of a teacher's aide. And Group C was a small class of approximately 15 students with one teacher. The results of the study found that students in the small class showed a onetime educational benefit in test scores as compared to students in the other two groups.

The questions raised by these and other results will require educational leaders to determine if the costs of smaller classes and the gains in achievement warrant the added expenditure of funds. Some school officials have determined that they can achieve the equivalent of small class size by the effective use of teaching strategies including technology and specific teaching techniques, such as computer-aided instruction, teaming, looping, and the efficient use of teacher aides.

Do we already have reduced class sizes? Even though pink slips have been delivered recently, data from the 2009 "Digest of Educational Statistics" (Table 64) indicate that while student enrollment in 2007 was 19.6% greater than in 1990, teacher employment was 32% greater. Since the beginning of this century, the comparable numbers are 4.4% for student growth and 8.1% for teachers. Perhaps some districts and schools are overstaffed.

BUSING

Public school districts with significantly high transportation expenses often have to subsidize their fleet operating expenses with funds that should be used for educational purposes. In attempts to reduce transportation expenses, some boards have implemented saving strategies such as using computer-aided technology to reroute buses minimizing the number of buses, drivers, fuel, and maintenance costs. Improved routing involves planning stops and changing schedules in relation to the various buildings. Generally, transportation operations are more efficient when school building opening and closing times are staggered to allow buses to run several routes each morning and evening. Staggered times are a must if multiple bus routes, per bus, are to be considered. One county district in Florida saved approximately $750,000 per year by using computer-aided transportation scheduling. Other efficiencies include establishing reasonable walking distances between bus stops, reducing courtesy bus riders (students within safe walking distances of their assigned schools), limiting specialized transportation services to only those students requiring such, and purchasing efficient vehicles (size, van vs. large passenger; gas vs. diesel; single purchases vs. group purchasing; in-house vs. contracted maintenance and compound storage of vehicles vs. allowing drivers to take them home). While numerous efficiencies can be developed in transportation services, they are typically inapplicable in very small districts.

ALTERNATIVE FORMS OF DELIVERY

Four-day weeks may save funds. Byron Elementary School, Peach County, Georgia, moved to 4-day weeks rather than lay off all of its music, art, and physical education teachers. School officials determined that about $400,000 a year in transportation and utility costs could be saved by moving to a 4-day week. Although the community and school leadership did not like this action, they decided that it was in the best interest of the students not to eliminate music, art, and physical education. They are holding on in hopes that the economy will improve and staff will not have to be furloughed.

Online education is very fast growing, in fact, so fast that the prediction is that half of high school students, by 2020, will be taking most of their training online. Educational leaders must prepare for this change, which will dramatically impact facilities, transportation, staffing ratios, human resources, and all the elements related to having students in a building. Will it be less or more expensive to educate students online? Already, much of the curriculum is developed, and some of it is free. Many school leaders are already deep into online education and are finding their way albeit somewhat slowly.

UNFUNDED MANDATES

The answer is simple. If funds are unavailable, mandates should not be implemented. If the state or federal government requires seat belts for buses, the funds to install them must be provided. If the pupil teacher ratio for primary grades is to be 20 to 1, then funds must be provided. When legislatures require all-day, everyday kindergartens, then the dollars must flow to support the requirement. If the economy turns unpleasant and tax levies fail, personnel on salary schedules providing for step or education increases may need to be suspended. School boards must live within their budgets just like everyone else. School leaders should work diligently to provide needed funds for reasonable operations, but when dollars are not available, changes in operation must be made.

COLLABORATION

School boards and community agencies must increase their level of collaboration so that tax dollars are spent with the maximum benefit afforded to students. Police, health, counseling, and other support agencies must continue to seek more and better ways to meet the needs of students and community members. Laws must be in place to encourage local governments to share resources. Local governments must be more aggressive in studying and implementing cooperative ventures such as between school and community: parks, pools, libraries, and transportation options. As an example, one community where I was a school administrator has three libraries within a 5-minute walk of each other. The community library is on the same grounds as an elementary school that has a first-class library and is within three blocks of the high school that has a state-of-the-art curriculum materials center. Obviously, it is possible to coordinate services in the community that could save taxpayer dollars.

MOVING FROM INPUTS TOWARD CONTINUOUS IMPROVEMENT

How can school boards move from simply adding more education inputs toward a system dedicated to *continuous improvement*? A process of continuous improvement is one in which everything is on the table and nothing is protected. This is how to move education forward over the long term. The key is to start from the core principles discussed by the Fordham Foundation including the following: Do not fund actions that have little or no evidence of success; eliminate unfunded mandates; promote experimentation with unconventional forms of schooling, such as science, technology, engineering, and mathematics (STEM) and Early College programs; and reward the risk takers for positive results. Boards must move from the status quo to a system that encourages and supports continuous improvement. Few schools or communities in this country have had success in raising the majority of its poor and minority students up to minimum performance standards, yet a few individual schools have made great progress on these dimensions, proving that success is possible.

INCREASED ANTI-TAX GROUPS

When the National Taxpayers Union, an advocacy group, states that nearly 60% of all American homes are assessed higher than they should be, citizens listen. A significant and growing national tension, especially in local communities, is on the verge of causing massive government deficits. States such as Massachusetts, Ohio, and California have essentially capped property tax growth due to increased evaluation; yet taxpayers in most other states are not as fortunate. Massachusetts's limit on property tax growth of a 2.5% increase per year moved the state from the second most taxed state to the 23rd. Government leaders in Ohio, especially school leaders, were not as fortunate as those in Massachusetts since the Ohio tax reductions requires no growth in income from increases in property values unless there is a vote of the people.

Educators could manage more effectively if school tax levies were not on the ballot every 3 to 5 years. Something like a 2.5% growth per year would work well in most school districts with the understanding that in lean income years, they might not receive any additional income.

The Lincoln Institute of Land Policy recently listed the median property tax in the United Stated at about 1% of value, or $1,000 per $100,000 of value. However, state taxes vary significantly. As an example, the 2007 Louisiana median real estate tax paid was $188 while the New Jersey median was over $6,300. Most citizens are not opposed to paying taxes, but they do push back during tough economic times, especially when assessed real estate values are not adjusted to market values. Taxpayers are looking for "fairer" ways to support government agencies that must be prepared to reduce spending in down markets. Most public agencies, especially schools, are not accustomed to such demands. How will school leaders change? What must they know and be able to do in order to ensure that their schools remain open to meet the basic needs of all students, especially in tight economic times?

UNION AND BOARD/ADMINISTRATION COOPERATION

Are unions and management willing to collaborate in ways that make it possible for schools to operate efficiently and effectively in both good and lean years? What is needed is better planning and anticipation of future forecasting. Decisionmakers must anticipate what the future might hold. The loss of or significant reductions in funds require school leaders to make improved choices for the future regarding funding needs, enrollment, increases, and/or decreases in staffing as well as the related expenditure connected to those areas.

It is not unheard of for educators to work fewer days per year for less pay, reduce fringe benefits, or agree to no raises, either step or for training or education, in an effort to balance school budgets. Still, it takes a cooperative relationship built on trust to allow something like this to happen. Trust building takes time and leadership must spend time nurturing relationships with faculty, staff, and community members.

With the average government employee making more than the average private employee, it will become more and more difficult to convince taxpayers to sustain the current funding model. It is often difficult for the taxpayer to understand how government employees receive good pay with exceptional benefits while they are fighting to make a fair wage with reduced benefits. Can this model survive, or will government employees have to start thinking about modest income increases and possible reductions in benefits that will allow for more efficient use of scare resources? Time will tell.

COUNTERPOINT: William L. Phillis
Ohio Coalition for Equity and Adequacy
of School Funding

School funding systems in states across the United States often result in vast inequities and gross, consequential inadequacies in educational opportunities. Currently, many governors and policymakers are attempting to resolve these inequities and inadequacies by establishing more robust standards and enacting more stringent accountability measures. These states are demanding improved educational outcomes, while decreasing state revenues to school districts. Local school leaders and educators are being blamed for less than stellar student performance when the inequitable, inadequate system is primarily to blame. Sufficient and adequate funding must be connected to standards and accountability to improve educational opportunities and student performance.

BACKGROUND

Years ago, a reporter asked this author how much it costs to educate students in public schools. The reporter was expecting a dollars-per-pupil answer and thus was frustrated by the response: "That depends on the educational opportunities provided, the characteristics and capabilities of the various students and the student outcomes expected." Students arrive at public schools with a wide range of social and educational needs, stages of development, capabilities, interests, and penchants for the learning experience. Therefore, students require varying programs and services to meet their individual educational needs. Requisite educational opportunities and prescribed student outcomes must be geared to the ever-changing socioeconomic environment, job market, and cultural factors; hence, the amount of funding that is sufficient and adequate depends on the social and economic order, as well as the needs of students.

SCHOOL FINANCE LITIGATION

The *sufficiency* and *adequacy* of school funding—sufficiency being "as much as is needed" and adequacy being "an ability to satisfy a requirement"—has been a burning issue in most states for decades. The school funding systems in at least 45 states have been challenged in court. Plaintiffs, typically, do not rush into litigation on school funding; rather, they research the matter and attempt to first resolve the issues with the executive and legislative branches. Courts have ruled in favor of the plaintiffs in about half of the cases, but even when they have not, litigation has tended to increase the level of state support.

State defendants in school funding cases typically argue that they have increased school appropriations beyond inflation year after year. Although this may be true, states' expectations of students and school boards increase year after year.

Some states have experienced multiple school funding cases that often take years. In New Jersey, for example, the litigation has been nonstop for 3 decades. Ohio has experienced two such cases, *Cincinnati v. Walter* and *DeRolph v. State*. Ohio's *DeRolph* case spanned nearly 12 years; however, the *DeRolph* decisions continue to influence Ohio's school funding reform efforts. The number and intensity of litigation indicates that the sufficiency and adequacy of school funding is, at least, suspect throughout the United States.

PROPERTY TAX DEPENDENCE CAUSES INEQUITIES

School funding systems in most states include property tax components significantly influencing the per-pupil revenues available to school boards. Fiscal capacity of school districts is typically measured by their property wealth per pupil. Thus, the pupil expenditures of boards are often directly related to districts' property wealth. This phenomenon is a common complaint of plaintiffs in school funding cases.

Data on expenditure per pupil indicate inequity in school funding and thus in the education system. Inequitable funding systems often correlate with wide variation in student and school performance, with disproportionate incidence of inadequacy in districts at the low end of the expenditure continuum. According to the National Education Association's figures in *Rankings and Estimates* (published December 2009), average expenditure per pupil among states in the 2008–2009 school year ranged from $17,289 in Rhode Island to $5,912 in Utah—a difference of $11,377. In Ohio, the expenditure variation among schools districts is from about $7,000 to more than $20,000—a difference of $13,000. Hence, the per-pupil expenditure variation among school districts in Ohio is similar to the variation among states. These enormous variations in per-pupil expenditures among states and within Ohio (and other states) point to flawed systems of school funding.

Although regional variations in property values, cost-of-doing-business, incidence of poverty, and other demographics would explain some of the disparity in expenditures per pupil among states, these factors do not explain all variations. It seems that some states provide greater educational opportunities than others. If the goal of respective school funding systems across the United States is to provide equitable and adequate systems, the expenditure data show that it is unmet. It is reasonable to contend that school funding is both insufficient and inadequate in many states, particularly in low expenditure districts.

DEFINITION OF TERMS

In this counterpoint essay, a common understanding of the terms *sufficient* and *adequate* can inform the discussion. *Sufficient* means "as much as is needed" while *adequate* means "able to satisfy a requirement." The emphasis is on what is necessary to meet students' needs and what satisfies constitutional requirements; to this end, all state constitutions impose responsibility for education on the state. Therefore, a discussion of this nature necessitates a consideration of the curriculum, programs, and services to which students are entitled. A discussion on the sufficiency and adequacy of school funding has limited value if the needs of students and the expectations that the social order holds for pupils are not considered. Sufficiency and adequacy of school funding are achieved when all students are afforded high quality educational opportunities and all children successfully meet the expectations of state officials and local educational communities.

OHIO IS TYPICAL

Regarding school funding data, since Ohio is typical of many states and is in the middle of the pack by many measures, these are referred to throughout the remainder of this counterpoint essay. According to the National Education Association's *Rankings and Estimates*, published in December 2009, Ohio's average expenditure per pupil was $9,358 in 2008–2009, which is 6% below the

U.S. median of $9,979. Ohio's average annual teacher salary for 2008–2009 was $54,656, compared to $54,319 for all states and the District of Columbia.

Ohio's expenditure for public K–12 schools (2006–2007) per $1,000 in personal income (2007) was $41 compared to the U.S. median of $40. Rhode Island had the highest expenditure ($53), while Arizona had the lowest ($28). These data show a significant difference among states in the percentage of personal income devoted to public education. This signals problems.

Ohio is presented as a poster child for school funding insufficiencies and inadequacies in the United States. The state is in the mid range of most factors related to school finance.

RESIDUAL BUDGETING IS THE PROBLEM

The historic approach to school funding in Ohio has been *residual budgeting*. This begins with a politically predetermined amount of state revenue for public K–12 education followed by allotting a portion each to basic student support and various categorical line items in the state budget, such as special education, gifted students, disadvantaged students, transportation, and school lunch. Typically, the predetermined pool of state funds is inadequate to cover the costs of high quality educational opportunities. Some, if not all, educational programs are shortchanged. The shortchanging of basic pupil support causes great disparity in educational programming from district to district. For example, in Ohio, fewer than 30% of identified gifted students receive special educational programming beyond regular classroom experiences, even though the state has funded a gifted appropriation line item for more than 3 decades. Obviously, there is a significant divergence between the actual cost of providing appropriate programming and the amount spent on gifted students.

The residual budgeting approach does not link the formulaic allocation to the actual cost of the components of high quality educational opportunities. Historically, Ohio has supplemented, to various degrees, local districts' efforts to provide educational opportunities for students. This approach, merely providing supplemental support, demonstrates that the state is neglecting its constitutional responsibility for securing "a thorough and efficient system of common schools throughout the state." It has contributed to the disparities and inadequacies characteristic of Ohio's public school system and provides evidence that sufficiency and adequacy in school funding have not been achieved.

FUNDING IS NOT CONNECTED TO STUDENT NEEDS

Numerous studies have concluded that Ohio's school system is inequitable and inadequate due to a lack of correspondence between the funding mechanism and the actual cost of appropriate education. One such study was conducted by the Joint Select Committee to Study Ohio's School Foundation Program and the Distribution of State Funds to School Districts. In the January 22, 1991, report of the committee's findings, it stated,

> The foundation's per pupil level should have some reasonable relationship to the cost of a quality basic program efficiently provided and some objective method of determining how it should be developed. The per pupil funding level is now set during deliberations on the biennial budget and is widely considered to represent a level determined almost solely by money available after deducting for other educational and non educational program costs. (Cupp & Wise, 1991, p. 6)

The state subsequently did little to connect the funding level with the "actual cost of a quality basic education" until the biennial budget for fiscal years 2010 and 2011.

Article VI, Section 2 of the Ohio Constitution, typical of education clauses in the other 49 states, clearly and definitely assigns the responsibility of securing a thorough and efficient system of public common schools to the state. The Supreme Court of Ohio, in the *DeRolph II* Syllabus, decreed that, "The attainment of efficiency and thoroughness is expressly made a purpose, not local, not municipal, but statewide." This constitutional declaration is an imperative consideration in determining the sufficiency and adequacy of school funding. A uniform high quality system throughout the state is a requirement placed on state government.

The state, in its quest for a uniform high quality system, must specify the educational opportunities required for 21st-century students and ensure that districts provide those opportunities. Otherwise, the inadequacies and inequities that have characterized the system will continue. Equally important, the state must establish expectations and accountability measures for students and for all segments of the educational delivery system. The educational opportunities, the expectations of students, and the educational delivery system must be aligned and coordinated with the funding system. The sufficiency and adequacy of school funding must be assessed in the context of educational opportunities that should be provided and the results expected.

EVIDENCE-BASED MODEL OF SCHOOL FUNDING CONNECTS THE DOTS

Public education reform measures, including the evidence-based model (EBM) for school funding, were incorporated in Ohio's budget bill for fiscal years 2010 and 2011. The EBM is premised on the constitutional requirement that the state will ensure high quality educational opportunities for all students. This model puts Ohio on the road toward a constitutional system of school funding that will be adequate and sufficient. However, until the model is perfected and fully funded, school funding will continue to be insufficient and inadequate. The EBM is being used in Arkansas, Wyoming, and North Dakota, as well as Ohio. Wisconsin and Washington are considering the use of the model.

At the very time Ohio is making a serious attempt to implement a historic new funding model, state revenues are in substantial decline. The downturn in the economy has the potential of derailing the state's movement toward a constitutional high quality system of education.

The total state revenue available in Ohio in fiscal year 2010, like in many other states, was about the same as in fiscal year 2000. Hence, the state lacks the fiscal resources to implement the new model appropriately. The funding structure is on the right track, but the funds are not available; thus, Ohio's public schools are still not funded sufficiently or adequately.

A notable feature of recent education reform legislation is the provision for the 28-member Ohio School Funding Advisory Council, which is required to make recommendations for the improvement of the EBM. The council's first report was submitted in December 2010, with subsequent reports due July 1 of each even-numbered year thereafter. The legislature had anticipated a need to keep the model aligned with student needs on a continuing basis.

This counterpoint essay argues that school funding in Ohio is neither sufficient nor adequate. However, if the EBM for school funding is completed appropriately and funded adequately, Ohio could become a national model for sufficiency and adequacy of funding. The EBM has the potential of correcting the flaws the Supreme Court of Ohio found in the school funding system. Yet as of this writing, school funding in Ohio remains neither sufficient nor adequate. The efficacy of Ohio's EBM relates to its approach to school funding beginning with the identification of the components of a high quality education. The funding level is determined by the actual costs.

The legislation establishing EBM provides for a phase in of the model. Guarantees and caps inherent in the legislation permit school boards to receive in the range of the same level of state funds they received the previous year. In contrast, most other state services were reduced to a funding level of about 70% of the previous year. Even with public education funding being an unquestioned top priority in Ohio, it is still not sufficient and adequate.

A RECORD OF NEGLECT

It is important to note that Ohio had a dismal record of neglect regarding sufficient and adequate funding for the public schools in the early years. The historical context of state neglect helps explain the current insufficiency and inadequacy of school funding.

A root cause of neglect may be a widespread misunderstanding of the locus of responsibility for public education. Notwithstanding the thorough and efficient clause of the Ohio Constitution, which puts the onus on the state, local districts have carried the dominant load of the financial burden for funding public schools during most of Ohio's statehood. In 1930, 80 years after the adoption of the "thorough and efficient clause," local property taxes supported 96% of the public education expenditures.

In the 1920s and early 1930s, funding for public schools reached a major crisis. Property values were declining, and taxpayers were defaulting on property tax bills. The state responded by enacting the school foundation program and a 3% sales tax to provide funding. Both provisions took effect in 1935. These actions reduced property tax support for school expenditures to approximately 50% of the total. The state maintained the 50–50 state–local portions until 1946, when the portion funded by property taxes began to increase. By 1965, property taxes supported 70% of the total public school expenditures. With the advent of increased federal funding and the Ohio income tax in 1972, the local portion of public school revenue declined to 57% in 1981. The local portion of public school revenue fluctuated between 60% and 46% since 1981 with a downward trend. In fiscal year 2009, the local percentage was 47.42, the state percentage 44.71 and the federal percentage 7.87. In only 2 of the years since 1981 has the total local revenue been less than the state revenue. The heavy dependence on property taxes for funding public schools results in gross inequities and egregious inadequacies in districts at the lower end of the property wealth continuum.

The Ohio experience of heavy dependence on property tax mirrors the nation's. According to the 2009 National Center for Education Statistics, *Digest of Education Statistics,* in 2006–2007, local tax revenue supported about 44% of the expenditures for public education in the nation. Local revenue in Ohio supports, as noted above, 47.42% of the expenditure for public education.

Property wealth has never been equally distributed among Ohio school districts. Currently, the range in property valuation per pupil among Ohio school districts is from a low of $42,335 to a high of $667,971 (Figure 11.1). With the elimination of the top and bottom 20%, the range is still startling—$88,000 to $209,000. The historical emphasis on property taxes in Ohio's school funding formula has caused wide variation in school districts' fiscal capacity, great disparities in expenditure per pupil, and thus great disparities in educational opportunities.

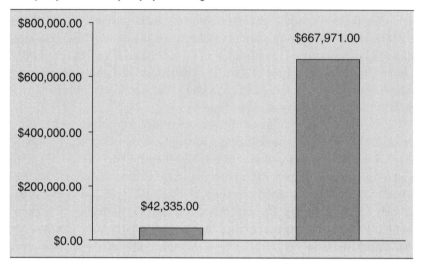

Figure 11.1

Property valuation per pupil among Ohio school districts in 2006–2007

Source: Data from the Ohio Department of Education.

GREAT DISPARITIES

The per-pupil expenditure in fiscal year 2009 ranged from $6,926 to $20,038 (Figure 11.2). The top 60 districts (10%) spent an average of $13,394 while the bottom 60 districts spent an average of $7,677. Ohio's expenditure-per-pupil data confirm that educational opportunities are unequally distributed. Even so, political officials in Ohio and many other states have failed to resolve the problems associated with the heavy dependence on property tax in school funding. Sufficiency and adequacy of school funding cannot be achieved until a state's funding system is less dependent on property tax. However, the EBM is on the right track to remedy this matter.

The traditional heavy dependence on property tax for school operations and facilities has spawned a misunderstanding that local funding comes with local control. The idea that local communities should determine the level of educational opportunities available to students by local tax effort is a prevalent notion. This notion would put each community, rather than the state, in charge of determining the standard of thorough and efficient.

THE LOCAL CONTROL MYTH

In 1979, the Supreme Court of Ohio, in *Board of Education of the City School District of Cincinnati v. Walter,* perpetuated the confusion regarding "local

Figure 11.2

Expenditure per pupil in Ohio in fiscal year 2009

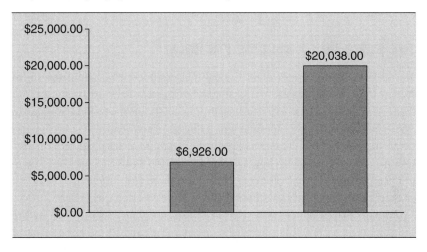

Source: Data from the Ohio Department of Education (2011).

control" and school funding. The Court stated, "We find local control to be a rational basis supporting Ohio's system of financing elementary and secondary education." The Court added, "We conclude that local control provides a rational basis supporting the disparity in per pupil expenditures in Ohio's school districts."

In *Walter*, the Court also endorsed the notion that school funding is a state-local partnership. According to the court, "Ohio has continued this financial partnership with local school districts until this present day." School funding can never be sufficient and adequate in Ohio or any other state as long as school funding is treated as a partnership between the state and local communities.

In contrast with *Walter*, in *DeRolph v. State* (1997), the same court noted the following:

> However, we admonish the General Assembly that it must create an entirely new school financing system. In establishing such a system, the General Assembly shall recognize that there is but one system of public education in Ohio. It is a statewide system, expressly created by the state's highest governing document, the Constitution. Thus, the establishment, organization and maintenance of public education are the state's responsibility.

DeRolph captured the plain, clear meaning of Article VI, section 2 of the Ohio Constitution. Sufficiency and adequacy of school funding will be elusive until Ohio's political figures fully embrace the constitutional requirement for a thorough and efficient system.

THE STATE MUST ASSUME ITS ROLE

Local school boards are in place to help deliver educational opportunities to students. These entities are political subdivisions of the state, established to deliver educational opportunities according to state statutes and standards. These subdivisions, although managed by locally elected citizens, are not partners with the state but are extensions of the state for the local delivery of educational opportunities. It should be clear that the state is responsible for a uniform system of school funding that is adequate and sufficient; otherwise, sufficiency and adequacy of school funding cannot be achieved.

Prior to the 1920s, the state highway system in Ohio was operated by the county governments with support from the state. The counties did not have equal financial capacity to construct and maintain state highways, even with financial support from the state. It became clear to all concerned that the state would have to assume responsibility for the state highway system to set forth a uniformly high quality highway system. That is what needs to happen with the state school system. That is what is envisioned by recent reform measures. The state must assume its constitutional responsibility to secure a thorough and efficient system.

Ohio has made some progress toward sufficiency and adequacy in terms of state priority and in the funding of school facilities. For example, Ohio's recent $23 billion school rebuilding program was prompted and spurred on by *DeRolph*. Since *DeRolph* in 1997, the 761 new or renovated building projects, serving 425,000 students in 260 school districts, have been completed. At the time of this writing, 136 buildings are under construction with another 164 facilities in active design. However, 112 other boards have been offered state funding for the construction of needed school buildings but have either chosen to postpone participation or have been unable to raise the required local share. This means that some students are being denied educationally adequate buildings because some local communities cannot or will not meet the state requirement for participating in the facilities program. Until this matter is resolved, sufficiency and adequacy of school funding is yet to be achieved in Ohio.

THE IMPORTANCE OF SUFFICIENCY AND ADEQUACY

The determination of sufficiency and adequacy of school funding is an exercise related to an assessment of the extent to which Ohio and other states secure high quality educational opportunities for all students more so than a statistical analysis of pupil expenditure and related school finance data. Sufficiency and adequacy of school funding will have occurred when the needs of all students are met regardless of their zip code. A practical result of sufficiency and adequacy in school funding is that students who move from any one district to any other district would experience uniformity in high quality educational opportunities.

From early colonial times, the need for the provision of public education has been articulated in consistent stipulations. An educated citizenry is requisite to a vital democratic society. In *Brown v. Board of Education* (1954), the U.S. Supreme Court ruled, "Where a State has undertaken to provide an opportunity for an education in its public schools, such an opportunity is a right which must be made available to all on equal terms" (p. 493).

Yet in 1973, when the Supreme Court had an opportunity to put some teeth in *Brown,* it backed away. In *San Antonio Independent School District v. Rodriguez* (1973), the Court refused to recognize education as a fundamental federal constitutional right of school children. Although the framers of the Constitution did not explicitly mention education, the aim and actuality of education is firmly embedded in the constitution of each state.

Since *Rodriguez,* most states have had school finance litigation. Plaintiffs in these cases have attempted to achieve school funding systems that result in equitable, adequate systems. Although the litigation has brought about greater funding to public schools by state legislatures, the systems typically do not connect the school funding levels with the needs of students.

To achieve uniform high quality educational opportunities throughout the nation, state governments must first clearly identify opportunity and performance measures, cost out those items, and provide funding. Although the new EBM in Ohio is on this appropriate track, sufficiency and adequacy will not be achieved until the model is completed, refined, and fully funded.

FURTHER READINGS AND RESOURCES

Baird, K. E. (2008). Federal direct expenditures and school funding disparities, 1990–2000. *Journal of Education Finance, 33,* 297–310.

Cupp, R., & Wise, D. (1991). *Report: Joint committee to study Ohio's school foundation program and the distribution of state funds to school districts.* Columbus: Ohio Legislative Committees.

Driscoll, L. G., & Salmon, R. G. (2008). How increased state equalization aid resulted in greater disparities: An unexpected consequence for the Commonwealth of Virginia. *Journal of Education Finance, 33,* 238–261.

Goldhaber, D., Dearmond, M., Player, D., & Choi, H.-J. (2008). Why do so few public school districts use merit pay? *Journal of Education Finance, 33,* 262–289.

Houle, D. (2007). *The shift age.* Available from http://www.Booksurge.com

Jefferson, A. L. (2008). Factors influencing educational opportunity in Ontario. *Journal of Education Finance, 33,* 290–296.

McKinley, S. K., & Phillis, W. L. (2008). Collaboration in search of a school funding remedy post DeRolph. *Journal of Education Finance, 33,* 311–330.

Monterey Institute's National Repository for Online Courses: http://www.monterey institute.org/nroc

Morse, J. F. (2007). *A level playing field.* Albany: State University of New York Press.

National Center for Education Statistics, Institute of Education Sciences, U.S. Department of Education. (2009, September). Table 64. *Digest of Educational Statistics.* Retrieved from http://nces.ed.gov/programs/digest/d09/tables/dt09_064.asp

Odden, A., & Picus, L. (2008). *School finance: A policy perspective.* New York: McGraw-Hill.

Ohio Department of Education. (2011). *Ohio's school foundation funding program: 2006–2007.* Columbus, OH: Author.

Speakman, S., Hassel, B., & Finn, C. (2005). *Charter school funding inequity's next frontier.* Washington, DC: Thomas B. Fordham Institute.

Thomas B. Fordham Institute. (2008, March). *Fund the child: Bringing equity, autonomy, and portability to Ohio schools.* Washington, DC: Author.

Wall, A., Frost, R., Smith, R., & Keeling, R. (2008). Examining a higher education funding formula in a time of shifting currents: Kentucky's benchmark approach. *Journal of Education Finance, 33,* 221–237.

COURT CASES AND STATUTES

Board of Education of City School District of Cincinnati v. Walter, 390 N.E.2d 813 (Ohio 1979).

Brown v. Board of Education, 347 U.S. 483 (1954).

DeRolph v. State, 677 N.E.2d 733 (Ohio 1997).

Robinson v. Cahill, 303 A.2d 273 (N.J. 1973a), *cert. denied,* 414 U.S. 976 (1973b).

San Antonio Independent School District v. Rodriguez, 411 U.S. 1 (1973).

Serrano v. Priest, 487 P.2d 1241 (Cal. 1971), 557 P.2d 929 (Cal. 1976), *cert. denied,* 432 U.S. 907 (1977).

Should governors and legislators "invest" in education?

POINT: Bob Taft, *University of Dayton*

COUNTERPOINT: William A. Proefriedt, *Queens College, City University of New York*

OVERVIEW

The history of American education is replete with legislative efforts to make schools and schooling accessible to all students. As early as 1647, Massachusetts created legislation, known as the Old Deluder Satan Law, requiring every town of more than 50 households to hire a teacher and for towns that exceeded 100 households to provide a Latin grammar school. More recently, the Race to the Top federal program provided competitive grants to "selected" states that evidenced a willingness to engage in reform practices that would enhance innovation and academic excellence.

Those who govern understand that an educated population is essential for democratic governance. As a result, legislators and other state policymakers have created laws such as those associated with compulsory school attendance and defining standards for what students should learn to enhance the capacity of communities to ensure that all children are properly educated.

Still, the issue of how much a top-down governmental approach should be used for educational problem solving remains unresolved, especially as an emerging era of smaller government intervention appears to be the clarion call of those right of the political center. Should governors and legislators be the ones who dictate accountability protocols and expectations? Or can those at the local level really monitor their educational efforts in ways that result in enhanced instructional practice and improved student learning? These types of questions are occurring at a time when the budget pressures on state legislatures have, quite simply, never been greater. With so many states facing significant amounts of red ink, can and should governors and legislatures really make a commitment to invest in education? Moreover, if they do make such investments, will they be able to honor the real and often financially significant mandates emerging out of policy?

In this chapter, the two contributors examine how and whether state level governmental leaders should be involved in shaping state and local educational practices. In the first essay, Bob Taft (University of Dayton and former Governor of Ohio) describes why governors should "invest" in education. For Taft, there is a direct connection between educational attainment and economic viability. For too long, the United States has been lagging educationally, and the consequences of that circumstance are now compromising the global competitiveness of the United States. In this regard, Taft notes that economic growth is tied to knowledge acquisition and information usage, and unless states as well their legislatures are able to expand significantly the number of students who succeed in school and excel in their studies, the prognosis for economic growth is bleak. According to Taft, students need to graduate from high school "college and career ready"; and it is the states, which have responsibility for funding and overseeing schools, that need to invest in education by engaging in practices and fostering reforms that truly ensure equitable opportunities for all students.

William A. Proefriedt (Queens College) has a different view. Proefriedt argues that governors and state legislators tend to overstate the power of schooling. True, good schools are important for any democracy; equally true, individuals are more than marketable commodities. Indeed, he asserts that legislators all too often overstate the role of schools and overpromise the connection between educational attainment and economic vitality. To Proefriedt, education is about much more than high value-added scores (strong student academic growth) or the number of college degrees granted. He points out that American communities are composed of citizens both young and old, and the challenge is to help all of them acquire the critical dispositions needed to question assumptions about how the marketplace should operate and to promote ways in which the lives of all can be improved.

What makes this debate so interesting is that the Lumina Foundation and others are now calling for even more young people to secure postsecondary credentials. Indeed, they have set a goal of having 60% of all 25- to 64-year-olds with some type of high quality postsecondary credential by the year 2025. To reach that goal, they want states to be more assertive in ensuring the college and career readiness of the young people exiting our schools. The expectation is clear, but can and should it be legislated, or does it make more sense to foster expectations through community engagement and consensus building without encouraging lawmakers to "legislate learning levels"?

In reading these two essays, consider these questions: First, are there negative consequences that result from legislative overzealousness such as No Child Left Behind or Race to the Top to make schools stronger and more accountable? Second, if governors or legislators did not assume responsibility for legislating learning, who would fill this void, and what might be the consequences?

Thomas J. Lasley, II
University of Dayton

POINT: Bob Taft
University of Dayton

In a knowledge-driven world economy, governors and legislators must invest in education to preserve the standard of living and quality of life we have enjoyed in the United States. Once a leader in providing educational opportunity to all citizens, the United States is falling behind other nations, which have recognized the benefits of highly educated workers and citizens. Of course, the 50 states have principal responsibility for elementary and secondary education in the United States; they must invest wisely to ensure that more students graduate from high school prepared to succeed in college, in good jobs, and as active, well-informed citizens.

ECONOMIC OPPORTUNITY

The continued growth of the American economy is essential to create good job opportunities for our citizens, to sustain our standard of living, and to provide a tax base to support vital public services such as education, health care, and our armed services.

Increasingly, our economy is based on knowledge and new information thereby placing a premium on the creation of a highly educated workforce. The number of manufacturing jobs continues to decline, and postsecondary education is a requirement for many that remain. There is a growing consensus, led by economists such as Gary Becker, that *human capital,* the knowledge and competencies of workers, has become the most important ingredient for creating economic prosperity. Good schools provide the foundation for the development of human capital.

At the same time, Americans live in an era of *globalization* made possible by rapid advances in computing and communications technology. Workers in one state compete not only with those in neighboring states, but also they compete with workers throughout the world, not just in manufacturing but also in such fields as software development, health care, call and service centers, claims processing, accounting, and research. In China alone, there are more than 600 research centers operated by multinational corporations. If states do not educate and train workers with the skills employers need, even more jobs will be moved elsewhere in search of talented workers.

CITIZENSHIP AND SOCIAL COHESION

A democratic society depends on educated citizens capable of making informed decisions and holding government leaders accountable for their performance. The Land Ordinance adopted by the U.S. Congress in 1785 set aside land in new states for public education, and the Northwest Ordinance of 1787 declared that since knowledge was necessary for good government, "schools and the means of education shall forever be encouraged." States bear the responsibility of providing the education necessary to prepare our youth for citizenship.

State investments in schools are also necessary to address a growing gap in earnings based on disparate levels of education. Earnings of college graduates compared to those with only a high school diploma have risen steadily for the past 3 decades. According to the U.S. Census Bureau, workers with a college degree earned almost twice as much as high school graduates in 2008. Hispanics and African Americans, the fastest growing part of our population, have the lowest overall level of educational attainment, a disparity that has potential adverse consequences for our nation's future cohesion and stability.

WHERE IMPROVEMENT IS NEEDED

High School Graduation

Too few students are graduating from American high schools. The United States ranks 18th among developed countries in high school graduation rates. Despite modest improvement over the past 30 years, only 7 out of 10 students graduate on time from high school. The on time graduation rate among Hispanic and African American students is even lower at just above 50% (Editorial Projects in Education staff, 2009). Students without high school diplomas are not prepared for most jobs in a knowledge-based economy. These young people are not qualified to enter college and are ill-prepared for any type of postsecondary education. Although a number of high school dropouts subsequently earn a General Equivalency Diploma (GED), or high school equivalent certificate, fewer of these students enter or graduate from college; and few are able to compete in a job market that requires 21st-century thinking skills.

There are high individual and social costs associated with those who fail to earn high school diplomas, as compared to high school and college graduates: lower lifetime earnings and higher rates of crime, unemployment, poverty, and public assistance. More than 70% of state prison and jail inmates have not completed high school (Harlow, 2003). Dropouts who are employed earn lower wages and provide less tax revenue to support public services at local, state, and federal levels. These young people are less likely to adopt healthy lifestyles, resulting in greater health care costs often borne by taxpayers. Finally, dropouts vote and volunteer at much lower rates than those with more education (Baum & Ma, 2007).

College Preparation and Degree Attainment

At one time, the United States led the world in college enrollment and completion, but other countries have been catching up and surpassing us. The United States now ranks 12th in the percentage of 25- to 34-year-olds who have a 2- or 4-year college degree with a rate of only 40%, according to the Organisation for Economic Co-operation and Development (OECD, 2009). While college enrollment has been increasing, the college completion rate remains low and has improved only modestly over the past decade. According to the OECD, the United States ranks 15th among 29 developed countries in that category: Only one out of every two students earns a bachelor's degree within 6 years of enrollment, and the 2-year college completion rate is even lower.

The failure of our schools to prepare students for college success is one important factor leading to low college graduation rates:

- Only 24% of high school students met college-readiness benchmarks on all four subjects on the 2010 American College Testing (ACT) college entrance exam according to ACT (2010).

- A third of 1st-year college students were enrolled in at least one remedial course in math or language arts during the 2007–2008 school year, and these students are less likely to graduate than their peers who are better prepared, according to the U.S. Department of Education National Center for Education Statistics.

- U.S. students fare poorly compared to those from other countries on international tests of math and science skills. For example, U.S. 15- to 16-year-olds ranked 22nd in science and 30th in math among students from 64 countries on the 2009 Programme for International Student Assessment.

The United States pays a big price for low college graduation rates. College graduates outperform high school graduates in lifetime earnings by wide margins and are less likely to be a burden on society due to unemployment or crime. They also tend to be more engaged as citizens—voting, volunteering, and donating blood at significantly higher levels.

In addition, there is strong evidence that the future growth of our economy will be impaired by low educational attainment. A recent study by the Center on Education and the Workforce at Georgetown University estimated that by 2018 the United States will need 22 million more workers with college degrees but will fall short of that number by at least 3 million at current college completion rates. Based on these data, the Lumina Foundation concludes that the United States should increase the share of younger workers with college degrees to 60% by the year 2025.

Shortages in certain highly skilled occupations such as nursing and information technology already force employers to recruit workers from outside the United States or move jobs to other countries. The United States continues to attract talented graduate students from overseas in scientific and engineering fields, but increasingly, these students return home with their degrees because of expanding job opportunities in developing countries. Clearly, the United States must raise the college graduation rate to compete for good jobs in the years ahead; and our progress will depend on making the kind of investments in elementary and secondary education that will enable more students to graduate from high school well prepared to succeed in postsecondary education.

MAKING GOOD INVESTMENTS IN EDUCATION
States Must Take the Lead

Since governors and state legislators have the primary responsibility for funding and overseeing public schools, they must take the lead in making the investments necessary to improve educational outcomes. With the exception of the large amount of onetime stimulus and incentive monies sent to the states in response to the 2007–2009 recession, the federal share of elementary and secondary school funding has not exceeded 10%. Given the magnitude of the federal budget deficit, it is not realistic to plan on higher rates of federal funding in future years.

The Right Kind of Investment

There is a debate among academic experts about whether *aggregate* increases in school spending result in improved student performance. Some note that inflation-adjusted, per-student spending has increased by 50% over the last 20 years with very little overall improvement in National Assessment of Educational Progress (NAEP) scores and high school graduation rates. Others point to significant gains in reading and math on NAEP among minority students over this time period as well as overall improvement on state assessments.

In any event, overall state and local expenditures on elementary and secondary education are likely to be constrained in the foreseeable future by severe budgetary challenges due to the recession and the slow pace of economic recovery. Nevertheless, states should continue to invest in schools to prevent budget cuts that harm learning, preserve equality of educational opportunities for students no matter where they live, and fund innovative reforms addressing low high school and college completion rates, which erode our ability to compete in the global economy.

Preventing School Budget Cuts That Harm Learning

School boards are cutting budgets across the country—freezing pay, reducing transportation, laying off personnel, deferring maintenance and technology purchases, cutting elective courses, and, in some cases, moving to 4-day school weeks. Many boards are at the point where it becomes impossible to make further reductions without adversely affecting student achievement in critical subjects, such as reading, writing, mathematics, and science. States should make sure districts have sufficient resources to prevent a decline in the quality of classroom instruction.

Preserving Equality of Educational Opportunity for All Students

In virtually every state, schools continue to depend, at least in part, on revenue from local property tax bases, which vary widely. State funding systems have evolved to compensate for such differences, providing more state aid to poorer districts in order to equalize educational opportunity and ensure adequate resources for each child's education no matter where they live. States should continue to make *equalizing* investments in education, from the standpoint of fundamental fairness and also to create the broadest possible pool of talented, knowledge workers to attract and retain good jobs.

Funding Innovative Reforms

For too many years, states have failed to make significant progress in graduating more students from high school well prepared for success in college and technically demanding jobs. Clearly, the status quo is unacceptable.

At the same time, a growing body of research is helping educators and policymakers identify the kind of investments in education that can make a difference in raising student achievement levels. Although some promising school reforms may not require new expenditures, most innovation is impossible without additional resources. Here are some prominent examples:

1. *High Quality Preschool Programs.* A significant amount of research shows that good preschool education programs are a cost-effective method of improving academic achievement in elementary school and increasing high school graduation and college enrollment rates. Yet about half of 3-year-olds and a quarter of 4-year-olds in the United States were not enrolled in public- or private center-based preschool programs in 2009. Unfortunately, children from poor families have lower rates of enrollment than those from families with higher-than-average incomes. In addition, quality standards for preschools remain low in a number of states. Until the recent recession, states were increasing their aggregate investment in preschool, but spending and enrollment declined in some states in 2009. Preschool is clearly one area in which state investments would bring positive returns in the form of student success.

2. *Teacher Quality.* Research studies have established that teacher quality is the most important in-school factor in student learning. States and school boards need to invest thoughtfully in the recruitment, nurturing, and on-the-job training of teachers. These efforts often involve the expenditure of funds.

Instructional experts have stressed the effectiveness of frequent, periodic assessments (*formative assessment*) of student learning and differentiating instruction to individual students based on the results of such assessments. Large numbers of teachers are unskilled in these strategies, and it is necessary to provide training for them, at a cost.

In a similar vein, a number of states have made steady progress in raising student proficiency levels in reading through reading institutes to help teachers understand the basic strategies for reading instruction. An alternative approach, placing highly trained reading coaches in schools to work with reading teachers, also involves an additional cost.

Comprehensive entry-year and residency programs connecting novice teachers with experienced and well-trained mentors can make a significant impact on new teacher quality and retention. This innovation also requires resources to free up experienced teachers to properly perform their mentoring duties.

Incentive pay programs are one promising strategy to recruit teachers for subjects such as mathematics and science where qualified teachers are in short supply and also to attract and retain effective teachers in the lowest performing schools where they are needed the most. This type of initiative involves additional investments since it is unlikely that the compensation of other teachers will be reduced to raise money for incentives.

3. *Building Better Data Systems.* The U.S. Department of Education and the Data Quality Campaign have called for states to build comprehensive

longitudinal data systems to measure student progress and inform educators on how best to use data to improve instruction. In particular, the ability to connect data on students' yearly growth in learning to specific classrooms and teachers has great potential for improving teacher evaluation and providing all students with effective teachers. Data systems have start-up and maintenance costs; and it will also be necessary to train teachers and principals to interpret and act on data.

4. *More Rigorous Standards and Better Assessments.* Academic standards established by the states to define what students should be able to know and do in each subject and grade level vary greatly in their rigor and alignment with what's needed for success in college and on the job. In 2009, almost all states agreed to participate in the Common Core State Standards Initiative that is developing common standards in mathematics and language arts that would be internationally benchmarked and aligned with college- and work-ready requirements. Implementing these new standards and developing new curriculum materials will involve an investment by the states.

In addition, new standards require new assessments. The federal government will award grants to groups of states to develop more comprehensive and meaningful assessments. The testing system would go beyond multiple choice questions and would seek to provide more timely and useful information to educators to drive student instruction. If states ultimately adopt common assessments for mathematics and language arts, there will be economies of scale that could reduce costs. However, in the meantime, there will be development and start-up expenses.

5. *Interventions for Low-Performing Schools and Districts.* School boards and states are required to intervene to improve persistently underperforming schools under the federal No Child Left Behind Act. Intervention may be in the form of teacher training, a new curriculum, replacing school staff, contracting out the operation of the school, or a state takeover. Yet there is insufficient funding and staffing at state and district levels to provide help to all schools currently in need of improvement. The federal government is proposing to limit mandatory intervention to the lowest performing 5% of schools. In any event, there will be a continuing need for additional resources to turn around failing schools.

6. *Providing Options for Children in Failing Schools.* One remedy for children in underperforming schools is to create options in the form of charter schools (autonomous public schools) or vouchers to attend private schools. Most states

authorize charter schools and a few have voucher programs. Even so, in most cases, states do not provide funding for these alternatives that is equivalent to spending in public schools. For example, the Knowledge Is Power Program (KIPP), one of the most successful operators of charter schools, must supplement public funding from private sources up to $1,500 per student per year. If states are serious about good alternatives for children in failing schools, then they will need to increase their support for charter schools and/or voucher programs.

7. *Science, Technology, Engineering, and Mathematics (STEM).* Individual states and the United States as a whole are not graduating enough students who are prepared for careers in fields requiring scientific, mathematical, and engineering training. As noted above, U.S. students do poorly on international tests in these subjects.

Many states are creating new STEM schools and STEM curricula to challenge and engage students. One national initiative, Project Lead the Way, which offers a high quality, inquiry-based preengineering curriculum, has been implemented in schools across the country. Such efforts that are designed to make U.S. students more competitive in the world economy to the benefit of all Americans will have to be sustained by continuing state and financial support.

EDUCATION MATTERS MOST

The United States rose to world prominence by investing in education, thereby creating a talented, knowledgeable workforce and sustaining a vibrant democracy. Today, as the nation struggles to compete in a global, knowledge-based economy, our educational progress has been lagging. Americans know a great deal about the kind of reforms that are necessary to prepare more students for successful futures. Governors and legislators should invest in education to accomplish this goal.

COUNTERPOINT: William A. Proefriedt
Queens College, City University of New York

Educational reformers of all political stripes, reflecting the larger culture, uncritically assume and anxiously articulate the purposes of schooling: to keep the United States competitive in the world marketplace and to move individuals up the socioeconomic ladder. It is not at all surprising, then, that point essay author Bob Taft enlists these ends as compelling reasons why states should invest generously in schooling and in a particular set of educational reforms. Schools and the teachers and students in them can accomplish wonderful things. States should continue investing in them. However, this essay addresses the question of what happens when we view education as almost exclusively aimed at economic ends.

Educators and the political figures that they enlist in our cause promise more than we can deliver in the economic arena. Educators badly overstate the efficacy of schooling in securing national and individual economic ends. The ubiquitous championing of education as the key to national prosperity and to the task of lessening our scandalous economic inequality allows us to sidestep controversial noneducational policies, which might more adequately address these problems. Worse, overwhelmed by this view of educational purpose, policymakers, citizens, teachers, curriculum makers, and most unfortunately, students at every level of schooling see schools as *only* instrumental to a career or as enhancing our gross national product. We have so saturated the public conversation about schooling with words signaling the twin ends of national economic prosperity and individual economic mobility that we have driven other more traditional and valuable ways of talking about and practicing schooling from the field. We need to recover ways of thinking about schooling in which young people are defined as *not only* human capital and nations as *not only* economic engines.

SCHOOLING FOR GLOBAL ECONOMIC COMPETITIVENESS

Taft worries that the United States is falling behind other countries in the quality of our schooling and in the numbers of citizens we graduate from our schools. He points out that we are in a worldwide competitive marketplace in which "*human capital,* the knowledge and competencies of workers, has become the most important ingredient for creating economic prosperity." Taft sees schools as the key to the production of human capital. According to him, we must invest wisely in them to maintain America's advantage in the world because without that advantage our present standard of living would deteriorate. He reminds us that the United States has slipped to 18th among developed nations in high school graduation rates and 15th in college completion rates, and he asserts that "the failure of our schools . . . is one important factor leading to low college graduation rates."

Taft also cites workforce studies showing we will need more workers with college degrees in the future, and he worries about the practice of recruiting students and workers in several fields from outside the United States. He argues that we must invest in the schools so that the schools can better prepare students for success in college. Taft worries further about the number of our students in college remediation courses and about our students' scores on international science and math tests. He worries that in the future our colleges will not produce enough graduates to fill jobs available in the economy.

I certainly agree that an educated workforce is a necessary part of any nation's effort to preserve its economic well-being. Still, I believe that he overstates the case for the centrality of the school in a national program to preserve and enhance our economic competitiveness with other nations. In attributing our employment problems exclusively to educational shortcomings, we fail to acknowledge more difficult choices that need to be addressed.

Andy Grove, the former CEO of Intel, notes that we take justified pride in the "knowledge workers" who have engendered enormously profitable high-tech start-ups. Our companies have developed the prototypes, but as costs in salary, health care, and pensions have risen, we have, Grove points out, in the interests of lower costs and higher profits for investors, moved the manufacturing of these prototypes offshore. This has led, Grove reports, to enormous job growth in China and job losses in the United States. We have produced high profits for individual companies derived from overseas manufacturing but mass unemployment in the United States. Not only do we lose an enormous number of jobs, Grove points out, but we lose also the kind of learning and context for more innovation, which goes along with the manufacturing process (Grove, 2010). However valuable more and better schooling may be, it would not seem to be the solution to the loss of our manufacturing base in the pursuit of individual profits for U.S. companies. Educational solutions are necessary but clearly not sufficient to the task of ensuring a decent standard of living for all in the nation.

SCHOOLS AS AGENTS OF ECONOMIC MOBILITY AND EQUALITY

Taft, to his credit, recognizes and wishes to do something about inequality in our society. He argues that state investments in schools are necessary to "address the growing gap in earnings based on disparate levels of education." To his credit also, Taft worries over the poor school performance of Hispanic and African American students. In recent years, individual states and the nation have taken this disparity with increasing seriousness. The federal No Child Left Behind Act wisely called for disaggregated results shedding light on the achievement levels of different groups of students. Taft points to the growth of differences in earnings between college educated and noncollege educated members of the workforce and reminds us that those who stay in school longer are more likely to adopt healthy lifestyles, vote more regularly, and volunteer to help in their communities more often.

The correlations between school success and lifetime earnings and a host of other valuable ends lead policymakers to conclude that we simply need to reform the schools so that they enable all students to finish high school prepared for success in college. They will then learn the 21st-century-workplace skills that will, in turn, allow them to match the earnings of other college-educated Americans. The policymakers reason that if the income gap is based on "disparate levels of education," we can close it by providing all with adequate schooling. Structures of income inequality in the larger society will simply disappear. This strikes me as illusory thinking. Schools can play an important role in social and economic mobility. Educational efforts alone, however, will not do the job.

Taft recognizes, first of all, that states should continue to make "equalizing investments" in schools to compensate for inequalities in per-pupil expenditures created by the local funding from property taxes. We seem unwilling as a nation to address even this matter of what he rightly characterizes as "fundamental fairness." Over decades, efforts to correct the vast differences in per-pupil expenditures between poor and affluent districts by appealing to equal protection clauses in the U.S. Constitution or in some state constitutions were unsuccessful. More recently, plaintiffs have made arguments for more equitable funding based on education clauses in state constitutions that place the burden on states to provide an adequate education for their citizens. These efforts have been arguably more successful, but despite state formulas meant to have an equalizing effect, school districts vary widely in the amount of money they spend per pupil. Legislators from wealthier districts find it politically precarious to vote for state funding formulas that redistribute revenues to poorer districts. Fundamental fairness in the matter of per-pupil expenditures has so far eluded most of the states and the nation.

Those who call for investment in the schools should be clear eyed about the extent to which school reforms can overcome the impact of poverty on children. Richard Rothstein (2004), while acknowledging that well-run schools can play a positive role in the lives of young people, targeted the illusory belief that school practices alone can close the "Black-White Achievement Gap." Rothstein looked with a wary eye at claims that a whole variety of improved school practices could compensate for the large differences in school success predicted by social class background. He found many of the reformers' claims to be misguided or fraudulent. At the same time, Rothstein suggested that we need to create social conditions under which altered school practices could be translated into genuinely educative experiences for those destined otherwise to lead constricted lives. He argued that policymakers at both the national and state levels may need to make hard choices between spending on new educational programs or on other approaches. Affordable and stable housing, Rothstein contended, is likely to contribute to the educational success of children. Living wage laws, creative jobs policies, the expansion of health care, laws encouraging union organizing and collective bargaining, changes in tax policies, and other nonschool policies could contribute effectively to both school success and individual social mobility.

In the end, though, however wise we may be in investing in policies and practices in school and out, we are still going to have large differences in school performance among students. The testing professionals are well aware of this predictable variability in large populations of students even when issues of race and poverty have been accounted for. We cannot flog all young people through an educational system and on to top jobs as creative entrepreneurs, knowledge workers, and engineers in the 20th-century workplace. Further, we are treated on an almost daily basis to new revelations from economic journalists about the extent of the growing inequality in our society. From 2002 to 2007, while the bottom 99% of incomes rose by 1.3% a year, the top 1% grew 10% a year. Its share of the national income during that period, James Surowiecki reported, doubled to 23% in 2007 (2010, p. 33). These kinds of inequities seem better addressed by tax reform than educational reform.

To think that the vast inequalities in income in our society will be significantly muted by educational policies seems unwarranted. We need a more humane set of public and private employment, income, fiscal, and tax practices. Efforts to achieve equality of educational opportunity are surely a part of any movement toward a more humane society, but if we fail to create a larger more economically democratic society outside the schools, individual school success will serve only as a further justification for the unconscionable income differences in the larger society. We will need home health aides as well as high-tech entrepreneurs. Regardless of their educational levels, we must figure out a way to pay them a living wage.

WHAT WORKS

It is easy to sympathize with governors and legislators, champions of education, who wish to be wise stewards of the public purse and to make what Taft calls "the right kind of investment" in the schools. Since Sputnik in the 1950s, they have watched educational leaders and national figures with an interest in schooling hop on and off a variety of reform bandwagons. Surely, there are better and worse ways of educational practice, and we should invest our public money where it has the best chance of supporting approaches that work well. Yet we ought not to set up illusory goals. The unkept promises of schooling have contributed already to a climate of hostility toward teachers and public education, which is likely to heat up as the promises multiply and remain unfulfilled. It is unlikely that a set of specific educational practices, *failing larger changes in the society,* will lead to dramatic changes in scores on standardized tests and college completion rates, to greater equality in the society, or to significant alterations in our gross national product.

Taft's championing of the expansion of preschool especially to poorer families is nothing but admirable. Financing the recruiting, training, mentoring, coaching, and other kinds of supportive structures for new teachers is, of course, unexceptionable. He is wise to focus his investment strategies on instructional efforts. Nonetheless, Taft then embraces a set of market-driven strategies that have of late defined what we mean by educational reform and that have driven other approaches from the field. Diane Ravitch (2010), in an extraordinarily detailed and well-argued book, called into question just the kind of "interventions" Taft endorses as worthy of state investment. Ravitch worried over a now dominant management approach that includes a heavy reliance on testing, competition, choice, incentives, sanctions, accountability, and data collection. She presented some painful examples demonstrating that solutions such as vouchers, contracting out schools to private companies, and developing charter schools have a mixed record at best. Many of these approaches are already mandated for failing schools by No Child Left Behind. "To date," Ravitch argued, "there is no substantial body of evidence that low-performing schools can be turned around by any of the remedies prescribed in the law" (p. 104).

Examining the practices of charter schools in urban settings, Ravitch (2010) worried that we may be creating a two-tiered system. "Now charters compete for the most successful students in the poorest communities, or they accept all applicants and push the low performers back into the public school system" (p. 146). Daniel Koretz has argued convincingly that policymakers have given too much credence to the accuracy of test scores. In the search for certainty in making high-stakes decisions, they have used or are planning to use test scores for high-stakes decisions about students, principals, teachers, and schools. Koretz sees these decisions as not only unwarranted by the accuracy of the tests but also as likely to generate inflated scores reached by undesirable behaviors ranging from teaching to the test to outright fraud.

Taft argues that the new Common Core State Standards adopted by most of the states will require funding for implementation and for the development of new assessments. There is much of worth in the standards and in the idea that we should have appropriate high expectations for students. When we have high expectations that students have the ability to reach, we motivate them toward achieving their goal; when we hold out expectations for students who do not have the ability to achieve them, we do them a disservice. The authors of the Common Core State Standards acknowledge that there are great differences in students' abilities. Yet they continue to argue that all students, including those with disabilities, should be held to the same standards. Students are not infinitely malleable, and a reform strategy that pretends they are is not likely to deliver on its promise.

OTHER WAYS OF TALKING ABOUT SCHOOLS

There is no question that schools can play a significant role in students' lives. Certainly, schools play an economic role, offering vocational options, providing a route toward a meaningful work life, and allowing students to survive and prosper economically. It is not unreasonable to guess that champions of generous educational funding also have experienced schooling as a path to self-understanding and to an understanding of the world around them. Certainly, Taft acknowledges that schools have other than economic purposes when he speaks of students succeeding as "active well-informed citizens" and when, echoing Jefferson, he acknowledges a democracy's need for "educated citizens capable of making informed decisions and holding government leaders accountable for their performance."

Perhaps Taft and so many other champions of educational reform today have chosen to emphasize schooling's economic aims because they believe such an emphasis to be the most credible with those who make budgetary decisions. In another century, perhaps saving our souls would have worked; in the second half of the 20th century, pointing to the Soviet threat loosened the purse strings; in ours, it is clearly saving our economic hides that carries the day.

Taft's choice of a rationale for investing in education reflects the dominant way we talk about schooling in our society. Our colleges endlessly peddle themselves to students as gateways to a career. No surprise then when the students are impatient with courses they perceive as irrelevant to their careers. The liberal arts professors, awkwardly, market their courses as the best preparation for the realities of the 21st-century global marketplace. John Dewey and W. E. B. Du Bois thought that schools at their best could lead students to better self-understanding and to a better sense of their own place in the world.

A serious education, rather than only preparing students for the 21st-century globalized marketplace might prepare them to question the ways in which that marketplace works and how it might be harnessed and altered to improve the human prospect. We need to shift from the notion of the individual as a marketable commodity to one in which students are defined as persons growing up in communities that are much more than economic engines.

FURTHER READINGS AND RESOURCES

American College Testing (ACT). (2009). *ACT national profile report—Graduating class 2009.* Iowa City, IA: Author.

American College Testing (ACT). (2010). *The condition of college and career readiness.* Iowa City, IA: American College Testing (ACT) College Board.

Baum, S., & Ma, J. (2007). *Education pays: The benefits of higher education for individuals and society.* New York: College Board.

College Board. (2007). *Education pays.* Washington, DC: Author.

Darling-Hammond, L. (2010). *The flat world and education.* New York: Teachers College, Columbia University.

Editorial Projects in Education staff. (Eds.). (2009, June). Diplomas count 2009 (The 4th annual report on graduation rates by *Education Week* and the Editorial Projects in Education Research Center [Special issue]). *Education Week, 28*(34).

Goldin, C., & Katz, L. (2008). *The race between education and technology.* Cambridge, MA: Harvard University Press.

Grove, A. (2010, July 1). How America can create jobs. *Bloomberg BusinessWeek.* Retrieved from http://www.businessweek.com/magazine/content/10_28/b4186048358596.htm

Harlow, C. (2003). *Education and correctional populations* (Bureau of Justice Statistics Special Report by U.S. Department of Justice). Washington, DC: Bureau of Justice Statistics.

Lips, D., Fleming, J., & Watkins, S. (2008). *Does spending more on education improve academic achievement?* Washington, DC: Heritage Foundation.

Lumina Foundation: http://Luminafoundation.org

The National Center for Public Policy and Higher Education. (2008). *Measuring up 2008: The national report card on higher education.* San Jose, CA: Author.

Organisation for Economic Co-operation and Development (OECD). (2009). *Education at a glance 2009.* Paris: Author.

Organisation for Economic Co-operation and Development (OECD). (2010). *PISA 2009 results: What students know and can do—Student performance in reading, mathematics and science* (Vol. 1). Paris: Author.

Ravitch, D. (2010). *The death and life of the great American school system.* New York: Basic Books.

Rothstein, R. (2004). *Class and schools: Using social, economic, and educational reform to close the Black-White achievement gap.* New York: Economic Policy Institute, Teachers College.

Surowiecki, J. (2010, August 16 & 23). Soak the very, very rich. *The New Yorker.* Retrieved August 29, 2011, from http://www.newyorker.com/talk/financial/2010/08/16/100816ta_talk_surowiecki

Will stronger business and corporate investment enhance public K–12 education?

POINT: Shaun C. Yoder and Susan R. Bodary,
Education First Consulting

COUNTERPOINT: Richard W. Van Vleck, *Oak Point Capital, LLC*

OVERVIEW

Follow the money. The infamous Deep Throat expression became popular in the 1970s following the release of *All the President's Men*, a film about the Watergate scandal, but following the money appears to be a timeless mantra. In education, the issue centers on adequately funding for public schools, with many in the education monopoly such as the unions and progressives asserting that there are too few dollars available while those who are outside of the K–12 structure, typically business leaders and some conservatives, suggesting that funds are more than adequate and are being either misspent or inefficiently used.

Complicating the funding picture is the challenge of educating the diverse student demographic that exists in the United States. According to 2007 U.S. Census data, the mean state and local revenue per pupil ranges from $17,552 in Vermont to $6,586 in Utah (Cavanagh, 2010). At first glance, it would appear that Vermont allocates generously the funds needed to ensure a quality education for all its students, while Utah seems to underfund its K–12 schools. In fact, though, according to the Education Law Center, Utah received an "A" for its per-pupil state and local funding allocations ($5,700, 0% poverty to $8,606, 30% poverty) while Vermont received a "C" ($15,802, 0% poverty to $15,344, 30% poverty) (Cavanagh, 2010).

The contentious issue is how communities can ensure that they have "adequate and sufficient" funds for effectively educating *every* pupil. Toward this end, some entrepreneurial educators and community leaders have sought to tap the resources of the corporate sector as a means of supplementing the resources available to schools. Geoffrey Canada and the Harlem Children's Zone initiative are perhaps the poster child exemplar for such an approach. Canada argues that the additional funding is essential for ensuring an extended school day, an 11-month school year and a wide variety of "incentives" to stimulate the interests of students in learning (e.g., trips to the Galapagos). He is seeking to break the cycle of poverty and to do that he supplements what the state of New York provides for both direct services and out-of-class expenses: New York spends approximately $14,000 per pupil (at 30% poverty level). Canada's message is compelling to some since Goldman Sachs pledged $20 million. Nevertheless, the question is whether such support is necessary or warranted. Does spending more money improve schools and student achievement? Further, should such corporate "investment" be encouraged? And will it make a difference?

In this chapter, the two essayists broach the question in different ways. Richard W. Van Vleck (Oak Point Capital) asserts that schools already have more than enough funds. On the other hand, Shaun C. Yoder and Susan R. Bodary (Education First Consulting) posit that business and corporate investment is essential to school improvement.

Van Vleck sees no compelling reason to enhance the funds available for U.S. schools. According to him, additional dollars will not improve student academic achievement and may even exacerbate existing inefficiencies in service delivery. Corporations and businesses have no charter to divert resources to public education and already do their share in terms of supporting education through the taxes they pay, argues Van Vleck, and the real key is to refocus the work of schools so that they emphasize academics, not social agendas; to increase competition by accelerating more "choice" options and proffer fewer mandated and costly union regulated work rules; and to channel more funds toward academic essentials and away from nonacademic programs.

Yoder and Bodary agree that there are significant problems confronting education and educators relative to student achievement and international competitiveness. However, these authors maintain that even with these challenges, a transformation can occur if the right type of investments are made and the appropriate types of engagement occur between businesses, corporations, and the education sector. With a real convergence of education in business sectors, Yoder and Bodary believe that the leadership position of the United States can be reestablished in a global economy.

In reading this chapter, consider the following questions: Spending for education has significantly increased over the past 40 years (150% in real terms), and if it is true that student achievement has remained stable (in areas such as mathematics and reading) during that time period, then does it really make sense to argue for more corporate investment in education? If student achievement has not improved despite more financial support from traditional sources, how should corporate leaders be involved to ensure that their investment does make a difference?

Thomas J. Lasley, II
University of Dayton

POINT: Shaun C. Yoder and Susan R. Bodary
Education First Consulting

Simply put, the answer to the question, Will stronger business and corporate investment enhance public K–12 education? is yes. To understand why, one must realize that *business and corporate investment in education* transcends mere financial support for programs or schools. In its most complete and dynamic form, it includes engagement through targeted corporate commitments of capital, staff, talent, and expertise strategically designed to enhance and accelerate America's public K–12 education system.

This holistic public-private partnership, or the convergence of education and business, is the key to strengthening American public education while preparing students for college and career in relevant ways. At least three significant benefits result from such a partnership: (1) systemic K–12 education policy reforms rooted in world-class research; (2) enhanced use of data, promoting student success; (3) and an aligned relationship between business and public K–12 education.

Analysis of each of these benefits presents a clear case as to why businesses and corporations should invest and engage in public K–12 education. However, before these benefits can be analyzed, it is necessary to understand the landscape of public education in the United States today and the challenges necessitating business and corporate investment and engagement.

CHALLENGES NECESSITATING BUSINESS INVESTMENT AND ENGAGEMENT

The United States once set the pace for public education across the world. Yet today, its education system faces three primary challenges: (1) fierce international competition, (2) stagnant student performance on national assessments and a persistent achievement gap, (3) and a looming fiscal tsunami.

Fierce International Competition

Similarly, more than 25 years ago, elected officials and policymakers feared that the United States was losing its position as the world's pacesetter, in part because of a growing recognition of the nation's mediocre education system and the rapid emergence of international competition from Japan (with its efficient production of automobiles) and Germany (with its quality production of machine tools). Hence, in 1983, the National Commission on Excellence in Education issued its report, *A Nation at Risk: The Imperative for Education Reform.* Created by T. H. Bell, the second U.S. secretary of education, appointed by President Ronald Reagan, the Commission brought forth five recommendations aimed at

1. strengthening high school graduation requirements,

2. clarifying standards and expectations for what students should know and be able to do,

3. expanding the school day and year,

4. enhancing teacher preparation, and

5. calling for citizens across the nation to "hold educators and elected officials responsible for providing the leadership necessary to achieve these reforms . . . and the fiscal support and stability required to bring about the reforms" (U.S. Department of Education, 1983, *A Nation at Risk*).

Not much has changed since 1983. Our nation's educational leadership position may even be in greater peril. Consider the following:

- In 2009, U.S. high school students ranked 30th of 65 countries and partner jurisdictions on the Organisation for Economic Co-operation and Development's (OECD) Programme for International Student Assessment (PISA) in mathematics, with an average score of 487, or 9 points below the OECD average.

- That same year, U.S. high school students ranked 20th of 65 countries and partner jurisdictions on the OECD's PISA in science, with an average score of 502, or 1 point above the OECD average.

- Interestingly, in 2006, nearly all of China's high school students studied calculus, compared to 13% of American students (Asia Society).

Figures 13.1 and 13.2 show 15-year-old student performance on the 2009 PISA mathematics and science literacy assessments across the top 40 participating countries or jurisdictions.

PISA mathematics and science literacy assessments can be used as proxies to determine how well the United States is preparing its students for success in college and career as measured against other countries. The results demonstrate that the foreign competition is exceeding our ability to prepare students

Figures 13.1 (left) and 13.2 (right)

15-year-old student performance on the 2009 PISA mathematics and science literacy assessments across the top 40 participating countries or jurisdictions

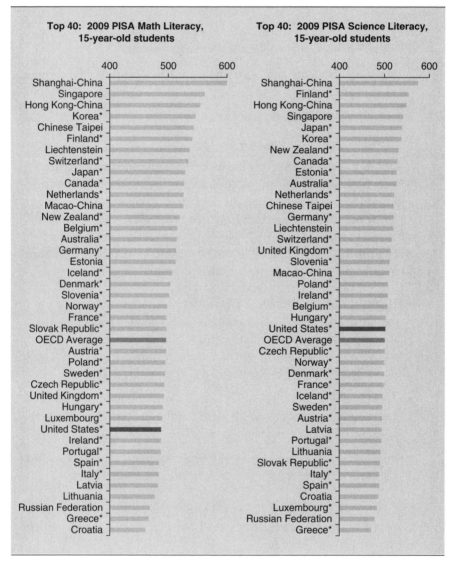

Source: OECD PISA 2009 Database. PISA 2009 Results: OECD 2010, Table I.A.; Comparing countries' and economies' performance.

* = OECD countries.

who are capable of filling high-tech, high-skill jobs. It is no surprise that international workforce trends reflect this unfortunate reality. In 2007, research and development R&D growth plans for 186 companies indicated that China and India would account for 31% of global R&D staff, up from 19% in 2004 (Hamilton & European Institute for Business Administration [INSEAD], 2006). This has resulted in the flight of high-tech jobs and research opportunities from the United States to other more talent-abundant countries.

More alarming still, many nations that outperformed the United States on PISA 2009 had lower per-pupil spending rates than the United States, raising serious questions about the efficiency and efficacy of America's public education system. Figure 13.3 shows that total expenditure by educational institutions per student from age 6 to 15 was highest in Luxembourg, the United States, Switzerland, and Norway. When examined in conjunction with Figures 13.1 and 13.2, it also indicates that at least 14 OECD countries spent less than the United States, but eclipsed U.S. performance in PISA mathematics and science. At least six of those countries spent less than the OECD average, including Germany, Korea, New Zealand, Hungary, Estonia, and Poland, and still exceeded U.S. performance (OECD PISA 2009 Database. PISA 2009 Results: OECD 2010, Table I.A. and PISA 2009 Results: What Makes a School Successful? – Volume IV; Table IV.3.21b, Cumulative expenditure by educational institutions: system level).

Stagnant Student Performance, a Changing Student Body, and an Achievement Gap

The National Assessment of Educational Progress (NAEP) reveals stagnant student performance across multiple measures over a 40-year period. Figures 13.4 and 13.5 offer a closer look at NAEP mathematics and reading assessments of 9-year-olds, showing little fluctuation in student performance and sluggish gains that never rise above the 250-point threshold.

Additionally, the characteristics of America's student body are rapidly changing, presenting new challenges to the system. Consider the following factors, which have bearing on student readiness and, ultimately, public K–12 education's ability to produce results (U.S. Department of Education, Institute of Education Sciences [IES], National Center for Education Statistics [NCES], 2008, "The Condition of Education 2008"):

- The percentage of school-age children living in families below the poverty threshold increased from 15% in 1979 to 21% in 1995; it then decreased to 16% in 2002.

Figure 13.3

Cumulative expenditure by educational institutions per student aged 6 to 15 (for 2007 in equivalent USD)

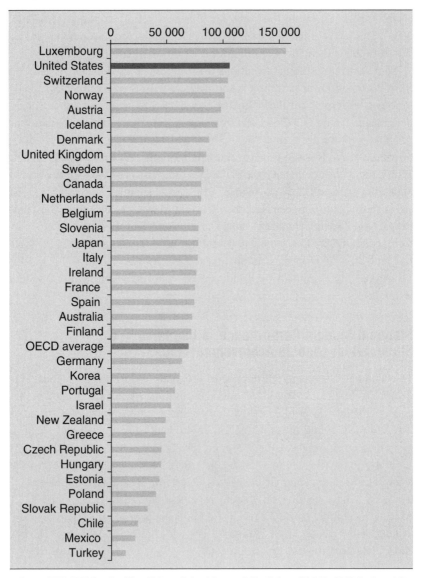

Source: PISA 2009 Results: What Makes a School Successful? – Volume IV; Table IV.3.21b, Cumulative expenditure by educational institutions: system level.

Figure 13.4

National Assessment of Education Progress (NAEP) reading and math performance

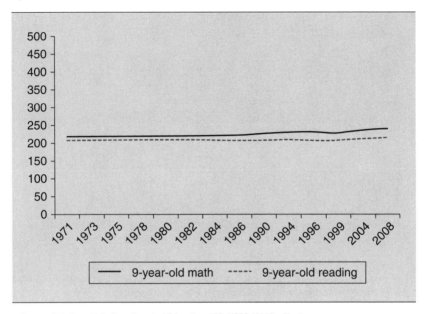

Source: Data from U.S. Department of Education, IES, NCES (2010a, May).

- The percentage of school-age children living in two-parent households decreased from 75% in 1979 to 67% in 2006.

- Another 23% of children lived with only their mother and 5% were in father-only households in 2006.

Figure 13.6 shows the racial and ethnic enrollment changes that have occurred since 1988. From 1988 to 2008, the number of White students in the nation's public schools decreased from 28.0 million to 26.7 million students, representing a decrease in enrollment from 68% to 55%. During that same time period, Hispanic enrollment increased from 4.5 million to 10.4 million students, doubling the percentage of Hispanics enrolled in elementary and secondary schools from 11% to 22%. The total number of Black students also increased from 6.8 million to 7.5 million, but their share of enrollment decreased from 17% to 16%. Hispanic enrollment surpassed Black enrollment for the first time

Figure 13.5

A closer look: NAEP reading and math performance

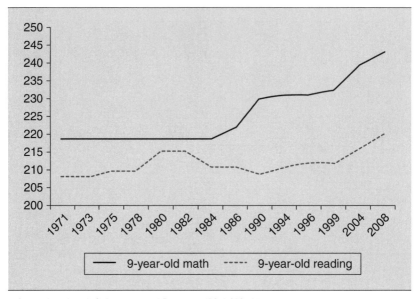

Source: Data from U.S. Department of Education, IES, NCES (2010a, May).

in 2002 and has remained higher in each year through 2008. While not included in Figure 13.6, in 2008, the combined enrollment of Asians, Pacific Islanders, American Indians/Alaska Natives, and students of two or more races made up about 7.4% of all students in public schools (U.S. Department of Education, IES, NCES, 2010a, "The Condition of Education 2010").

Finally, state and national student assessments expose America's battle with a persistent achievement gap, separating the lowest performing student subgroups from the highest performing student subgroups. Figure 13.7 shows 9-year-old student performance in reading, disaggregated by the three largest student racial and ethnic groups—White, Black, and Hispanic. It uncovers significant achievement gaps that have existed for nearly 40 years. Since 1999, reading performance in every student group increased. As noted in Table 13.1, year 2008 represents the peak of performance for all student groups in reading. Despite these gains, however, significant achievement gaps still persist: 21 points separate the performance of White students from Hispanic students and 24 points separate the performance of White students from Black students.

Figure 13.6

Racial and ethnic enrollment in public schools (in millions)

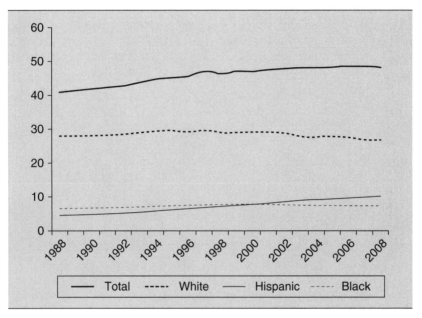

Source: Data from U.S. Department of Education and IES National Center for Education Statistics (2010a, May, Table A-4-1).

A Looming Fiscal Tsunami

Over the past 45 years, government spending on public education has been increasing at a rate that cannot likely be sustained in the current economic climate. Today's public elementary and secondary schools operate through a mixture of state, local, and federal funding (U.S. Department of Education, IES, NCES, 2008). Since the 1970s, the state and local share of funding has been roughly split at 45%. The federal share has been approximately 10%. From 1961 to 2006, public K–12 per-pupil education expenditures have nearly quadrupled (in constant 2007–2008 dollars), as depicted in Figure 13.8. From 1990 to 2006, per-pupil expenditures increased from $7,749 in 1990 to $10,041 in 2006, a jump of nearly 30% over 16 years. Figure 13.8 demonstrates that public schools' per-pupil real-dollar revenues have increased almost every year over the past 45 years. These dollars kept coming even when the economy, as measured by gross domestic product (GDP), turned downward (Hess & Osberg, 2010).

Figure 13.7

National Assessment of Education Progress (NAEP) 9-year-old reading performance

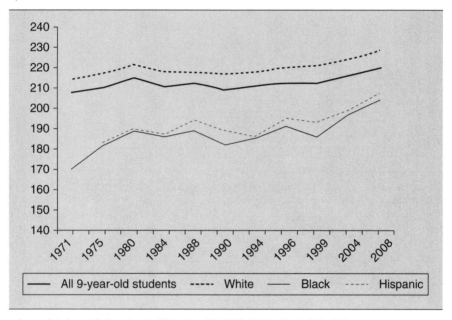

Source: Data from U.S. Department of Education, IES, NCES (2009a, March, Table 116).

In their chapter in *Stretching the School Dollar* (2010), James Guthrie and Arthur Peng suggested that America's public schools face a "forthcoming fiscal tsunami." They noted that even when controlled for inflation, school spending has been increasing substantially for a century. "The number of school employees relative to the number of students has followed a similar trajectory over the past five decades" (p. 19), and "a unique set of constitutional, structural, financial, and political arrangements has, up to now, ensured that school systems and professional educators are buffered from revenue losses when the economy declines" (p. 20). "Such was the past" (p. 20), wrote the authors who suggested this funding trend will slow, if not fully reverse itself, in the midst of the Great Recession and state budgets that struggle to keep the lights on at the state house.

Table 13.1

National Assessment of Education Progress (NAEP) 9-year-old reading performance

	1990	1994	1996	1999	2004	2008
White	217	218	220	221	224	228
Black	182	185	191	186	197	204
Hispanic	189	186	195	193	199	207

Source: Data from U.S. Department of Education, IES, NCES (2009a, March, Table 116).

Figure 13.8

U.S. per-pupil spending on public primary and secondary education

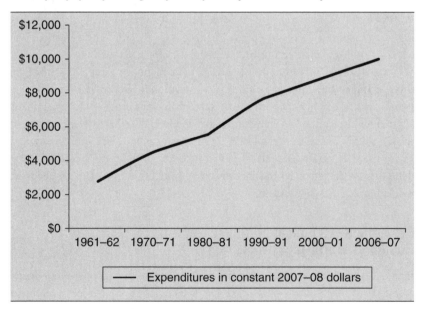

Source: Data from U.S. Department of Education, National Center for Education Statistics. (2011). *Digest of education statistics, 2010* (NCES 2011-015), Table 190.

THE NECESSITY OF A PUBLIC–PRIVATE PARTNERSHIP

With growing international competition, stagnating student performance, a persistent achievement gap, and a pending fiscal crisis, it is clear that something must be done to transform America's public school system. A public-private partnership can prove to be the linchpin to such transformation. The problems facing public K–12 education can be solved only by innovative, transformative, and entrepreneurial steps—those that are second nature to businesses and corporations and require their leadership, investment, and engagement. The convergence of education and business will turn America's public education system around and drive it back to global dominance.

THE BENEFITS OF BUSINESS AND CORPORATE INVESTMENT

Public-private partnerships resulting from generous corporate contributions to enhance and transform public K–12 education have been well publicized in recent years. For example, in 2008, AT&T launched its 4-year, $100 million Aspire program to focus on the high school dropout crisis. In 2009, Time Warner Cable launched its 5-year, $100 million Connect a Million Minds initiative to inspire students to pursue learning opportunities and careers in science, technology, engineering, and mathematics (STEM).

Such business investment and engagement in public education produces three primary benefits: systemic K–12 education policy reforms rooted in world-class research; enhanced use of data, promoting student success; and an aligned relationship between business and public K–12 education. Any of these three benefits alone would make a strong case for business investment and engagement in public education. When taken together, these benefits clearly demonstrate that stronger business and corporate investment and engagement will enhance public education.

Systemic K–12 Education Policy Reforms Rooted in World-Class Research

In April 2009, McKinsey & Company, a global strategic and operational consulting firm, released a report titled *The Economic Impact of the Achievement Gap in America's Schools*. Funded and performed independently by McKinsey, the report injected a sense of urgency into a problem that had grown stale. The report discussed the issue in a new way, quantifying the economic toll of the nation's achievement gap. Essentially, it concluded that the gap in academic achievement between children in the United States and their counterparts in other countries cost the U.S. economy as much as $2.3 trillion in economic output in 2008.

The report also explained that if our nation's long-standing achievement gap between Black and Hispanic student performance and White student performance had been closed in 2008, GDP would have been as much as $525 billion higher, or 2% to 4% of GDP. Likewise, closing the performance gap between low income students and the remainder of the student population would have increased GDP in 2008 by as much as $700 billion, or 3% to 5% of GDP. These gaps, noted McKinsey, underline the staggering economic and social cost of underused human talent.

McKinsey's report did more than just energize elected officials, policymakers, and educators to ramp up efforts to close the achievement gap at all levels. It also articulated why businesses and corporations should invest in public education. What's more, the report brought external thinking and expert analysis into a community long known to be inward looking.

McKinsey is but one example of how corporate investment in public education can produce world-class research that in turn spurs systemic K–12 education policy reform. The business community as a whole is deeply invested in education policy, providing external political support for innovative, transformative, and entrepreneurial education policies. For example, the Business Roundtable (BR) has been engaged in strengthening education policy for decades.

BR, as noted on its website, is an association of CEOs of leading U.S. companies that employ nearly 12 million people and have revenues exceeding $6 trillion a year. It was established in 1972 with the belief that "in a pluralistic society, businesses should plan an active and effective role in the formation of public policy."

BR has been especially active in the realm of education policy. BR's Education, Innovation and Workforce Competitiveness initiative has produced powerful education policy leadership, leading the way on standards-based reform efforts and placing STEM education front-and-center in the nation's education policy agenda. In its latest "Roadmap for Growth" document, BR calls for a partnership between the nation's business community, the White House, and Congress and issues the following recommendations to the federal government:

- Improve mathematics and science education by investing in basic research in the physical sciences and engineering and renewing and funding the America Competes Act

- Improve K–12 education by modernizing and strengthening the Elementary and Secondary Education Act, including internationally benchmarked standards and assessments, better measures of performance for teachers and administrators, and a greater focus on STEM

- Expand incentives both for innovation and for scaling up proven programs in K–12 education such as Race to the Top, Teacher Incentive Funds, and Investing in Innovation and expansion of high quality charter schools

- Promote a Race to the Top competition for 2- and 4-year colleges that focuses on completion rates and attainment of credentials valued by employers

Through the examples of McKinsey & Company and BR, it is clear that one of the primary benefits of corporate investment and engagement in public education is world-class research that triggers systemic policy reform. The analytics, skills, and thought-leadership that the business community brings to bear on education policy are valuable and ultimately transformative.

Enhanced Use of Data, Promoting Student Success

In 2005, Nationwide Insurance, America's sixth largest auto and homeowner insurer, headquartered in Columbus, Ohio, formed a partnership with Columbus City Schools. In conversations with Superintendent Gene Harris, Nationwide's then-CEO Jerry Jurgensen, learned that the district was inundated with data from the state of Ohio, but it did not have the internal expertise to analyze, interpret, and apply the data. To address this issue, Jurgensen loaned a group of Nationwide information technology (IT) professionals to Columbus City Schools to distill the data and present it to educators in a one-page format. The one-page distillation presented student feeder patterns for specific school buildings in the district. Educators in the building used the information to identify incoming student-learning deficits and surpluses and to target support services where needed.

Five years and nearly $4 million later, the one-page data distillation project for nine schools has evolved into the All-School Improvement Plan (ASIP) that enables the use of academic achievement data at the district, school, and teacher levels. These data are organized to facilitate the identification of priority areas for improvement, especially for those schools in turnaround status [*Fifth to First: Ohio's Race to the Top*, Section (C)(3): Using Data to Improve Instruction, Narrative (C)(3), page C3-2]. The system enables educators to identify their high priority challenges and to select specific evidence-based strategies to address each challenge. Educators then develop an implementation plan for the strategies and track the implementation of the plans. The process is complete when new achievement scores populate the system and educators are able to see if their strategies resulted in improved academic performance.

Nationwide's commitment to Columbus City schools is one example of how business is partnering effectively with public education to support the smarter use of data. At the national level, the Bill & Melinda Gates Foundation is working with the National Student Clearinghouse on a new pilot program to track postsecondary outcomes of high school students in three states.

While not a business or corporation, the Bill & Melinda Gates Foundation was founded in the late 1990s by Microsoft founder Bill Gates and funded from profits of the Microsoft Corporation, making it a conduit for business and corporate investments. This foundation holds education as one of its key focus areas and in 2009 invested more than $373 million in strategic education initiatives.

One of those strategic education initiatives is the National Student Clearinghouse Pilot Project. The Clearinghouse seeks to link K–12 and post-secondary data in a set of high quality, actionable reports that can be used by schools, districts, and states to improve the college readiness and success of their students. Ultimately, the Clearinghouse will help school districts accurately gauge the college success of their graduates by answering a series of key questions:

- How many high school graduates enroll in college?

- Do they persist and graduate from college?

- How long does it take them to earn a degree?

- Which colleges do they most commonly attend?

- Did any students go on to college who started 9th grade in the school district but did not graduate?

Such questions provide school districts with feedback and insight necessary to evaluate and calibrate programs to ensure maximum student success.

Both Nationwide and the Bill & Melinda Gates Foundation are providing a needed service for school districts lacking the tools and expertise to evaluate and analyze student data and use them to drive instruction and supports. This is yet another benefit of corporate investment that systemically improves public K–12 education.

An Aligned Relationship Between Business and Public K–12 Education

In July 2008, GE Lighting signed a lease agreement with the Cleveland Metropolitan School District to host the 10th grade class of MC²STEM High School at GE Lighting's Nela Park. The vision for the school—located on GE Lighting's corporate campus—is to expose high school students to "innovation, imagination and the corporate world," preparing future engineers and scientists. This is the first known high school in the nation to be integrated into an industrial campus (McClellan & Timan, 2010).

To help launch the school, GE Lighting committed nearly $500,000 from 2008 to 2010. The year-round school operates in four 10-week intervals, with three weeklong breaks at the end of each period. The school's curriculum is project based and focuses specifically on energy and sustainability. There are no admission requirements and student credit is based on mastery, not seat time. The approach is aligned not only with the needs of the 21st century, but also it is fully informed by the business world, significantly ratcheting up the relevance factor for students.

Perhaps the most valuable attribute of the school is the GE volunteers, who have contributed over 5,500 hours to the students over the past 2 years. These volunteers have been recognized both internally and externally for the service they performed for MC²STEM High School.

GE Lighting's partnership with Cleveland Metropolitan is a national exemplar. In addition to working closely with students at MC²STEM High School, GE Volunteers also devote a great deal of time and effort to working with students throughout the school district. They serve as tutors, mentors, and educators in elementary and high schools, create "science projects in a box" for elementary school students, and host a "Youth Empowerment Summit" to help students identify their future goals and to learn how to pursue those goals.

GE Lighting is not the only business engaging in STEM education. Businesses across the nation are currently partnering with K–12 education, institutions of higher education, and philanthropy to build, connect, or enhance STEM schools or programs through emerging networks. In Ohio, Battelle and Procter & Gamble are engaged in the Ohio STEM Learning Network (OSLN). In New York, Time Warner has instituted the Connect a Million Minds project, and in Massachusetts, Raytheon is involved with the STEM model project. These initiatives aim to share best practices and design elements across the connected schools and programs to help improve public schools. Likewise, the programs and initiatives align students' education with the needs of the modern economy.

The above examples demonstrate the third primary benefit of business investment and engagement in public education: alignment of the education of the nation's students with the needs of the business community. Such alignment produces a workforce prepared to meet the needs of the modern economy, making public education significantly more valuable and relevant to its students.

CONCLUSION

America's public K–12 education system faces serious challenges and is in need of transformation. Such a transformation requires the investment and engagement of committed businesses and corporations. The three primary benefits discussed above demonstrate the positive impact the private sector can have on public education in the United States. And this is just the beginning. The true convergence of education and business, through lasting public-private partnerships, can restore America's leadership position in the global economy.

COUNTERPOINT: Richard W. Van Vleck
Oak Point Capital, LLC

An affirmative answer to the question, Will stronger business and corporate investment enhance public K–12 education? has at its foundation five premises:

1. That public K–12 schools need more funding

2. That more funding will drive improvements in student academic achievement

3. That funding from businesses and corporations would be large enough to make a difference in the funding of public K–12 schools

4. That an attributable financial return would accrue to businesses and corporations, providing the incentive to invest in public K–12 education

5. That businesses and corporations have an obligation, or at least a legitimate role, in providing funds for public K–12 education

The purpose of this essay is to refute these premises and assert that businesses and corporations should not provide funding for public K–12 education.

DO PUBLIC K–12 SCHOOLS NEED MORE FUNDING?

Funding for public K–12 schools in the United States is at an all-time high and is rising rapidly. From 1970 to 2007, cumulative U.S. funding for public K–12 education was $9.1 trillion, growing at a compound annual rate of 7.1%, according to the U.S. Department of Education's Institute of Education Sciences (IES), National Center for Education Statistics, or NCES (2009b, Table 26). In 2007–2008, combined public K–12 funding at federal, state, and local levels totaled $583 billion. This represents an increase since 1997–1998 of 75%, adding $249 billion to public K–12 funding in just 10 years, doubling the rate of inflation. Appropriations for the U.S. Department of Education jumped from $6.9 billion in 1980 to $37.9 billion in 2008, growing at a compound annual rate of 6.3% (U.S. Department of Education, n.d.).

These rapid increases are not being driven by growing public K–12 student enrollment but by more spending per student. Public K–12 enrollment grew from 47.2 million in 1997 to 48.6 million in 2007 (U.S. Census Bureau, n.d.), a compound annual rate of 0.3%, one twentieth of the rate of funding growth in the same period. The driver of the funding growth is the rapid increase in average national expenditure per pupil, which grew from $6,189 in 1997 to $9,154 in 2005–2006 (U.S. Department of Education, IES, NCES, *Digest of Education Statistics 2008* [2009a], Table 181), a compound annual rate of 5.0%, again almost doubling the inflation rate.

The United States spends more per pupil on secondary education than all of the 30 nations in the Organisation for Economic Co-operation and Development (OECD), except Luxembourg, Switzerland, and Norway. In the most recent year reported, 2006, U.S. per-pupil secondary education spending was 35% above the OECD average and 27% above the average of the 10 largest and most diverse OECD countries (OECD, 2009, *Education at a Glance 2009*, Table B1.1a). Further, as a percentage of gross domestic product (GDP), the United States spends more than all OECD nations but Denmark, Korea, New Zealand, the United Kingdom, and Switzerland, and the United States spends 18% more than the OECD average (OECD, 2009, Table B2.1).

While it could be argued that more government funding should be provided, it cannot be concluded that U.S. public K–12 education is underfunded. By measures of absolute dollars spent, the growth of dollar spending, the growth of per-pupil spending, per-pupil spending compared to other advanced economies, and spending as a percentage of GDP compared to other advanced economies, the United States fully funds public K–12 education and is on a course to spend even more.

WILL MORE FUNDING DRIVE IMPROVEMENTS IN STUDENT ACADEMIC ACHIEVEMENT?

Despite the dramatic funding increases for U.S. public K–12 education in the last 40 years, there has been almost no measurable improvement in student academic achievement.

The National Assessment of Educational Progress, the only nationally representative assessment of student academic achievement, has been measuring student performance continuously since the 1970s. It shows little to no improvement in achievement by 12th graders in foundational academic subjects, as shown in Table 13.2.

The College Board provides long-term trends in college readiness, as measured by Scholastic Aptitude Test (SAT) scores. Corrected for the 1995 recentering of the SAT scale, critical reading achievement appears to have declined since 1972, while mathematics shows little improvement, and writing scores are basically unchanged (see Table 13.3).

American College Testing (ACT) Inc. provides trends in college readiness, as measured by ACT scores. From 1996 to 2009, composite scores are unchanged, and subject matter scores show slight improvements for mathematics and English but similarly slight declines for reading and science, as shown in Table 13.4.

Table 13.2

Average scale score change over time

Subject	Time Period	Average Scale Score Change
Reading	1971 to 2008	From 285 to 286
Mathematics	1978 to 2008	From 300 to 306
Science	1996 to 2005	From 149 to 146
Writing	1998 to 2007	From 148 to 152

Source: U.S. Department of Education, IES, NCES (2011).

Table 13.3

Mean SAT score change over time

Subject	Time Period	Mean SAT Score Change
Critical Reading	1972 to 2009	From 530 to 501
Mathematics	1972 to 2009	From 509 to 515
Writing	2006 to 2009	From 497 to 492

Source: Data from the College Board (n.d., Table 2).

Table 13.4

Average ACT score change over time

Subject	Time Period	Average ACT Score Change
Reading	1996 to 2009	From 22.5 to 22.3
Mathematics	1996 to 2009	From 21.5 to 21.9
English	1996 to 2009	From 21.5 to 21.7
Science	1996 to 2009	From 22.1 to 21.7
Composite	1996 to 2009	From 22.0 to 22.0

Source: Data from ACT, Inc. (2000, Summary); ACT, Inc. (2009, Table 1.4).

Average U.S. public secondary school freshman graduation rates have remained unchanged for the last 17 years, with the 1990–1991 graduation rate at 73.7% and the 2006–2007 graduation rate at 73.9% (U.S. Department of Education, IES, NCES, *Digest of Education Statistics 2009,* Table 105, 2010b).

International comparisons of U.S. student academic achievement show a similar pattern of little progress. The OECD's Program for International Student Assessment (PISA) is the world's most comprehensive test of student achievement; it measures 15-year-old student academic performance every 3 years in OECD countries and other countries. Table 13.5 shows that compared to other OECD countries, U.S. academic achievement is poor and deteriorating.

Table 13.5

Changes in PISA test scores over time

	2000		2003		2006	
	U.S. Rank	**Score**	**U.S. Rank**	**Score**	**U.S. Rank**	**Score**
Reading Literacy	15 of 27	504*	15 of 29	495*	No Test	No Test
Mathematics Literacy	18 of 27	493*	24 of 29	483**	25 of 30	474**
Science Literacy	14 of 27	499*	19 of 29	491**	21 of 30	489**

Source: Data from Organisation for Economic Co-operation and Development (OECD) Programme for International Student Assessment (PISA) (2000, 2003, 2007a, 2007b, & 2007c).

*Difference from OECD average not statistically significant. ** OECD average wtih statistical significance.

The International Association for the Evaluation of Educational Achievement's Trends in International Mathematics and Science Study (TIMSS) is an assessment of math and science achievement of students in grades 4 and 8 in 36 countries around the world conducted every 4 years. U.S. 8th grade student achievement is shown to be near the bottom and with relatively little change, compared to 15 of the most advanced nations (see Table 13.6).

The leading independent measurements of U.S. public K–12 academic performance and the leading comparisons of international public K–12 academic performance show that U.S. absolute and relative performance has been stagnant. This lack of U.S. absolute and relative performance improvement has happened despite 40 years of aggressive funding increases that have placed U.S. public K–12 education funding among the highest in the world.

It must be concluded that increased funding is not a driver of academic performance improvement and that sustaining policies that continue to add funding to U.S. public K–12 schools is simply unjustifiable, if the purpose is to improve student academic achievement.

WOULD FUNDING FROM BUSINESSES AND CORPORATIONS BE LARGE ENOUGH TO MAKE A DIFFERENCE?

Leaving aside for the moment whether businesses and corporations should provide funding for public K–12 education, it is useful to examine whether U.S. businesses and corporations could provide enough additional funds to make a difference in public K–12 academic achievement.

Table 13.6

Changes in rank and score on Trends in International Mathematics and Science Study (TIMSS), 1995–2007

	1995		1999		2003		2007	
	U.S. Rank	Score	U.S. Rank	Score	U.S. Rank	Score	U.S. Rank	Score
Mathematics	9 of 15	492	12 of 15	502	10 of 15	504	9 of 15	508
Science	7 of 8	513	11 of 15	515	10 of 15	527	11 of 15	520

Source: Data from International Association for the Evaluation of Educational Achievement (2009).

The source of such funding would be corporate profits. During the period from 2000 to 2009, average total annual profits for Fortune 500 companies were $414 billion (Tully, 2007, 2009, 2010). Spending a proportion of this total to augment public K–12 funding requires diverting the funds from growth-driving corporate investment and from distribution to shareholders. This sets a practical limit on the amount that corporations could provide for public schools due to intense pressures to drive corporate growth and to reward shareholders with dividends.

Assuming that the practical limit is 10% of corporate profit and that every firm in the Fortune 500 was willing to divert this much to public K–12 schools, it would add $41 billion per year to public education funding—clearly a substantial amount. But compared to the $583 billion provided to public education from government sources in 2007–2008, corporations would be increasing total funding by only 7.6%. Given consistent findings that additional funding does not improve public K–12 academic performance, one could infer that this small incremental increase would not drive meaningful increases in U.S. educational achievement.

Although the Fortune 500 companies' providing 10% of their profits to fund public K–12 education would likely not have a material impact on U.S. educational achievement, it would have a hugely adverse impact on corporate shareholders.

Shareholder wealth is determined by the number of shares that are owned and the price of the shares, with share price being driven by corporate earnings. Share prices have historically averaged 16.4 times corporate earnings (The Big Picture, 2005), although the range swings widely at any point in time. This means that on average, an additional dollar of corporate earnings per share translates into $16.40 of additional share price, at the historical average. Conversely, if corporate earnings fall by a dollar, it translates into a share price drop of $16.40. Because of this price-earnings multiplier effect, corporate shareholders are extremely sensitive to corporate earnings per share.

Were the Fortune 500 companies to divert $41 billion, or 10% of their earnings, to fund public K–12 education, the earnings available to shareholders would fall commensurately by $41 billion. This would cause the prices of Fortune 500 shares to fall. Due to the price-earnings multiplier, the value of all of the Fortune 500 companies' shares would fall by 16.4 times the $41 billion, or $679 billion, due to the lower share prices. It is inconceivable that shareholders would tolerate such a reduction in their personal wealth, especially for the purpose of adding to the fully funded U.S. public K–12 education system with little chance of improved academic performance from their additional funding.

WOULD AN ATTRIBUTABLE FINANCIAL RETURN ACCRUE TO BUSINESSES AND CORPORATIONS, PROVIDING THE INCENTIVE TO INVEST IN PUBLIC K–12 EDUCATION?

Business is an economic activity to increase the wealth of its owners by investing funds with the prospect of generating future financial returns commensurate with the risks undertaken. To put funds at risk, shareholders require corporate investments to have direct and quantifiable financial returns over a specified time period and at a level that adequately compensates them for the uncertainties associated with the amount and the timing of the returns. A proposed allocation of corporate funds that cannot satisfy these criteria does not provide the incentive required to allocate the funds and does not qualify as an investment.

Allocating corporate funds to public K–12 education contradicts the economic tenets of corporate purpose. It is difficult to find any mechanism through which corporate spending to improve the academic achievement of public school graduates would drive any directly measurable incremental financial returns to a corporation.

Such returns would have to be in the form of measurable increased revenues, reduced expenses, or reduced investment. It is hard to imagine how corporate funding for public K–12 schools would drive any amount of measurable, incremental corporate sales and revenues in a predictable time frame. The only expense reductions that could be imagined would be reducing corporate expenses for employee training or hiring. However, establishing a direct link between public school funding and the amount of reduced training or hiring expense is remote. Further, the dollar reduction of corporate training or hiring expense would have to be many times greater than the dollar amount spent for public education for it to satisfy the economic return criteria to qualify as an investment—again, a very difficult linkage to imagine. Funding public education as a way to reduce some form of corporate investment is even more difficult to envision. Moreover, all of these problems identifying the amount of direct financial benefits are compounded by the additional difficulty of determining the timing of when such economic benefits would occur. Due to these problems, the allocation of corporate funds to public K–12 schools does not constitute an investment.

Privately owned businesses are not under the stricter financial constraints of publicly traded corporations. Were the owner of a privately held business to allocate corporate funds to public K–12 education, it would be a gift or a charity, not an investment for the reasons described above. The incentives for such funding would fall along the lines of community leadership or "giving back," of which both have the feel of self-aggrandizement for the owner as the core incentive.

The efficacy of using increased funding to improve student achievement is shown to be poor. Further, the efficiency of providing funding to public K–12 education is also poor, given that only 52% of public K–12 expenditures are for instructional purposes, which is now lower than it was in 1990 (U.S. Department of Education, IES, NCES, 2009b, Table 174). Even for privately held businesses, the rationale to divert corporate funds to public K–12 education is extremely weak.

The inability to identify any directly attributable economic benefits to corporate shareholders or owners of privately held businesses from an allocation of funds to public K–12 education means that such funding fails to qualify as an investment and cuts against the economic purpose of business. This lack of economic return provides no incentive for corporations or businesses to allocate funds for this purpose.

DO BUSINESSES AND CORPORATIONS HAVE AN OBLIGATION, OR AT LEAST A LEGITIMATE ROLE, IN PROVIDING FUNDS FOR PUBLIC K–12 EDUCATION?

Although businesses and corporations have a clear interest in improved U.S. public K–12 educational achievement, they have no role in producing it. Milton Friedman, the Nobel Prize–winning economist, perhaps said it best: "The social responsibility of business is to increase its profits" (1970). By this, he meant that the purpose of businesses, especially public corporations, is to "make as much money as possible [for their shareholders] while conforming to the basic rules of the society, both those embodied in law and those embodied in ethical custom." This mission obligates businesses and corporations to restrict their interests and activities to producing economic results that benefit the interests of their shareholders. Diverting corporate funds to any purposes other than current or future shareholder returns is to be essentially confiscating money from the owners. This fully applies to providing corporate funds to public K–12 education.

If some shareholders feel that additional funds should be provided to public education, then they can sell their shares in the corporation and donate the proceeds as the appropriate way to provide the additional funding they want. Since some or even many shareholders are likely not interested in providing additional funding to public education, a corporation that provides direct funding for this purpose is acting in conflict with the interests of those shareholders, and such actions should not be undertaken.

Friedman acknowledges that the shareholder-wealth-generation purposes of corporations must comply with the law and with ethical customs. One of the critical legal obligations that corporations fulfill is to pay taxes. During the period from 2000 to 2009, U.S. corporate income taxes totaled $3.1 trillion (U.S. Department of Commerce, Bureau of Economic Analysis, n.d., Table 1.10). The United States has the highest federal corporate income tax rate among the 30 OECD countries, at 35%. Combined with top state corporate income tax rates, the United States has the highest overall corporate tax structure, with government taking up to 41.5% of corporate income (Tax Foundation, 2009). Thus, through corporate income tax payments at federal and state levels, U.S. corporations and businesses are providing and will continue to provide funding to the public K–12 education system at a rate higher than their OECD corporate competitors. By fulfilling their tax obligations, corporations have no further obligation or role in providing funding for public K–12 education.

CONCLUSION

U.S. public K–12 schools are fully funded, and further funding can be expected not to improve student achievement, based on decades of empirical evidence. Funding from businesses and public corporations would constitute charitable giving, not investment, and would not be large enough to materially change U.S. public K–12 academic performance. Through the highest corporate income taxes in the world, corporations and businesses already fully satisfy any role that could be expected of them to help pay for public K–12 schools. Therefore, U.S. corporations and businesses should not provide additional funds to enhance public K–12 education.

Enhancing U.S. public K–12 education requires policies other than seeking additional funding from corporations and businesses. Policy alternatives that should be considered include

- refocusing public K–12 schools' mission to building demonstrable skills in foundational academic subjects and doing less social work,

- channeling public K–12 school funds into the classroom and away from noninstructional bureaucracies and nonacademic programs,

- eliminating union-driven work rules, which block the ability of state and local governments and boards of education from making the changes needed to improve the efficacy and efficiency of principals and teachers in K–12 public education, and

- accelerating the emergence of more alternatives to near-monopoly government K–12 schools so that the cost-reducing and quality-increasing dynamics of American competition can be realized.

FURTHER READINGS AND RESOURCES

American College Testing (ACT), Inc. (2000). *2000 national score report* (Summary: Five year history of college-bound students' scores). Iowa City, IA: Author. Retrieved from http://www.act.org/news/data/00/00data.html

American College Testing (ACT), Inc. (2009). *ACT profile report—National: Graduating class 2009* (Table 1.4: Five year trends—Average ACT scores by level of preparation, p. 8). Iowa City, IA: Author. Retrieved from http://www.act.org/news/data/09/pdf/National2009.pdf

Asia Society. (2006, May). *Math and science education in a global age: What the U.S. can learn from China.* New York: Author.

Auguste, B. G., Hancock, B., & Laboissiere, M. (2009, June). The economic cost of the US education gap. *McKinsey Quarterly.* Retrieved from http://www.sefi.be/wp-content/uploads/McKinsey%20-%20the%20cost%20of%20the%20US%20edu%20gap%20June%202009.pdf

The Big Picture. (2005, August 27). *Earnings or multiple expansion?* Retrieved June 9, 2011, from http://bigpicture.typepad.com/comments/2005/08/earnings_or_mul.html

Business Roundtable: http://businessroundtable.org

Cavanagh, S. (2010, October 12). Study challenges states on "fairness" of funding. *Education Week.* Retrieved October 29, 2011, from http://www.edweek.org/ew/articles/2010/10/12/08fairness.h30.html?qs=funding+of+education

The College Board. (n.d.). *College bound seniors—2009* (Table 2: Mean SAT scores of college-bound seniors, 1972–2009). New York: Author.

Friedman, M. (1970, September 13). The social responsibility of business is to increase its profits. *New York Times Magazine.*

Guthrie, J. W., & Peng, A. (2010). A warning for all who would listen—America's public schools face a forthcoming fiscal tsunami. In F. M. Hess & E. Osberg (Eds.), *Stretching the school dollar: How schools and districts can save money while serving students best* (pp. 19–44). Cambridge, MA: Harvard Education Press.

Hamilton, B. A., & European Institute for Business Administration (INSEAD). (2006). *Innovation: Is global the way forward?* Retrieved from http://www.boozallen.com/media/file/Innovation_Is_Global_The_Way_Forward_v2.pdf

Hess, F. M., & Osberg, E. (Eds.). (2010). *Stretching the school dollar: How schools and districts can save money while serving students best.* Cambridge, MA: Harvard Education Press.

International Association for the Evaluation of Educational Achievement. (2009). *TIMSS 2007 international science report.* Chestnut Hill, MA: TIMSS & PIRLS International Study Center, Boston College.

McClellan, J., & Timan, A. (2010, October). [Imagination @ Nela Park—GE Lighting and MC²STEM Partnership]. Unpublished raw data.

National Commission on Excellence in Education. (1983). *A nation at risk: The imperative for educational reform.* Washington, DC: Author.

Organisation for Economic Co-operation and Development (OECD). (2000). *Knowledge and skills for life—First results from the OECD Programme for International Student Assessment (PISA) 2000* (Figure 2.4: Multiple comparisons of mean performance on the combined Reading Literacy Scale; Figure 3.2: Multiple comparisons of mean performance on the Mathematical Literacy Scale; & Figure 3.5: Multiple comparisons of mean performance on the Scientific Literacy Scale). Paris: Author.

Organisation for Economic Co-operation and Development (OECD). (2003). *Learning for tomorrow's world—First results PISA 2003.* Paris: Author.

Organisation for Economic Co-operation and Development (OECD). (2007a). *PISA 2006: Science competencies for tomorrow's world: Executive summary* (Table 4: Range of rank of countries/economies on the Reading Scale; Table 5: Range of rank of countries/economies on the Mathematics Scale; Table 2: Range of rank of countries/economies on the Science Scale). Paris: Author.

Organisation for Economic Co-operation and Development (OECD). (2007b). *PISA 2006: Science competencies for tomorrow's world: Vol. 2. Data* (Table 6.2c). Paris: Author.

Organisation for Economic Co-operation and Development (OECD) Programme for International Student Assessment (PISA). (2007c). *PISA 2006: Science competencies for tomorrow's world* (Vols. 1–2). Retrieved from http://www.oecd.org/document/2/0,3343,en_32252351_32236191_39718850_1_1_1_1,00.html#Vol_1_and_2

Organisation for Economic Co-operation and Development (OECD). (2009). *Education at a glance 2009: OECD indicators* (Table B1.1a: Annual expenditures on education institutions per student for all services). (2006). Paris: Author.

Organisation for Economic Co-operation and Development (OECD). (2010). *PISA 2009: What students know and can do: Student performance in reading, mathematics, and science.* Paris: Author.

Tax Foundation. (2009, December 2). *National and state corporate income tax rates, U.S. and OECD countries—2009.* Washington, DC: Author.

Tully, S. (2007, April 15). A profit gusher of epic proportions. *Fortune.* Retrieved August 29, 2011, from http://money.cnn.com/magazines/fortune/fortune_archive/2007/04/30/8405391/index.htm

Tully, S. (2009, April 21). Pop! Went the profit bubble. *Fortune.* Retrieved August 29, 2011, from http://money.cnn.com/2009/04/16/news/companies/tully_profitbubble.fortune/index.htm

Tully, S. (2010, April 15). Fortune 500: Profits bounce back. *Fortune.* Retrieved August 29, 2011, from http://money.cnn.com/2010/04/13/news/companies/fortune_500_profits.fortune/index.htm

U.S. Census Bureau. (n.d.). *Statistical abstract of the United States: 2010* (Table 220: Enrollment in public and private schools: 1970–2007). Washington, DC: Author.

Retrieved August 29, 2011, from http://www.census.gov/prod/2009pubs/10statab/educ.pdf

U.S. Department of Commerce, Bureau of Economic Analysis. (n.d.). *National income and product accounts table* (Table 1.10: Gross domestic income by type of income). Retrieved April 25, 2010, from http://www.bea.gov/national/nipaweb/TableView.asp?SelectedTable=51&Freq=Qtr&FirstYear=2009&LastYear=2011

U.S. Department of Education. (1983, April). *Recommendations: A nation at risk: The imperative for educational reform.* Retrieved from http://www2.ed.gov/pubs/NatAtRisk/index.html

U.S. Department of Education. (n.d.). *Education department budget history table: FY 1980—FY 2009 president's budget.* Washington, DC: Author.

U.S. Department of Education, Institute of Education Sciences (IES), National Center for Education Statistics (NCES). (2008, June). *The condition of education 2008.* Washington, DC: Author. Retrieved from http://nces.ed.gov/pubs2008/2008031.pdf

U.S. Department of Education, Institute of Education Sciences (IES), National Center for Education Statistics (NCES). (2009a, March). *Digest of Education Statistics 2008.* Washington, DC: Authors. Retrieved from http://nces.ed.gov/pubs2009/2009020.pdf

U.S. Department of Education, Institute of Education Sciences (IES), National Center for Education Statistics (NCES). (2009b). *Digest of Education Statistics 2008* (Table 26, Table 174). Washington, DC: Author.

U.S. Department of Education, Institute of Education Sciences (IES), National Center for Education Statistics (NCES). (2010a, May). *The condition of education 2010.* Washington, DC: Author. Retrieved from http://nces.ed.gov/pubs2010/2010028.pdf

U.S. Department of Education, Institute of Education Sciences (IES), National Center for Education Statistics (NCES). (2010b). *Digest of Education Statistics 2009* (Table 105: Averaged freshman graduation rates for public secondary schools, by state or jurisdiction: Selected years, 1990–01 through 2006–07). Washington, DC: Author.

U.S. Department of Education, Institute of Education Sciences (IES), National Center for Education Statistics (NCES). (2011). *Nation's report card (2010).* Washington, DC: Author.

14

Are parents appropriately involved in decisions regarding standards and accountability?

POINT: Rodney Kennedy, *First Baptist Church Dayton*
COUNTERPOINT: Kerry C. Coovert, *University of Dayton*

OVERVIEW

In the 1960s, James Coleman conducted groundbreaking research demonstrating the importance of parents and the family. For Coleman and others who were working with him, the family constituted the most powerful and significant influencer in terms of student academic achievement. Coleman did not assert that teachers were unimportant; he simply argued that parents and families were more important. There clearly is a relationship between family income and the intellectual capital that young persons possess when they enter school. In recent decades, researchers have repeatedly documented the way in which parent socioeconomic status correlates with student academic achievement.

In the United States, there is an achievement gap between and among students from different racial and ethnic groups; there is also an achievement gap between our most affluent and most needy students. The United States is not the only country that evidences such a gap, but some other countries have been able to address the problem in ways that clearly demonstrate that it is solvable. Finland, for example, evidenced a strong achievement gap in the 1970s, a gap that was correlated to family socioeconomic status. Part of the Finnish success story is attributable to the fact that schools began to embed a large number of services such as health services that do not rely exclusively on families or parents to provide. In other words, in some situations, the social network is sufficiently strong to ensure that all children have opportunities for preschool, adequate housing, and the ability to live in home situations where there is a certain minimal living allowance.

What is emerging are indicators of how and whether parents should be relied on as significant providers of the education of their children. Is it the parents' responsibility to educate the child or is it that of societies? Should parents have a strong voice in what happens at school to their children or are classrooms the domain of teachers? Another question asks whether those teachers should be the ones who dictate what children learn and how they learn it. As education has emerged as a profession or semiprofession, the decision making of teachers has been treated more like that of other professionals such as doctors and lawyers with the result that teachers view their specialized expertise as sufficient and appropriate in determining what children need. In this way, parents can inform what teachers do, but the teachers have the professional obligation to dictate on the part of larger social communities what children need to know in order to enter the world of work.

Rodney Kennedy (First Baptist Church Dayton) takes the view that parents should be "activist voices" in the education of their children. To Kennedy, parental participation in school governance is critical just as parent involvement in the life of their children is imperative. In fact, he posits that schools are diminished when there is not widespread and significant parent involvement in the decision-making process. Kennedy does not assert that parents should control what happens in school. Even so, he does contend that parents know what is best for their children and that they need to have their voices heard and recognized by the educators who are working with their young.

Kerry C. Coovert (University of Dayton) takes a different view, contending that parents clearly have the right to be advocates for their children but that advocacy should never move to the point where parents "own" the education of their children. She adds that there are now common academic standards for most of the 50 states and there are now defined expectations for what students should know to be college and career ready. For Coovert, the issue is that teachers have the responsibility for ensuring that students possess the requisite knowledge for academic success. Coovert maintains that parents can voice their concerns and their ideas but ultimately it is the teachers, as professionals, who are held accountable for ensuring that students receive the educations they need to compete in the complex society that they will enter.

In reading this chapter, consider the following four questions. First, should parents be given the opportunity to actively shape and determine what happens in schools? Second, should teachers accommodate what they do to those parental expectations? Third, what does it mean to be a professional? Fourth, if teachers are professionals, how do they then accommodate the concerns and interests of parents?

Thomas J. Lasley, II
University of Dayton

POINT: Rodney Kennedy
First Baptist Church Dayton

Parents should not allow education professionals to be the ones to exclusively dictate issues around standards and accountability. Research demonstrates consistently that parental involvement is one of, and perhaps the key, determinative factor in the education of students. Yet this finding, accepted as a truism, does not resolve the tensions in an ongoing debate about the quality, quantity, and focus of parental involvement. For example, there are serious questions about the role of parents in issues of standards and accountability. Thus, the argument here insists that parental focus on issues of standards and accountability helps the development of strong academic performance by American students. Having parents present for school functions is important, but it does not go far enough. What parents need is empowerment, a sense of ownership, and a way to know that their voice matters in the serious issues of school governance.

Standards are defined as the skills and conceptual understandings that children should possess and the things they should know by the end of each academic year. Academic standards have been largely produced by professional educators without much input from parents. Standards generally include three basic components: *content* that tells what students should know and be able to do, *performance* that tells how students will demonstrate ability to meet the standards, and *proficiency* that indicates how well students have learned the content.

Kids spend about 70% of their waking time outside of school, making parental involvement more vital to academic success. The earlier in a child's development parental involvement begins, the more powerful the effects in terms of a young person's intellectual growth. Studies have shown that more than 85% of the general public believes that support from parents is the most important way to improve the schools.

Although the role and influence of standards and accountability continues to generate debate in the United States, support for standards and accountability has become rather universal. Federal, state, and local school boards have put in place vigorous standards and accountability, and readers can see from other essays in this book, there is now a move toward common academic standards, especially in reading and mathematics.

CRITICISMS AND BENEFITS OF PARENTAL INVOLVEMENT

School officials often raise objections to parent involvement in terms of their participation in the development of standards and accountability. Educators feel that parents do not have enough training to make decisions about a school's curriculum, although surveys of parents indicate that the majority of them feel they are capable of making sound decisions about what students should learn and what academic outcomes should be expected.

Participation of parents would help eliminate assumptions parents and school personnel have about one another's motives, attitudes, intentions, and abilities. School personnel would benefit from the parents' ability to serve as resources for the academic, social, and psychological development of their children (because of their interaction with children over time).

The usual objections revolve around issues of parents not being professional educators, not understanding the purpose and goals of standards, and not knowing how to apply standards to the educational process. Allowing parents to have voice and vote in such a central issue of education, such as standards and accountability, may well serve as a motivating factor to increase parental involvement. When people know that they are appreciated and that they are a part of important decisional processes, schools will move to a more democratic, open, and trusting environment between teachers and parents.

Parental participation in school governance is a critical issue. Parents should be allowed and encouraged to help make program decisions around issues of standards, accountability, goal setting, development and implementation of program activities, assessment, personnel decisions, and funding allocations. The more democratic and parentally involved the process, the more successful the school will be.

Without question, this is the most controversial area of proposed parental involvement. No one disputes that parents should be involved in school activities and homework, but lines are drawn and territories are protected when the suggestion is made that parents should have an active role in setting standards. Here there occurs reluctance on the part of professional educators, such as principals and teachers.

No one questions the importance of parental involvement. No one suggests that there is enough parental involvement. Parental involvement must go beyond traditional forms of participation, such as attending school functions, parent-teacher conferences, homework help, and fund raising activities.

Over the last 18 years, I have addressed more than 250,000 parents in 42 states. During this time, I discovered that parents are intentionally and intensely involved in the academic lives of their children. Parents care deeply about the academic performance of their children. Parents want to know how they can do a better job. While parents can react in negative ways to change, and some parents did so at the advent of stronger standards and accountability, they have come to accept these factors as essential to academic success.

In interviews with public school administrators, Title I supervisors, and parental involvement coordinators, the number one complaint has been how difficult it is to get parents involved. The argument here is that a more democratic, more participative form of engagement will help to alleviate this problem.

CONNECTING PARENTAL INVOLVEMENT TO STANDARDS AND ACCOUNTABILITY

Parental involvement is the key to a school's success. This oft-repeated phrase has become a truism and almost a dead metaphor because of the difficulty of translating the truth of the statement into accountability and action by the schools and parents. American parents become less involved as children get older, and this indifference may translate into student indifference, which begins to be evidenced in middle school. Laurence Steinberg (1996) observed that "national studies of American families show that parental involvement drops off precipitously between elementary and secondary school—precisely at the time when youngsters' susceptibility to peer influence is rapidly rising" (p. 142). Parental involvement in parent-teacher conferences, homework, and study skills at home can expand to also include parental involvement in academic standards and accountability. A process determined collaboratively with parents can outline agreed on expectations and accountability for all stakeholders in the school.

Building on a democratic, dialogic model of communication developed by Stanley Deetz (1995), the argument for parental input in standards and accountability suggests that more democratic communication processes implemented in school relationships with parents is a vital first step to academic success. The best way to make progress in America's schools is to engage parents in all issues of academic success, particularly issues of standards and accountability. Using a communications model, Deetz outlines the case for parental involvement in standards and accountability. Analogically, the transformation of business through a communication model will also transform schools, and parents are the key. Parental involvement with standards and accountability begins with the recognition that parents are essential *stakeholders* (they have a stake in the educational process). Therefore, at a minimum, parents should have some representation rights. If this basic right is expanded to include direct decisional influence by parents, then it can lead to greater effectiveness in meeting the goals of the school.

What evolves is a stakeholder model of school decision making that explores growing diversity, needs to pay attention to more basic everyday negotiation processes, reviews control systems within schools that hamper stakeholder representation, and explores new conceptions of interaction that are likely to improve collaborative decision making within schools. This analysis can help improve the growing attempts in schools to respect diversity and achieve a higher level of participation.

We need widespread parental participation in the decision-making processes within schools because diverse group participation in school decisions will lead to better decisions. Parents can make good collaborative decisions in relationship with professional educators if given the chance and a forum. Decisions about standards and accountability influence the everyday lives of students and parents, but these decisions are outside the realm of democratic processes. When we ask fundamental questions about where decisions about standards and accountability are being made, we learn they are mostly made by legislators and professional educators. If the critical decisions about education are made without the input of parents, then we are sacrificing a valuable and critical mass of information. I am suggesting a model where schools become a place where we explore and develop choices for all. Social, cultural, and psychological factors will be more readily integrated into designing portfolios for an increasingly diverse student population and their learning, with appropriate input from parents.

Democratic skills are learned and cannot be separated from the practice of communication. This means working with parents to develop listening skills, negotiation skills, cooperation, facilitation, and group creativity. A powerful by-product of this kind of cooperative team building among educators and parents will be the rise of trust, credibility, and understanding. As Aristotle demonstrated, one of the most powerful elements of persuasion is ethos, and at the heart of ethos is the ability to inspire trust in others, believability, and a sense that everyone is looking out for the best interests of everyone else. In this model, the more democratic the process and the less autocratic the school leaders, the more success students will have.

Adopting a dialogical, democratic communication model will mean making fundamental changes in the educational status quo. By replacing a top-down decision-making process (with limited parent involvement) with a bottom-up process (more parent involvement), better results will be obtainable in schools.

The social structure of the school should grow from the bottom rather than be enforced from the top. Quality information must be widely distributed. The more parents participate in the setting of standards, the more parents know about the purposes and goals of standards, and the more parents will participate in helping their children meet standards. Knowledge is power.

One of the best ways to build trust relationships in schools is for parents to be treated by school professionals as a fixed asset. An adversarial role between teachers and parents hurts the school environment. By including parents in governance issues, administrators, teachers, and parents can better identify and work collaboratively toward common goals. This means the open sharing of all information with parents. Decision making in this communication model is based on consensus through a series of joint teacher-parent committees known as *accountability rings*. Increased shared accountability has the effect of demanding more from teachers and parents.

Since teaching, learning, and testing are designed to connect to the academic standards, does it not follow that parental involvement should connect to the academic standards? Parents and educators can develop a plan for parental involvement in the standards. For example, as parents learn more about the diversity of different cultures, they can develop home teaching strategies around the learning styles of their children. Lisa Delpit (1995) argued that we are part of a "culture of power." Issues of power are enacted in schools, their governance, their rules, their standards, their methodologies, and their success or failure. One culture has most of the power in this culture of power, and they make the rules. Unless we are willing to acknowledge the existence of the culture of power, we will be unable to grant representation to the multiple voices of other cultures that have little or no power.

By involving parents in issues of standards and accountability, we take one step toward the more effective sharing of power and the more effective education of students from diverse cultures. Cultural issues are a part of this equation. Unless we work to overcome the power of the privileged, we will not be able to adequately educate children of other cultures. Delpit (1995) noted,

> In the educational institutions of this country, the possibilities for poor people and for people of color to define themselves, to determine the self each should be, involve a power that lies outside of the self. It is others who determine how they should act, how they are to be judged. When one "we" gets to determine standards for all "wes," then some "wes" are in trouble. (p. xv)

Not only should educators encourage parents' questions about and interest in the academic standards, but they should also involve parents in the process.

The more parents participate in and have a voice in setting standards, the more prepared they will be to help their children achieve content, performance, and proficiency standards.

Parental involvement in standards and accountability will serve the general purpose of giving parents understanding and purpose. Parents will know the direction that teachers are taking and be better prepared to implement standards and accountability for academic success. In other words, parents will be more involved in a process when they have had a vote and a voice in how the standards and accountability issues have been determined. Rather than a top-down version of education, involved parents will offer a top-up perspective. Professional educators, more aware of the issues of home and community, will be better able to craft standards and accountability factors.

PARENTS AS STAKEHOLDERS

As an argument from the lesser to the greater, consider one example from Glasgow Middle School, Baton Rouge, Louisiana. The principal recruited a school improvement team composed of administration, teachers, and parents. The team produced a collaborative document that guided the school in reaching its goals and that collaborative document was the result of the collective input of all the different stakeholders, not just selective ones.

What this model of a school improvement team accomplished in measurable effectiveness, success, and achievement can be expanded to encapsulate issues of standards and accountability. Representative parents and teachers can work with the administration to increase understanding and implementation of standards and accountability across the board, and many have called for this type of collaboration. Thomas Lasley, Thomas Matczynski, and James Rowley (2002) noted, "American teachers need to work more collaboratively with both parents and their teacher colleagues" (p. 15).

A 1994 plan, called an educational "Marshall Plan," produced a set of national educational goals. One of the ambitious goals in this plan is the following: Every school will promote partnerships that will increase parental involvement and participation in promoting the social, emotional, and academic growth of children. However, the United States has not increased the percentage of schools reporting that parent input is considered when making policy decisions in three or more areas. In the area of these kinds of partnerships, the nation has made no measurable progress over the last 10 years. For instance, when members of the school improvement team observe teachers, one result will be a greater sense of accountability among teachers. While some teachers may not support having parents observe their instruction, there is nothing a teacher does in her classroom that a parent shouldn't see or experience. The sense of ownership among parents also increases the trust level between parents and teachers. As Deetz (1995) said, "Morally and practically, we [educators] must expand the capacity to represent a larger set of stakeholders and their values" (p. 5).

Increasing the number of stakeholders means the active consideration of *forums* and *voice*. Issues of forum consider who should be involved regarding which issues at which time. Issues of voice consider the openness of the discussion, the processes in the formation of meaning, and the possibility of forming new social relations. Issues of voice are becoming more and more significant.

The question we must address is, Are school decisions and agreements achieved through open equable negotiations, stakeholder participation, and democratic processes or through acts of domination and control? The former ensures the participation of parents; the latter necessarily means that they are excluded.

Managerial control systems hamper important negotiations and have led to decisions that have been bad for many legitimate stakeholders. Parents feel excluded because they are not part of the primary decisional processes for their children. The leading school controls today are consent processes. Consent describes the variety of situations and processes in which parents actively, though unknowingly, accomplish the interests of others in the faulty attempt to fulfill their own interests. Parents are complicit in their own victimization. With consent, rather than having open discussions in which different and conflicting needs are brought to expression and negotiation, the discussion is closed, or there appears to be no problem in need of discussion.

By developing a multiple stakeholder model of school decision making around issues of standards and accountability, educators will send a message that parental involvement is more than window dressing, more than attending meetings and serving as cheerleaders. In this model, negotiations are imperative. What results? Parents know and trust that their voice counts and will be heard.

A model of interaction will help school leaders explore how we handle consent processes, diversity issues, trust issues, and communication problems. The result will be educators and parents who will more openly engage in fundamental social decisions about how best to govern the school.

The goal of this model is to increase cooperation and representation on a grand scale. The wider stakeholder participation envisioned in this argument is well within reach. All we lack is the will, the commitment, the courage to overcome communication strategies built on top-down management, issues of control and consent, and protection of territory by professional educators.

My concern is parental representation in decision making around issues of standards and accountability. Who is involved? What kinds of things are decisions about? What is the process of deciding? The model suggested here includes parents as stakeholders in issues of accountability and standards, enlarges the realm of decisional consideration, and seeks innovative collaborative decisions based on the articulation of shared and group and/or individual specific goals.

A team approach is essential for this model. When parents and educators agree to work from explicit decisional contexts, participation is robust and better decisions are made.

CONCLUSION

In summary, here are some initial organizing principles that serve as a good initiation to how such a partnership in a stakeholder, democratic process would work:

1. Treat parents as a fixed asset. Provide opportunities for them to maximize their contributions and value to the school. Provide training and skill development for parents.

2. Base decisional processes on teams, which will attempt to identify and work collaboratively toward common goals of relationship building, trust, and nonadversarial relationships. Educators should allow parents to observe teachers in class settings.

3. Openly share all information with all stakeholders, especially parents.

4. Make decisions based on consensus through a series of formal joint educator-parent teams or decision rings. As stakeholders in the operation of school, parents will participate in educational decisions as full partners including the standards and accountability issues. This step eliminates the usual complaint that decisional authority cannot be located on lower levels because parents are ill informed, not interested, or lack the necessary professional credentials.

5. Educator-parent teams will be the basic building blocks of the school organization.

6. Encourage everyone's efforts toward the common goals of achievement, academic success, meeting and exceeding standards, and holding all stakeholders accountable for outputs.

7. Rather than simply ask parents to think and act like owners, treat them as owners and assure them of a higher status.

8. Agree to hold everyone to schoolwide goals, not because they have bought in or consented to them, but because they chose them. This sort of widespread participation in decisional processes keeps educators accountable to all stakeholders, up and down the organization. There will also be gains in terms of high parental satisfaction, commitment, and loyalty. In a diverse culture, there is no such thing as too much information, too much participation, and too much democracy.

9. Expect the process to be uneven and even messy at times. The ultimate benefit will come in the kind of long-range relationships based on trust, openness, and honesty produced between teachers and parents working together on the same team for the educational success of their students and children.

COUNTERPOINT: Kerry C. Coovert
University of Dayton

The Elementary and Secondary Education Act (ESEA) was enacted in 1965 to provide assistance from the federal government to children who were disadvantaged and to address areas of concern in such areas as rural and urban school systems. ESEA was reauthorized as the controversial No Child Left Behind Act (NCLB) and signed into law by President George W. Bush in January 2002. The NCLB brought more focus on standards in each of six subject areas and measures of accountability of the skills in addition to the content required to be successful in these subjects as well as after high school graduation. The standards and accountability measures were meant to provide the educational field with more focus for teaching, but also they were meant to involve parents in the educational process by providing information on the quality of the schools and its teachers as well as learning outcomes of each student's achievement.

The NCLB Act, or ESEA, is now in the proposal stages to be reauthorized again under the Obama administration. With the possible reauthorization of the NCLB Act, or ESEA, issues of standards and accountability continue to bring many questions to the field of education. Some of those questions surround the responsibility for achievement in learning. More specifically, a key question concerns who is responsible for the academic achievement of children? Put another way, this question asks, who is responsible for making sure that children meet the standards and how those who are responsible for this are held accountable. It is obvious that school boards, educational administrators, teachers, and other staff are involved in this process. However, in an ever-changing society that melds technology, culture, and diversity, it is important for educators to keep in mind that parents must play central roles in the education of their children. In fact, research continuously shows that parental involvement can be an important piece in the academic success of children. Yet in spite if this notion, parents do not have a clear understanding of standards, accountability, and what their role is in a standards-driven school reform. This, in turn, does not provide a way for parents to be able to become involved in the process of education and help to support the success of their children in classrooms.

STANDARDS

As stated, educational officials put standards in place so that expectations are kept high in all school systems, including those in which students may struggle due to economic disadvantages and/or due to a lack of resources. The standards indicate defined levels of educational skills, content, and quality. The standards that have been put in place guide teachers in what content to deliver, what skills to teach, and when it is a developmentally appropriate time to implement these standards in instructing students. To be able to support the academic success of children, teachers must be able to incorporate these standards with research-based teaching strategies. At the same time, standards are not meant to constrict teaching but to provide a multitude of ways for students to demonstrate their academic abilities. The ability of students, coupled with their knowledge of the standards, is to be measured by achievement assessments as a way to monitor a given student's progress against that of other children of their age and grade level. It is part of the professional obligation of teachers to understand defined academic standards and to be able to use them as a guide to demonstrate tangible growth in student learning as measured by achievement assessments. It is the responsibility of teachers to ensure that all children are able to progress along the academic continuum no matter what school system they are teaching in or the previous academic successes, or lack thereof, of students.

Parents, on the other hand, can use standards as a point of entry into the education of their children. Understanding and becoming familiar with the standards for their children can often be used to hold teachers accountable based on the quality of education that teachers provide. Moreover, the standards and assessments provide more than just a grade. The standards provide the information necessary for parents to make informed decisions about the education of children and opportunities to collaborate with teachers on how to support the continued learning of their children in their homes. It is an opportunity to talk with the teacher and not just to be talked to. However, these standards are interwoven into a complex system of reform that is confusing and can sometimes be overwhelming for most parents, especially for those in low income communities and/or families where English is not the primary language. This should neither deter parents from trying to understand the process nor should it deter educators from providing resources for parents to become involved; yet it does suggest certain limits for parental involvement. These limits also define the parameters of appropriate parental involvement.

While educational leaders need to put measures in place to break down the possible barriers between teachers and parents, parents must be willing to join in partnerships with educators to become active participants in the education of their children in addition to understanding and appreciating the limits of their involvement. Having parents become more familiar with the standards can provide better understandings of what their children are learning. Moreover, this increased level of understanding can open avenues of communication between parents and teachers. However, this deeper level of understanding should not provide license for parents to perceive that they control the learning process. Instead, parents must be helped to understand that they are partners, not "directors," of the academic progress of their children.

ACCOUNTABILITY

At the same time that they are becoming familiar with the standards, parents should begin to understand how accountability works. Accountability focuses on the academic performance of students and on overall performance of schools, such as improvement overall in attendance, knowledge of content, graduation rates and the like, reporting of outcomes of achievement results, improvement that is continuous over time, and consequences that are put in place for schools with poor student performance. Unfortunately, accountability is another area that is often mystifying to parents.

Parents understand that teachers are held accountable for all students' learning and education, but they may find this process perplexing. Teachers are now responsible more than ever before for what is being taught in the classrooms and whether students walk away with understandings of the content and skills needed to succeed in school and beyond. This is a component that is definitely a part of teachers' responsibilities as professionals. Teachers should be held accountable in some way for the quality of education they provide. Parents, on the other hand, should be accountable for knowing school data, understanding teacher quality within their schools and districts, and being able to make informed choices for the education of their children.

It is important for parents to believe that standards need to remain high and someone should be responsible for the results. Even so, parents typically are not well informed on the data provided to the general public concerning account-ability measurements and their outcomes. To ensure the academic success of their children, parents must have better understandings of the data provided to make informed educational decisions and to be able to collaborate with educa-tors while demonstrating their support for teachers. However, this is not an easy thing to do. Data are not reader friendly, information is not easy to find unless individuals know what they are looking for, and the data provided can be over-whelming. Since even some teachers struggle to understand the data results, expecting parents to know what they are looking at is unreasonable. Learning what the data mean and explaining them to parents is important in order to help them to become active participants in the education of their children.

Parents should advocate for school environments that welcome their par-ticipation and understanding from their perspective. For example, many par-ents simply do not know they have a right to be heard and need to be a part of understanding the educational goals and outcomes of their children. Parents should also be actively involved with educators regarding how their children will meet state and national standards, particularly those for those students in honors courses, gifted programs, special education, Title I, and/or remedial classes. Again, educational leaders fall short of explicitly providing this infor-mation for parents, which in turn makes them fall short of supporting the educational success of their children.

Based on the results of the accountability measures, parents have a right to choose different schools if assessment and school data results indicate that their children are attending low-performing schools. In other words, low-performing schools are those failing to achieve adequate yearly progress consistent with the provisions of NCLB. Educators in schools that are in this position must com-municate the assessment results to parents while providing supplemental edu-cational services to support the achievement of students in need of additional assistance. In this event, parents must be able to make informed decisions based on their knowledge of standards and the outcomes of accountability.

As the accountability provisions of the NCLB, and perhaps state, laws kick into play, parents must be aware of their options and what services their chil-dren are entitled to so that their children receive the educations to which they are entitled. Without having familiarity with the educational process of their children, which includes standards and accountability, parents can make poor decisions, thereby, further impeding the academic progress of their children. In this regard, while many parents know that school choice exists, they do not understand its parameters. As noted earlier, parents often lack clear understandings of their roles in standards-driven school reform. It is imperative, then, that parents begin to become more involved and familiar with this reform so that they not only better educate themselves but also help to ensure the success of their children. Further, it is imperative for parents to understand the limits of their involvement: they are partners, not owners, of the education that their children receive in schools.

In looking at parental involvement in schools and the standards and accountability process, which guides them, it is obvious that there are many pros to parental involvement and their focus on what occurs in schools. Schools can reach higher levels of achievement and student attendance when leaders have greater communication with teachers and provide parents with better choices for providing quality educations for their children. Yet as stated earlier, some boards, or other school level leaders, in addition to other local, state, and federal governmental officials do not always make this an easy process.

At present, parents are not involved in schools as much as they once were. The challenges of family life are becoming more difficult for parents, especially those in high poverty environments. Families are dealing with busier schedules and households where both parents are working full-time outside of their homes. In addition, increasing numbers of children come from single-parent family homes where the balance of raising a family is placed on one parent. The process of standards and accountability has added another challenge, one that can be confusing and can cause parents to become inactive in or disengaged from the education of their children. While education is seen as a tool for success, and most parents agree with this notion, over time, many parents don't spend enough time focusing on school environments and the process that guides learning to ensure the success of children being raised in those environments. In essence, there are real or perceived limits emerging around what parents can do to ensure the readiness of their children to learn.

PARENTAL LIMITS: AN EXAMPLE

Those who believe in the power of parents often fail to appreciate the significant body of research evolving around early learning. Early childhood education continues to be an educational stepchild despite the fact that the return on investment (ROI) is the most significant for any portion of the P–16 pipeline. Dollars invested with early learning pay dividends, for children and for society.

Indeed, some estimate that the ROI for each dollar invested in early learning ranges from about $2 per child to as much as $17 per child.

Those who push for parental education often fail to understand just how compromised the educational experiences are for children from higher poverty families. Simply stated, far too many high poverty families are unable to ensure the kindergarten readiness of the children they raise. Go to any, and I emphasize *any*, high poverty school district that uses kindergarten assessments to measure kindergarten readiness and compare children who come from non-regulated care environments to those from regulated facilities—you will see a difference in the readiness of the children. Simply put, one will see that the children who have received quality early learning care are, in general, much better prepared to be ready to learn when they begin kindergarten and formal schooling: They possess more of the literacy, numeracy, and socioemotional skills essential for school success. Parents in poverty confront ongoing survival demands. Those demands have the ability to compromise their capacity to raise their children to ensure their readiness to learn when they come to school.

I am *not* suggesting poor parents do not love or care for their children: They do! What I am suggesting is that they have a myriad of survival demands on their lives that mitigate significantly their ability to provide the type of early educational experiences and/or resources their children require. In essence, parents are not, on the whole, the best educational providers, particularly for children in poverty. The demands created by limited financial resources coupled with time constraints (working two jobs) make reading to and problem solving with their child difficult, if not impossible. Teachers (trained early learning professionals), not parents, are the ones who should direct the educational process for our youngest learners. With well-trained, well-educated teachers, our youngest higher poverty learners will receive the same benefits as those coming from affluent homes.

CONCLUSION

Laws and policies in education are ever-changing and can be difficult to understand. Despite the challenges facing families today, it is an essential responsibility of parents to focus on education. Parents need to become advocates for partnerships with school officials even when education officials may not take the initiative. However, parents need to understand the limits of their involvement, especially in a pluralistic society, where individuals' values come into conflict with one another and especially in a society that places economic demands on them that compromise their ability to really "invest" in their child's education.

Teachers are professionals and should be supported with this in mind. Teachers have been trained to teach all children and to provide them with a quality education. Parents must act as advocates for their children who should, and must, hold schools accountable for the achievement of all students. Additionally, parents should provide social and emotional home environments that support the content and skills being taught in classrooms but should limit their involvement to advocacy rather than direct interventions. In light of how many different parental perspectives exist in any school, it is virtually impossible for teachers to function effectively if parents individually attempt to intervene on behalf of their child or define the teaching that should occur in classrooms. This is the role of professional educators who serve in our schools and who will work with parents to ensure that each child is ready to learn at school.

Further Readings and Resources

Deetz, S. (1995). *Transforming communication transforming business: Building responsive and responsible workplaces.* Cresskill, NJ: Hampton Press.

Delpit, L. (1995). *Other people's children: Cultural conflict in the classroom.* New York: New Press.

Greene, L. (1998). *A parent's guide to understanding academic standards.* Washington, DC: Association for Curriculum and Development, Council for Basic Education.

Lasley, T. J., Matczynski, T. J., & Rowley, J. B. (2002). *Instructional models: Strategies for teaching in a diverse society.* Belmont, CA: Wadsworth.

National Coalition for Parental Involvement in Education. (n.d.). *Developing partnerships.* Retrieved from http://www.ncpie.org/DevelopingPartnerships

National PTA. (n.d.). *Topics.* Retrieved from http://www.pta.org/topics.asp

Steinberg, L. (1996). *Beyond the classroom: Why school reform has failed and what parents need to do.* New York: Touchstone.

U.S. Department of Education. (n.d.). *Elementary & secondary education: Regulations—Editor's picks.* Retrieved from http://www2.ed.gov/policy/elsec/reg/edpicks.jhtml?src=ln

INDEX

Note: Bolded numbers refer to volume numbers in the Debating Issues in American Education series.